Union Recognition

Several thousand new trade union recognition agreements have been signed since 1997, representing a major development within industrial relations in Britain. This has resulted from the interaction of union organising efforts and the statutory union recognition provisions of the Employment Relations Act 1999. However, for trade unions recognition alone is not enough, for a vital issue is whether, having gained union recognition, trade unions are now effectively delivering upon the promises and prospects of union recognition.

The essays in *Union Recognition* examine the substantive outcomes of these new agreements in regard to union representation and collective bargaining. In particular, the impact on terms and conditions of employment, employers' behaviour and strategy, the nature of the union–management bargaining relationship, and the building of workplace unionism are explored. While the collection focuses primarily on Britain, the germane issues are also looked at in the context of Australia, Canada and the USA. Conceptually and theoretically, *Union Recognition* offers contributions which develop our understanding of the relationship between workplace and national unionisms and of mobilisation theory.

Gregor Gall is Professor of Industrial Relations and Director of the Centre for Research in Employment Studies at the University of Hertfordshire, and editor of *Union Organizing: campaigning for trade union recognition* (Routledge 2003).

Routledge research in employment relations

Series editors: Rick Delbridge and Edmund Heery

Cardiff Business School, UK.

Aspects of the employment relationship are central to numerous courses at both undergraduate and postgraduate level.

Drawing from insights from industrial relations, human resource management and industrial sociology, this series provides an alternative source of research-based materials and texts, reviewing key developments in employment research.

Books published in this series are works of high academic merit, drawn from a wide range of academic studies in the social sciences.

1 **Social Partnership at Work**
Carola M. Frege

2 **Human Resource Management in the Hotel Industry**
Kim Hoque

3 **Redefining Public Sector Unionism**
UNISON and the future of trade unions
Edited by Mike Terry

4 **Employee Ownership, Participation and Governance**
A study of ESOPs in the UK
Andrew Pendleton

5 **Human Resource Management in Developing Countries**
Pawan S. Budhwar and Yaw A. Debrah

6 **Gender, Diversity and Trade Unions**
International perspectives
Edited by Fiona Colgan and Sue Ledwith

7 **Inside the Factory of the Future**
Work, power and authority in microelectronics
Alan Macinlay and Phil Taylor

8 **New Unions, New Workplaces**
A study of union resilience in the restructured workplace
Andy Danford, Mike Richardson and Martin Upchurch

9 **Partnership and Modernisation in Employment Relations**
Edited by Mark Stuart and Miguel Martinez Lucio

10 **Partnership at Work**
William K. Roche and John F. Geary

11 **European Works Councils**
Pessimism of the intellect optimism of the will?
Edited by Ian Fitzgerald and John Stirling

12 **Employment Relations in Non-Union Firms**
Tony Dundon and Derek Rollinson

13 **Management, Labour Process and Software Development**
Reality bytes
Edited by Rowena Barrett

14 **A Comparison of the Trade Union Merger Process in Britain and Germany**
Joining forces?
Jeremy Waddington, Marcus Kahmann and Jürgen Hoffmann

15 **French Industrial Relations in the New World Economy**
Nick Parsons

16 **Union Recognition**
Organising and bargaining outcomes
Edited by Gregor Gall

Also available from Routledge:

Rethinking Industrial Relations
Mobilisation, collectivism and long waves
John Kelly

Employee Relations in the Public Services
Themes and issues
Edited by Susan Corby and Geoff White

The Insecure Workforce
Edited by Edmund Heery and John Salmon

Public Service Employment Relations in Europe
Transformation, modernisation or inertia?
Edited by Stephen Bach, Lorenzo Bordogna, Giuseppe Della Rocca and David Winchester

Reward Management
A critical text
Edited by Geoff White and Janet Druker

Working for McDonald's in Europe
The unequal struggle?
Tony Royle

Job Insecurity and Work Intensification
Edited by Brendan Burchell, David Ladipo and Frank Wilkinson

Union Organizing
Campaigning for trade union recognition
Edited by Gregor Gall

Employment Relations in the Hospitality and Tourism Industries
Rosemary Lucas

Union Recognition

Organising and bargaining outcomes

Edited by Gregor Gall

Routledge
Taylor & Francis Group
LONDON AND NEW YORK

First published 2006
by Routledge
2 Park Square, Milton Park, Abingdon, Oxon OX14 4RN

Simultaneously published in the USA and Canada
by Routledge
270 Madison Ave, New York, NY 10016

Routledge is an imprint of the Taylor & Francis Group

Typeset in Garamond by Wearset Ltd, Boldon, Tyne and Wear
Printed and bound in Great Britain by MPG Books Ltd, Bodmin

British Library Cataloguing in Publication Data
A catalogue record for this book is available from the British Library

Library of Congress Cataloging in Publication Data
A catalog record for this book has been requested

ISBN 0-415-34336-4

Contents

Tables

Contributors

Professor Bob Bruno, Professor of Industrial and Labor Relations, University of Illinois at Urbana-Champaign

Alex Bryson, Principal Research Fellow, Policy Studies Institute

Fiona Colgan, Senior Research Fellow, Centre for Equality Research in Business, Working Lives Institute, London Metropolitan University

Chris Creegan, Senior Research Fellow, Centre for Equality Research in Business, Working Lives Institute, London Metropolitan University

Professor Gregor Gall, Professor of Industrial Relations, University of Hertfordshire

Paul Gollan, Associate Fellow, London School of Economics

Professor Gerry Griffin, Professor of Management, Division of Business and Enterprise, University of South Australia

Professor Edmund Heery, Professor of Employment Relations, Cardiff University

Dr Jane Holgate, Research Fellow, Queen Mary, University of London and London Metropolitan University

Lisa Jordan, Director of Gender and Diversity Programs, University of Minnesota

Dr Sonia McKay, Senior Researcher, Working Lives Institute, London Metropolitan University

Dr Sian Moore, Senior Researcher, Working Lives Institute, London Metropolitan University

Professor Joseph B. Rose, Professor of Industrial Relations, DeGroote School of Business, McMaster University

Melanie Simms, Lecturer in Industrial Relations, Warwick Business School, Warwick University

Dr Alan Tuckman, Senior Lecturer in HRM, Nottingham Business School, Nottingham Trent University

Dr Michael Whittall, Research Fellow, Nottingham Business School, Nottingham Trent University

Hannah Wood, Research Fellow, Working Lives Institute, London Metropolitan University

Abbreviations and acronyms

ACM	Association of College Management
AEEU	Amalgamated Engineering and Electrical Union
AEP	Association of Educational Psychologists
AEU	Amalgamated Engineering Union
AFA	Association of Flight Attendants
AFL-CIO	American Federation of Labor – Congress of Industrial Organizations
ALGUS	Alliance and Leicester Group Union of Staff
Amicus	General union active in manufacturing and the public sector (formed from the merger of AEEU and MSF)
AMO	Association of Magisterial Officers
ANSA	Abbey National Staff Association
ASLEF	Associated Society of Locomotive Engineers and Firemen
ASTMS	Association of Scientific, Technical and Managerial Staffs
ATL	Association of Teachers and Lecturers
AUEW	Amalgamated Union of Engineering Workers
AUT	Association of University Teachers
BACM-TEAM	British Association of Colliery Management – Technical, Energy and Administrative Management
BALPA	British Air Line Pilots Association
BDA	British Dental Association
BECTU	Broadcasting, Entertainment, Cinematograph and Theatre Union
BFAWU	Bakers, Food and Allied Workers Union
BSU	Britannia Staff Union
CATU	Ceramic and Allied Trades Union
Connect	The union for professionals in communications
CSP	Chartered Society of Physiotherapy
CWU	Communication Workers' Union
EIS	Educational Institute of Scotland
Equity	British actors' association
ERA	Employment Relations Act 1999
FoC	Father of the Chapel

FTO	Full-time officer (of a trade union)
GMB	General, Municipal, Boilermakers and Allied Trade Union: Britain's general union
GPMU	Graphical, Paper and Media Union
GSA	Guiness Staff Association
HCSA	Hospital Consultants and Specialists Association
IPMS	Institution of Professionals, Managers and Specialists
ISTC	Iron and Steel Trades Confederation
IUOOC	Inter Union Offshore Oil Committee
IUHS	Independent Union of Halifax Staff
KFAT	National Union of Knitwear, Footwear and Apparel Trades
MSF	Manufacturing, Science, Finance Union
MU	Musicians' Union
NACO	National Association of Co-operative Officials
NAHT	National Association of Head Teachers
NATFHE	The University and College Lecturers' Union
NGSU	Nationwide Group Staff Union
NUJ	National Union of Journalists
NULMW	National Union of Lock and Metal Workers
NUMAST	National Union of Marine, Aviation and Shipping Transport Officers
NUS	National Union of Seamen
OILC	Offshore Industry Liaison Committee
PAT	Professional Association of Teachers
PCS	Public and Commercial Services union (formed from the merger of PTC and CPSA unions)
POA	Prison Officers' Association
Prospect	Skilled union for technical and administrative staffs (formed from the merger of IPMS and EMA)
RBA	Retail Book Association
RCM	Royal College of Midwives
RMT	National Union of Rail, Maritime and Transport Workers
SHA	Secondary Heads' Association
SocAuth	Society of Authors
SSTA	Scottish Secondary Teachers' Association
STUC	Scottish Trades Union Congress
T&G	Transport and General: Britain's biggest general union
TASS	Technical, Administrative and Supervisory Section (of AUEW)
TGWU	Transport and General Workers' Union
TSSA	Transport Salaried Staffs' Association
TUC	Trades Union Congress
UCAC	Undeb Cenedlaethol Athrawon Cymru
UCATT	Union of Construction, Allied Trades and Technicians
UFS	Union of Finance Staff

UNIFI	The union for staff in financial services
UNISON	Britain's public sector union
USDAW	Union of Shop, Distributive and Allied Workers
WERS	Workplace Employee Relations Survey
WGGB	Writers' Guild of Great Britain

Foreword

No one should underestimate the current challenge facing the UK union movement to recruit new members and extend the collective bargaining coverage. In recent decades, trade union membership has declined by five million. While in 1979, terms and conditions of nearly 80 per cent of the UK workforce were determined by collective agreements or Wages Councils' orders, collective bargaining coverage now stands at only 36 per cent, the lowest level of any country in the European Union.

Nevertheless, there are clear signs for optimism for trade unions, as highlighted by case studies in this collection. In recent years unions have signed over 800 new recognition agreements. Membership levels, which were in free fall during the 1980s and 1990s, have stabilised and are rising amongst women. Union density is on the increase in some sectors, and there is growing evidence that unions are beginning to rebuild their influence in the workplace and beyond.

A range of factors have contributed to this nascent revival, including the more positive political environment, a tighter labour market and increased public sector spending and employment. The improved legislative framework and the increased focus on organising and recruitment throughout UK unions have also played an important role. The introduction of statutory recognition legislation in the Employment Relations Act 1999 has supported unions' organising initiatives at an enterprise level and created new opportunities to achieve recognition. The legislation has been successful not just in terms of statutory recognition awards at the Central Arbitration Committee (CAC) but also, more significantly, in terms of a 300 per cent increase in voluntary recognition agreements signed in recent years, very few of which would have been likely without the availability of recourse to a legal route.

Encouragingly, there is also evidence that some employers who were initially hostile to the concept of negotiating working conditions with a union have been pleasantly surprised by the experience and have engaged in genuine collective bargaining. Others, though, remain reluctant to do more than the bare minimum required by the law. Yet despite the success of the scheme, it has not in itself led to a significant extension of collective bargaining coverage in the UK. This would never be achieved by a scheme which is entirely reliant on majority membership and/or proven support. It has, however, as some of the following chapters demonstrate, provided an essential part of the organising and recruitment strategies of unions.

Whatever limited revival there has been in unions' fortunes in recent years, it still leaves no room for complacency. Unions recognise that they have to raise their game if they are going to move beyond the current stable platform and really turn the tide in membership and collective bargaining coverage.

This will involve a significant cultural change, with a refocusing of resources into organising activities, increased cooperation between unions and a more effective use of employment law to support organising and bargaining agendas. The TUC's new Organising and Representation at Work Task Group, established in 2004, has been charged with three key tasks in this area. First, the new task group takes on the mandate of the former New Unionism Task Group to support union efforts to organise and recruit in key sectors, companies and communities, by helping unions improve recruitment, training and support for workplace reps and by promoting trade unionism to underrepresented groups such as women, black and young workers, and those working in so-called atypical employment. There are plans to build on initiatives such as the Organising Academy, which has been the most visible expression of increased and continued investment to organising in recent years. Since it opened its doors in 1998, the Academy has trained nearly 200 Academy Organisers – with just over half of those going through the programme being women, and some 55 per cent being aged under thirty.

The second key task is to assist unions in benefiting from new employment legislation to support the wider organising and bargaining agendas. The Employment Act 2004 strengthens the statutory recognition scheme in a number of key respects, including new laws regulating the intimidatory actions of employers once a statutory ballot has been announced, and improved rights for unions to communicate with workers once a recognition claim has been admitted by the CAC. The ERA recognition scheme, however, is only one source of support for unions. The new Information and Consultation Regulations and procedures for handling collective grievances in workplaces also provide opportunities to organise in workplaces and to extend and deepen the bargaining agenda.

Third, the TUC will continue to campaign for and to promote strengthened employment law. The Warwick Accord agreed between the Labour Party and affiliated trade unions proffers a number of important initiatives, one of the most interesting of which is proposals for developing sectoral forums comprised of employer and union representatives from different low-paying and low-skilled sectors of industry. If such forums are given teeth and become effective vehicles for the regulation of working conditions and employment relations, they could help to address the current democratic deficit and underdeveloped management skills, particularly in smaller firms.

In developing this future agenda, unions recognise the importance of learning from previous experience. By drawing on experiences of UK unions, and of international counterparts, this collection of chapters makes a valuable contribution to the debate by identifying some union organising and bargaining initiatives and approaches that have proved successful, and those that have failed to yield results.

Brendan Barber, General Secretary, TUC

1 Introduction

The fruits of labour?

Gregor Gall

Since 1995, the point at which the influence of the Labour Party's commitment once in office to legislate for a statutory means to gain union recognition began to take effect on the industrial relations climate in Britain (Gall 2004b), over 2,800 new recognition agreements have been signed (Table 1.2). These agreements cover around 1,200,000 workers and involve many large and well-known employers (Table 1.2). This represents a major development within trade unionism and the compass of industrial relations in Britain, broadly speaking being the outcome of the interaction of the introduction of union organising efforts and the statutory recognition provisions of the Employment Relations Act 1999 (ERA). For trade unionism, this advance is a potentially vital defence against decline, both in terms of offsetting current decline and providing a bridgehead for taking further corrective action. The collection *Union Organizing: campaigning for trade recognition* (Gall 2003a) contained a number of overviews and case studies of the processes by which unions attempted to gain, and gained, union recognition. With many of the tranche of new agreements now several years old, it is now appropriate to begin examining the results and outcomes of these agreements. This point has recognised by union leaders such as Derek Simpson and Tony Woodley, respectively Amicus and TGWU general secretaries (in A. Murray 2003: 124 and *Tribune* 27 June 2003) and some academics (e.g. Gall 2003d: 243, 2003f, 2004c; Markowitz 2000: 130). There are a number of salient areas for investigation here. Among the most obvious are the substantive outcomes of recognition and collective bargaining vis-à-vis terms and conditions of employment; employers' behaviour and strategy in responding to the challenge posed by union recognition; the nature and processes of the bargaining/union–management relationship; and the building of workplace union presence (membership, organisation, activity) and its relation with national trade unionism. For our purposes here, these broadly concern union resources, union processes and union outcomes (Willman and Kelly 2004: 4–5).

Consequently, this collection has two main themes. The first is an examination of the fates and fortunes of the new recognition agreements as outcomes in themselves. They warrant examination for, since 1995, some

16 per cent of union members are now covered by recognition where they were previously not. Analysis of new agreements will help the process of assessing (a) the resultant state of the union movement as it attempts to rejuvenate itself, (b) the behaviour of previously non-union employers in dealing with trade unionism when managerial practice has been dominated by non-unionism, and (c) the extent to which democracy and collective participation now exist in the workplace. For trade unionists, a vital issue is whether, having gained recognition, trade unions are now delivering upon the promises and prospects of recognition. Workers and union members do not prize recognition in itself as an institutional 'right' but rather view it in terms of what benefits it may bring. For unions, the potential to retain the relatively recently recruited members (under the new recognition agreements) and to recruit others in the future, primarily but not exclusively outside in-fill recruitment, will depend upon how effective unions are – or are seen to be – in realising the benefits of union membership. Therefore, the collection will provide the first assessment of these and other related issues. In a sense, much of the future of the union movement can be viewed through the prism of these new agreements. The second theme is an examination of the new recognition agreements as a quasi-distinct development within contemporary trade unionism. It can be contended that the processes and dynamics of workplace trade unionism under new recognition agreements are discrete from those comprising, and taking place within, long-standing workplace trade unionism under long-standing recognition agreements. For example, workplace unionism under the new recognition agreements may be more youthful, vibrant and challenging (to management and national union) than that under long-standing recognition agreements, the former arguably being free of inertia, bureaucratisation and conservatism.

Conceptually and theoretically, this collection seeks to develop our understanding of the relationship between workplace and national unionisms and of mobilisation theory as a result of analysing the above two themes. Although the focus of the collection largely concerns Britain, the issues are also germane to other countries. In terms of declining membership, organising approaches, statutory recognition provisions and limited legal and public policy support for collective bargaining thereafter, and what may be termed the 'Anglo-Saxon' model of trade unionism, the countries of Australia, Canada and the USA have been chosen to help develop some points of departure for contextualisation and comparative analysis. Of course, there are also potentially useful dissimilarities between the countries, such as different dominant state and employer policies towards trade unionism, varying union strength and differences in union approaches to utilising statutory recognition provisions. In regard of the latter, for example, in Canada the overwhelming majority of recognition is derived through statutory means. In Britain, the overwhelming majority of recognition is through voluntary means, and lying somewhere in between is the situation in the USA. These chapters, then, are capable of providing foundations for insights into the situation in Britain as well as illuminating the more generic issues.[1]

Substantive content

The new recognition agreements present opportunities and challenges, some of which are new, some of which are existing, for the union movement. To begin understanding these issues, consideration of a number of related aspects is necessary. These are:

- The process by which recognition was gained, involving (a) the degree of member involvement and mobilisation, (b) the degree of national union control and influence, and (c) the role of state bodies such as the Advisory, Conciliation and Arbitration Service (ACAS) and the Central Arbitration Committee (CAC), where each is considered with a view to its respective influence on post-recognition outcomes.
- The complexion of the recognition agreement itself (e.g. traditional, partnership, 'sweetheart', single-union), again in terms of influencing post-recognition outcomes.
- The bargaining outcomes themselves, such as recognition agreements as partnership agreements leading to mutual gains, de facto enterprise unionism or union marginalisation, or, by contrast, traditional agreements leading to strong bargaining relationships and industrial conflict. From this, the bargaining relationship can be judged to be one based on either 'integrative' or 'distributive' bargaining (Walton and McKersie 1965; Chamberlain and Kuhn 1965).
- The possible differential impact on bargaining processes and outcomes as a result of recognition being secured through the statutory procedure as opposed to voluntarily.
- Whether unions have been able to create the 'self-organised' organised (*sic*) workplace within the remit of the espoused 'organising culture' or whether the more historically dominant 'servicing' relationship between members and union lay officials/full-time officers (FTOs) continues to exert more influence. Specifically, this aspect concerns whether, with an increasing number of recognition agreements but not a net and immediate increase in income from new members, unions are able to offer sufficient resources to help establish the 'organised' workplace.
- Whether, and to what extent, tension or compatibility exists between the workplace union and the national union over bargaining agenda and *modus operandi* where the workplace unionism is relatively new and fresh but the national union is older and more experienced.
- The determinants of improvements, reductions and stagnation in workers' pay and conditions in relation to the results of collective bargaining, union strength, employer choice, employer resource and the

prevailing state of labour and product markets. To put it simply and for the unions, what is the 'union mark-up' or 'premium'?

- Whether, and to what extent, the union has been able to achieve 'employee voice', justice and fairness in the workplace.

In addition to examining these outcomes in themselves, another way by which to make an assessment would be to compare these outcomes to those from older, existing recognition agreements. However, the data required to carry out this task is not readily available. It may be that some such data emerges from WERS5, for some of the workplaces used may comprise those with new recognition agreements. We do, however, know that on one calculation the 'union mark-up' or union wage premium has declined significantly in recent years from 13 per cent in 1994 to 3 per cent in 2001 (Bryson and Gomez 2002: 61). This should serve to temper the extent of any expectations of the likely gains under the new recognition agreements, both in terms of wages and, probably, for wider remuneration and other conditions of employment.

What defines and characterises new recognition agreements?

This section discusses the implications for a workplace union of its move from the situation of campaigning for, and gaining, recognition to one of providing representation and conducting bargaining. The employer's agreeing to recognition is thus a cusp that represents a significant transition. (For the sake of simplicity at this point and throughout this section, it is reasonably assumed that little or no de facto representation or bargaining took place prior to recognition and that employer resistance after recognition is negligible. Consequently, we can envisage a simon-pure categorisation and change of function.) In doing so, and in examining the outcomes of the new recognition agreements, it is imperative to have a sense of what comprises and defines a new agreement (where recognition has never or has not recently existed). Thus, a 'new' agreement can be defined as one that is between 0 and three years old. This allows for the first series of annual negotiations over wages and conditions, the implementation of new grievance procedures, the union facing employer demands for the first (post-recognition) time for changes in work organisation (task or temporal) and so on, as well as the process of the settling-down of relations between employer and union. The danger in defining a new agreement much beyond three years is that this would gradually lose the colourations that could be characterised as 'new' and, conversely, increasingly contain the colourations typifying more-long-standing agreements.

In considering the engagement of the workplace union (aided or led by the external union, whether local, regional or national) in these activities, the conceptual framework must be able to take account of the specificity of the dynamics and forces comprising, and acting upon, new recognition agreements. One way in which this may be done is to interrogate the issues on the heuristic premise that the new recognition agreements are founded upon new workplace unionism which has a marked tendency to display more vibrancy, independence and spontaneity compared to long-standing recognition agreements and thus (more) long-standing workplace unionism. The other side of this is that new recognition agreements are founded upon new workplace unionism that may be thought of as being free(r) from certain constraints found, or found to be more pronounced, in long-standing recognition agreements and thus (more) long-standing workplace unionism. Primarily, these constraints consist of settled relationships with employers and national unions that may be regarded as tending towards inertia and stasis through demobilisation, routinisation, bureaucratisation and incorporation by comparison to the dynamics under new workplace unionism. Even where the campaign to gain recognition has taken a significant period of time (see Gall 2004b: 262), so that the workplace unionism has had a lengthy period of existence prior to recognition, the change from non-recognition to recognition, representation and bargaining still represents a momentous juncture.[2] In this regard, workplace unionism, for the moment all other things being equal, may be viewed as passing through a number of sequential stages, each of which has its own specific dynamics: birth, growth, consolidation, and then either stasis and renewal or atrophy.[3]

So the move from pre-recognition to post-recognition comprises two specific, but closely related, aspects. This first is that the workplace union experiences a change in situational purpose. The second is that its relationship with the employer changes from relative illegitimacy to relative legitimacy. Alongside and ensuing from the increase in *relative* legitimacy is the *relative* increase in stability for the workplace union where it attains a regularised and fuller relationship with the employer (see Gall 2003b: 6–8 for a discussion of what recognition involves).

Taking the first aspect, the workplace union is primarily consumed by its drive towards a single moment, namely, that of gaining recognition as a means of opening up the possibility of extensive representation and bargaining. That single moment is a definite point in time and an endpoint in itself, albeit as a means to a further end. The mobilisation to gain recognition is of a singular and narrowed nature, where collectivism and solidarity were created for that certain purpose. Save the minority of cases where gaining recognition involved the deployment of industrial action, the aggregation of membership and worker support for the purposes of membership audit or workplace ballot to gain recognition is not necessarily likely to involve particularly high levels of collectivism and solidarity. By contrast, once recognition has been gained, the process of then engaging in representation and bargaining is multifaceted, indefinite and continuous, requiring multiple, unending and more varied applications and mobilisations of the workplace union within a regularised and institutionalised setting. Gaining recognition involves the creation of a single alliance throughout the workforce, with workers and members having different reasons for, and attaching different priorities to, wanting recognition. Representation and bargaining will seldom involve the same degree of unity and purpose again, for differing and sectional concerns will come to the fore when and where the workplace union addresses different issues and demands. Put another way, the rhythm of union life is now different because the existence and rationale have moved from one of campaigning primarily for recognition based on the foundation of recruitment, where all other activities are subordinate, to one of attempting to engage in effective bargaining and representation. Therefore, it should not be assumed that the nature of the mobilisation undertaken to gain recognition can be directly replicated once recognition has been gained or is directly transferable or even appropriate for conducting representation and bargaining. It is easiest to pose these issues where union activity consists of building up membership and worker support for the purposes of an audit or ballot, but does not involve much in the way of representational work, union education and structure building.

Looking at the second aspect, the consequence of gaining recognition involves a trajectory towards normalisation, institutionalisation, routinisation and regularisation of the relationship between the union and employer, with implications for the union as an institution and as its members. The rhythm of union activity becomes bound up with, and often centred round, a routine of (union) meetings that feed into, and respond to, union–management meetings. The latter comprise exercises in information dissemination, consultation, negotiation and representation. Some of these meetings are scheduled in advance or expected at certain times, like annual wage negotiations. Consequently, a greater sense of distance can open up between the 'union' – consisting of the union reps or FTOs – on the one hand, and the members on the other, because there is now less importance attached to what the union does of its own volition and initiative. Moreover, the tasks and processes of bargaining and representation in the first instance reduce the significance of membership involvement as a specialisation of task and expertise develops in the form of the union reps and union lay officers. Often it appears that the functions of, and tasks undertaken by, the union reps are the sum of the union's activity. This is accentuated where there is facility time for the union reps.

This broad characterisation can now be fleshed out to take account of the likely micro-scenarios that can be envisaged after recognition has been gained. First, for union members, these include the possibility of heightened expectations of what is to come in terms of benefits, feelings of elation, enthusiasm and excitement, and a sigh of collective relief which may precipitate demobilisation and reflect exhaustion, as well as an anxiety about 'what is next?' and about lack of bargaining skills. Second, for the union as an institution, these include the resource implications of servicing new agreements while organising further and additional recognition campaigns elsewhere, the necessity and desirability of delivering upon promises and pledges, achieving and maintaining membership involvement and participation in the face of pressures towards demobilisation, and providing training and guidance for inexperienced and unfamiliar lay office-holders. Of course, the approaches and goals of 'servicing' and 'organising' would imply different accents on these particular issues. Third, for the employers, no matter what their intentions, considerable amounts of time, energies and resources will be spent gearing up to face the new challenge. With regard to the employers trying to control the union and the bargaining process, these may include creating demobilisation, incorporation, attitudinal restructuring and marginalisation. Within these or other confines, employers will also seek to establish a stable bargaining relationship based on trust, familiarity and experience of each other and the settling-down of the relationship into acceptable format, spirit and parameters.

While the preceding discussion represents a heuristic device to explore the salient issues, it is incomplete in a number of respects. First, it has not, as it were, factored in the influence of the nature of procedural recognition agreement signed by the national union on behalf of the workplace union. Possible dimensions here include constrained unionism following a 'sweetheart' or 'partnership' deal, compared to more robust unionism under a traditional recognition agreement. But such formal agreements do not govern social processes like collective bargaining for a number of reasons. Amongst these are that such documents represent a statement of intent, not actuality, and the balance of forces between employer and union at the point of signing (and not thereafter). Second, the discussion did not take cognisance of the ramifications of the external socio-economic environment, whether micro-, meso- or macro-, vis-à-vis labour and product markets, company restructuring and so on. Third, it was assumed that no pre-recognition representation or bargaining took place. This was to pose the issues starkly for the purpose of clarification. However, such de facto representation or bargaining can, and does, take place. Consequently, it may provide the basis for post-recognition representation or bargaining in terms of mobilisation, articulation and collectivism, and the skills and experience contained therein. The same kind of point can be made about employer opposition in the pre-recognition period. Where recognition is won or conceded, previous experience of employer resistance may provide some form of inoculation. (But by the same token, no prior bargaining taking place as a result of employer resistance may mean that in these cases many of the previous considerations are not relevant.) Fourth, it is plausible to suggest that young workplace unionism may require greater help and resources from the national union in its initial stages because it is relatively inexperienced and underdeveloped in representation and bargaining. After a period of time, the workplace may then develop the requisite skills and experience. So these qualifications enrich our understanding of the potential resultant diversity after recognition has been gained.

A typology of variation

In an attempt to bring some of these processual issues together and to give an indication of the complexity of possible outcomes and the forces accounting for them, the following typology is put forward. In the current context of union weakness and quiescence, and also more generally speaking, the key single influence on the process and outcome of the post-recognition period is held to be that of the employers, in terms of their superior financial, ideological and organisational resources. These influence the employers' values and goals, and their strategies and tactics towards recognition. However, interaction with the agency of trade unionism can support, alter or ameliorate the approach of the employer. With this in mind, the typology is conceptualised around three components:

Intention denotes both employer's and union's initial behaviour regarding the positions they adopt in entering the 'recognition process', such as what they seek (recognition, non-recognition), type of recognition (voluntary/semi-voluntary/statutory, full/partial, partnership/traditional) and how they go about seeking this (dialogue, mobilisation, partnership, confrontation, using state agencies).

Process denotes the relational aspects of the interaction of each party's behaviour on the other party, consequent upon their intentions, which help to explain the success or failure of each party in attaining its goals. These may include one party being superordinate and the other subordinate so that the outcome reflects the prevailing balance of power, as well as attitudinal restructuring and compromise, where the process of interaction leads to moderation of, or alteration in, each party's behaviour and goals. Therefore, 'process' denotes the complex interaction where the parties' intentions may be realised as well as where a party's intentions may be changed as a result of proactive and reactive responses from the other party. Attitudinal restructuring may be 'positive' as well as 'negative', conscious as well as unconscious.

Outcome relates not merely to agreement to recognise or not and the content of the formal procedural agreement where recognition is gained, but also the substantive and relational outcomes following these, such as bargaining outcomes and de facto working relationships judged in terms of 'integrative'/'cooperative' or 'conjunctive'/'distributive' bargaining (Walton and McKersie 1965; Chamberlain and Kuhn 1965).

The possible influence of the arena in which recognition has been gained, namely voluntarily, semi-voluntarily, semi-statutory and statutory, has been referred to previously. From these components, several critical junctures can be identified: the process of discussing the recognition claim, agreement to recognition or not, negotiation of procedural agreement, substantive and relational outcomes of recognition and non-recognition. In each, there are slightly different dynamics and forces operating (for example, the decision to recognise may or may not imply a certain type of procedural agreement), suggesting large degrees of indeterminacy to each juncture.

In terms of the generic outcomes, the key terms used in the typology need to be defined. While providing a definition of *partnership* is problematic, it can be suggested that at base, it will at least involve a consciously adopted approach of (supposed) cooperation and mutual benefit with attendant outcomes, sometimes known as a 'productivity coalition'. *Traditional* refers to the fact that the spirit, process and content of the bargaining relationship are based on pluralism and distributive bargaining and includes the possibility of industrial action within certain limits. *Oppositional* refers to not only a heightened sense of distributive bargaining but also that of a state of stalemate, sporadic guerrilla warfare and semi-permanent conflict. Without stipulating every possible outcome, the main outcomes where recognition has been gained are outlined. For example, the prospect of the emergence of a genuine partnership outcome from a full statutory application is very small.

So to recap, variation in relational outcomes is both possible and probable. However, the typology does not provide for a means by which to account for how the workplace union develops its bargaining agenda and general outlook. Setting aside the influence of differences in union politics and ideology in accounting for variation in these concerns, research in the USA suggests that the type of approach unions take in organising recognition campaigns has a significant influence on the post-recognition period with regard to the nature of the workplace union, membership participation and its bargaining prowess (Markowitz 2000). In a retail operation and a manufacturing plant in the early 1990s, Markowitz found that the process of member participation in the campaign holds out the possibility of creating higher degrees of attachment, consciousness, democracy and self-efficacy thereafter. In the 'union as business' approach, worker/member involvement was limited to gathering the required signatures and union cards to gain recognition under FTO direction. This can be characterised as a top-down, externally dominated approach that severely limited membership involvement and resulted in members seeing the union in the post-recognition period as a business service which has been bought. Thus, it was understood to be the union's job to deliver improvements where the union was an external third party whose professional services had been hired. In essence, union members are de facto consumers. This distant relationship led to the pursuit by the union of what it regarded as the best interests of the membership, but the members disagreed, leading to dissatisfaction. By contrast, the 'union as workers' approach saw workers/members participating in and taking a leading role in campaigning for recognition, as well as helping to determine the bargaining agenda. This resulted in expectations of continuing membership control and democracy after recognition that did not materialise, because the union decided that it could not continue to provide the same level of resources to facilitate the organising. This led to alienation

Table 1.1 Typology of bargaining relationship outcomes

Arena/category	*Partnership*	*Traditional*	*Oppositional*
Voluntary and semi-voluntary	*A* results from a partnership intention and process on the part of both parties. *B* results from the imposition of a partnership intention and process by the stronger party on the other party (equally possibly employer or union). *C* results from the traditional intentions of both parties that are moderated by attitudinal restructuring in the recognition process.	*A* results from a traditional intention and process on the part of both parties, or the imposition of a traditional intention and process by the stronger party on the other. *B* results from the partnership intentions of both parties which are eroded through attitudinal restructuring involving the uncovering of significant conflicts of interests in the recognition process.	*A* results from an unwilling employer, with an intention to resist, being forced to concede recognition by dint of union strength. This unwillingness to recognise continues in the post-recognition period and relations are polarised by the recognition process. This leads to protracted difficulties in producing a procedural agreement and 'surface' or 'bad faith' bargaining or de facto non-recognition or only partial recognition.

Statutory and quasi-statutory	*D* results from a traditional intention and process on the part of the union wherein the inevitability of recognition as a result of union strength leads to a pragmatic but agnostic employer then adopting a partnership perspective in the signing of an agreement and the post-recognition period.	*C* results from a traditional intention and process on the part of the union wherein the experience of the union through attitudinal restructuring leads to an employer with the intention of militant oppositionalism then adopting a traditional perspective in the signing of an agreement and the post-recognition. *D* results from a traditional intention and process on the part of the union wherein the experience of the union through attitudinal restructuring leads to a pragmatic but agnostic employer then adopting a traditional perspective in the signing of an agreement and the post-recognition period.	*B* results from an unwilling employer, with an intention to resist, being forced to concede recognition by dint of union strength, demonstrated through some usage of the statutory procedure. This unwillingness to recognise continues in the post-recognition period and relations are polarised by the recognition process. This leads to protracted difficulties in producing a procedural agreement and 'surface' or 'bad faith' bargaining or de facto non-recognition or partial recognition.

Note
The typology allows for using 'organising for partnership' where a partnership-subscribing union uses organising techniques to compel a resistant employer to accept recognition based on partnership (cf. comment in Danford 2004:199). Examples are Amicus-AEEU, Community (and formerly its major pre-merger constituent, the ISTC) and USDAW.

and divisions amongst the members and ultimately an attempt by some workers to derecognise the union. The former approach could be said to be a 'servicing' approach, while the latter is an 'organising' approach.

Limitation on space in this introductory chapter does not allow for the working into the typology of the processes by which union agendas and outlooks are determined and brought to the bargaining table. Although arguably of less complexity because of the absence of democratic process, neither does space allow for this exercise on the part of the employers. Nonetheless, it is important to acknowledge the significance of the prior processes that have an influence on the two parties' behaviour towards each other.

The practice of collective bargaining after recognition

One of the most obvious points of departure by which to begin examining the outcomes of the new recognition is to take the recognition agreements themselves as a guide to consequent action and behaviour. And here there is likely to be a considerable diversity in what agreements look like. This can be gauged in a number of ways. Of the 1,846 new agreements signed between 6 June 2000 and 31 December 2004, 198 of these have been signed as a result of the statutory provisions (ranging from involving CAC applications onwards to statutory awards) where the CAC recognition awards comprise just pay, hours and holidays. Of all the new recognition agreements signed between 1995–2003, ACAS has been involved in only 27 per cent of these, so that its possible influence in determining the recognition agreement is limited to this tranche. Again, of all the new recognition agreements signed since 1995, some 7 per cent are for partial recognition and only 19 per cent are known to be called partnership agreements. Therefore, the remaining ones are likely to comprise traditional recognition agreements, that is, for full recognition based on bilateral mechanisms, and not partnership agreements. But the term 'traditional' covers a plethora of scopes of bargaining across issues like pay, hours, holidays, redundancy and entitlements as well as rights to information and consultation (see Gall 2003b). But this also means that these agreements are less likely to cover the issues comprising the new bargaining agenda, such as equality, personal development, training, lifelong learning, information disclosure on corporate social responsibility and corporate governance.

Although the majority of the recent recognition agreements have come into existence since 2000 (see Table 1.2) and can be said still to constitute 'new' as per the definition presented above, some limited research has already been conducted into the outcomes of these new agreements, in general terms (see Gall 2001b, 2003c: 92, 2003f, 2004a, 2004c; Gall and McKay 2001:106–7, Moore *et al.* 2004), in call centres (Kelly and Badigannavar 2004: 38–44); in electronics (Findlay and McKinlay 2003a: 123–7); and in transport (Wills 2003: 147). These studies have highlighted the relative successes of unions in gaining improvements in terms and conditions of employment in some cases, *as well as* the considerable difficulties in building and/or maintaining coherent and healthy union organisation and, in particular and following from this, mobilising union resources to gain bargaining objectives in other cases.

Where frustration at lack of union progress has existed, member support has been likely to ebb. Often lack of such progress has been intertwined with low levels of membership participation and extra-workplace union support in the face of employer intransigence. The phenomena of workplace union demobilisation and disorganisation after gaining recognition and following changes in activist personnel, membership turnover and FTO support identified by Kelly and Badigannavar (2004: 38–44) and Wills (2003: 147) can be found elsewhere (Gall 2005b). In some cases, resuscitation has been possible (Gall 2005b). Between 1995 and 2003, a small but significant extent of employer resistance in post-recognition situations has been identified (Gall 2004a). This resistance ranges from cases of using surface bargaining, deploying 'constrained recognition agreements' (Gall and McKay 2001: 106), and utilising competing non-union means of representation. Between 2000 and 2004, industrial disputes comprising ballots for, and the taking of, strikes and industrial action have occurred amongst 24 per cent of the 379 known cases of bargaining outcomes in cases of new recognition agreements (Gall 2005b; see also Gall 2003f, 2004c). This suggests that a strand of employers has been prepared to engage in the utmost opposition to genuine bargaining, that some workplace unions have risen to the challenge facing them in a combative manner and that these union members have exhibited higher expectations than employers were prepared to meet.

This contemporaneous field of study must then be situated in the literature which concerns the inherent nature of trade unionism and collective bargaining under capitalism (see, *inter alia*, Anderson 1967; Beynon 1984; Hyman 1983, 1989; and Kelly 1988). Here the limitations and constraints of trade unionism, and of the conditions under which trade unionism operates, are prioritised in the understanding of the behaviour of trade unionism within systems of industrial relations and collective bargaining. These concern the 'stunted' aspirations of trade unionism, the enforced nature of compromises, and the institutionalisation and bureaucratisation of means and methods of operation within defined arenas of activity. The import of this is that the new recognition agreements should be inserted into our wider and more long-standing understanding of the political economy of trade unionism and collective bargaining. To do otherwise would be ahistorical and non-materialist.

Broadening out to wider issues

The future of trade unionism and the future for trade unionism

In what sense may it be productive to view the new recognition agreements and the trade unionism contained therein as representing or embodying the future of, and for, trade unionism? It is commonly accepted that the strength and success of current 'union revitalisation' projects in Australia, Britain, Canada and the USA, broadly defined as attempts to rejuvenate unions and re-establish their influence in new and traditional sectors of economic activity, is relatively limited. Consequently, the concept of the 'representation gap' (Towers 1997) is still salient. Nevertheless, any progress made in reducing the 'representation gap' and any 'lessons' contained therein may be viewed as providing 'pilot' projects on workplace unionism from which 'best practice' about, and guidance on, future activities can emerge. For others, such as activists, inspiration and models may be provided with the inducement of a demonstration effect. Put bluntly, the quintessential issue here is, do the new recognition agreements contain the seeds of a 'new order' or do they merely reflect the '*ancien régime*'? This is to think in similar terms to the way Fairbrother (2000) posed the issue of the possibility of 'union renewal' developing from the existing terrain of trade unionism. On a different level, if a sufficiently large tapestry of new recognition agreements with successful bargaining outcomes can be created, the potential exists to rejuvenate national unions not only in terms of practice but also resources (members, activists, finance, expertise, etc.).

A slow train coming to a halt?

Progress for trade unions in Britain in gaining further new recognition agreements has waxed and then waned, as Table 1.2 indicates, even though derecognition is now almost unheard of. The number of agreements gained by 2004 had fallen back to below the level of the lift-off achieved in 1999. Broadly speaking, and whilst recognising that the situation is a dynamic one, the primary explanations for this concern four factors. First, unions' using-up of their strongest cases with which to go forward in the voluntary and statutory arenas. Second, the difficulty for unions in replenishing their stocks of strong cases. Third, the decline in the size of the pool of the more union-receptive non-union employers. And fourth, the increasing predominance of the more anti-union employers amongst the remaining milieu of non-union employers (see also Gall 2004b). Indeed, not only has the level of new agreements being signed fallen markedly, but the reliance of unions on the CAC to achieve those that are has also increased and significantly so (last column of Table 1.2). A good example of the overall character and outcome of the recognition campaigns comes from the GMB, which between 1999 and 2001 ran sixty-three recognition campaigns in its Liverpool, North

Table 1.2 New trade union recognition agreements, 1995–2004

Year	*Number of new recognition deals*	*Known numbers covered by new recognition deals (from number of cases*	*Number of cases of derecognition*	*Known numbers covered by derecognition deals (from number of cases)*	*% cases where CAC application used to gain voluntary agreement*	*% of deals which are CAC awards*	*% of new recognition deals where CAC used directly or indirectly*
1995	88	27,404 (64)	66	15,931 (42)	n/a	n/a	n/a
1996	86	26,377 (64)	54	16,851 (46)	n/a	n/a	n/a
1997	109	24,509 (75)	31	4,362 (17)	n/a	n/a	n/a
1998	128	39,820 (68)	7	432 (4)	n/a	n/a	n/a
1999	365	130,446 (265)	11	1,210 (9)	n/a	n/a	n/a
2000	525	156,745 (452)	4	1,700 (3)	0	1	1
2001	685	122,033 (425)	5	108 (1)	3	3	6
2002	388	201,053 (224)	9	760 (3)	5	9	14
2003	259	78,053 (206)	4	100 (1)	8	12	20
2004	239	39,702 (208)	2	340 (2)	6	13	19
Total	2,872	846,142 (2,051)	193	41,794 (128)	n/a	n/a	n/a

Source: Author's own work (see, for example, Gall 2004b for methodology).

Note

By taking the known number of workers covered from 71 per cent of the new agreements and averaging up from this for the remainder, around 1.2 million workers are covered by all the new agreements.

Wales and Irish region. Of these, only seven gained recognition and only four remained as campaigns thereafter (Gall 2003g: 199).

Such a trajectory in gaining new recognition agreements is paralleled by movements in aggregate union membership and aggregate bargaining coverage (Tables 1.3, 1.4, 1.5) in that union effort to offset and end downward movement has been achieved, but this has been small-scale, fragile and

Table 1.3 Union membership and density in Britain, 1997–2004

Year	*Certification Office*	*Labour Force Survey (members in employment)*	*LFS density (%) (by employees in membership)*	*TUC membership*
1997	n/a	6.643m	30.6	6.756m
1998	n/a	6.640m	30.1	6.754m
1999	7.795m	6.622m	29.8	6.764m
2000	7.852m	6.636m	29.7	6.816m
2001	7.898m	6.558m	29.3	6.721m
2002	7.779m	6.577m	29.2	6.685m
2003	7.752m	6.524m	29.3	6.690m
2004	7.735m	6.513m	28.8	6.423m

Sources: Certification Office *Annual Report* (various), Palmer *et al.* 2004:14 and TUC *Annual Directory* (various).

Note

Differences in data-gathering methods can lead to different figures and estimations.

Table 1.4 Union coverage from the Labour Force Survey, 1996–2004

Year	*No. of employees having union members present in workplace*	*% of employees working where a union is present in the workplace*	*No. of employees whose pay is affected by collective agreements*	*% of employees whose pay is affected by collective agreements*
1996	11.144m	50.3	8.243m	37.2
1997	11.105m	48.9	8.198m	36.1
1998	11.130m	48.0	8.177m	35.3
1999	11.439m	48.7	7.274m	36.2
2000	11.684m	49.1	7.269m	36.3
2001	11.611m	48.3	7.215m	35.7
2002	11.769m	48.6	7.273m	35.7
2003	11.759m	48.8	7.236m	36.0
2004	11.664m	48.4	7.225m	35.0

Source: Palmer *et al.* (2004: 34).

Note

The data before and after 1999 is not directly comparable as a result of changes in questions and methods of calculation.

Table 1.5 British Social Attitudes surveys: workers in workplaces with recognition

Year	*1983*	*1984*	*1985*	*1986*	*1987*	*1989*	*1990*	*1991*	*1993*	*1994*	*1995*	*1996*	*1997*	*1998*	*1999*	*2000*	*2001*	*2002*
%	66	63	62	62	62	58	58	58	56	54	55	50	50	49	47	48	47	49

Source: Alex Bryson, Policy Studies Institute, personal email communication, data run from British Social Attitudes surveys, 24 March 2004.

Note
Data unavailable for 1988 and 1992.

possibly temporary. With regard to membership, through increased union recruitment activity within a more favourable environment (economic, legal, political), more workers have joined unions, but the aggregate high point is little higher and is not necessarily permanently so. With regard to bargaining coverage, some year-on-year and sizeable increase has been achieved but the size of the labour force has grown, so reducing proportionate coverage, and some of the increase in bargaining coverage is attributable to the increased size of the public sector workforce.

Workplace and national unionism

Previous critical work on trade unionism in Britain (e.g. Darlington 2002; Fairbrother 2000) has often privileged workplace unionism over national unionism by, *inter alia*, dint of its closeness to grass-roots members and its alleged dynamism resultant from being located at the points of production, distribution and exchange. This is contrasted with national unionism as an organisation-cum-institution and its necessary bureaucratism resulting from routinisation and regularisation at several steps removed from members. Much of this debate concerns identifying the 'way forward' and is predicated to greater or lesser degrees on counterpoising the golden age of vibrant shop steward organisation in manufacturing in the 1960s and 1970s with the malaise within national unions since the early 1980s. However, the period of the last two decades is arguably better viewed in a way which emphasises the mutual interdependence of workplace and national unionism, notwithstanding historical and contemporary tensions, because of the severely weakened capacity of contemporary trade unionism per se in Britain. Amongst the key considerations here are not just depleted union presence and membership, with consequences for unions' resource bases, but the decline in labour movement activism and labour movement activists, mirroring and being bound up with the decline in left-wing organised political activism. Workplace unionism needs national unionism, and vice versa, in a much more tangible and immediate way than for a long time. Workplace unionism needs the financial, ideological and organisational support and coordination of national unionism. Meanwhile, national unionism cannot continue to float nonchalantly above the aggregation of workplace unionism because its strength and credibility are being called into question, and because these ultimately rest on workplace unionism. The key relationship in the union is, arguably, thus a vertical one in this context. Previously, workplace unionism was able to aggregate its power independently by horizontal links, e.g. combine committees and shop steward committees. This suggests that the relationship between workplace and national unionism is a historically contingent one, where the strength of certain processes and forces affecting the relationship vary over time. The implications of this intra-union interdependence suggest that to view contemporary trade unionism through the lenses of, or as in pursuit of, 'organising' or 'servicing' is limited in its analytical usefulness.

Applying mobilisation theory to trade unions

Union Organizing (Gall 2003a) attempted to use mobilisation theory, following Kelly (1998), to help interpret and analyse the processes by which unionisation and recognition campaigns come into being, develop and succeed, particularly in terms of workers developing grievances and constructing and mobilising the necessary power resources to seek redress for grievances vis-à-vis employers. This collection attempts to take this theory forward by developing its usage with regard to understanding union behaviour. Specifically, unions are viewed as sites of social and political struggle (workplace, branch, region, industry, national) where union members, most likely the activists, are often engaged in internal union struggles with fellow members at different levels and sections in the union to develop a consensus, whether proactive or reactive, around not only bargaining agendas but also the *modus operandi* for achieving consequently agreed goals. In this dual-focused struggle, lay union officers have to navigate the currents of fatalism, passivity and individualism amongst members and other activists. Added to this relationship is another factor, namely, the influence of the national union, which may been seen to act as a quasi-separate, quasi-external party to the workplace union. In this, the national union may, broadly speaking, 'help' or 'hinder' the formulation of policy and means by members by virtue of its resources (ideological, financial and organisational) as well as interests (common, compatible, conflicting with those of workplace unionism). Activists and members will seek either to gain the support of the national union in their endeavours and on their terms or, where interests and views clash, ignore or marginalise the influence of the national union. Of course, the genesis of bargaining agendas is not solely the preserve of workplace unionism but also derives from extra-workplace campaigns created by a milieu of activists within national union policy circles. Consequently, compatibility and commonality of interests may ensue between the dichotomies (workplace/extra-workplace, workplace union/national union). Where existing lay officers are long-standing and distanced from the membership, members may need to struggle to get union activists to take up their bargaining agenda. Suffice it to say that, under whatever scenario is envisaged, mobilisations to construct alliances and agendas are necessary. The significance of this discussion is that alongside the union struggle to attain improved conditions of employment vis-à-vis the employer, another more primitive and fundamental (internal union) struggle takes place to determine agenda and *modus operandi*. Without the latter, the former will not take place, although the two may develop in a parallel manner and may influence each other in a mutually conditioning manner. Ultimately, without strength in building union power resources through the primitive struggle, unions will be ineffective in the struggle with employers.

However, there is another significant aspect to the salience of using mobilisation theory to understand trade unionism. This concerns the workplace lay activists and office-holders that possess the *social capital* (Findlay and McKinlay 2002) that is capable of, and necessary for, recruiting, organising, motivating and leading workers and members in the workplace on a day-to-day and immediate basis. The issue for mobilisation theory is to understand how and why these activists emerge and can be developed, and their relationship to FTOs. A number of questions initially arise here. *Inter alia*, and often by contrast with 'ordinary members', do activists have a sharper sense of injustice? Do they have a *Weltanschauung* based on identifying social injustice and seeking its abolition? What are the triggers for moving to become an activist? Are there different qualitative types of activists? And what role do FTOs play in identifying, grooming and developing activists? The decomposition of the social democratic project in Britain and elsewhere means that the most obvious source of existing and potential activists no longer exists to anything like the same degree as previously, either in quantitative or qualitative terms (that is, in terms of motivation). It almost goes without saying that the far left at present and in the foreseeable future cannot fill this in both quantitative (numerical) and qualitative (credibility, ability to relate to) terms. The social movements of anti-globalisation/anti-corporatism/anti-capitalism and for fair trade, social justice, community resources, environmental protectionism, peace and disarmament might in hypothetical terms provide some source of replenishment. But care has to be exercised here in speculating whether they can do so for, amongst many reasons, their social composition is different and collectivism in the workplace is not an important part of their rationale and means. This brief consideration of the role of activists, leaders and internal union political and participative processes stands in the light of the acknowledgement that these areas need to be filled out with mobilisation theory (Gall 1999, 2000b; Kelly 2000).

Finally, and given the variations in dynamics and situational contexts of the social processes of collective bargaining under the new recognition agreements, there is a large, but not infinite, number of possible outcomes. Therefore, diversity and complexity of outcomes must be acknowledged to be the hallmark of the phenomena under study. But it is believed that mobilisation theory offers the best single available means by which to understand this rich diversity with a view to developing an action-based framework for practice.

Chapter content and structure

This opening chapter has sought to provide a base on which the following chapters stand, by establishing and elaborating on the themes that are subsequently examined and discussed. It has provided a number of contentions and scenarios that can be examined. But it has also sought to discuss the salient issues in a generic and stand-alone manner. Consequently, given its wide-ranging scope, not all the issues discussed and questions raised will necessarily be addressed or answered in any great detail (cf. comments in Carter 2004 and Danford 2004). The first four substantive chapters (Chapters 2–5) provide a foundation on which the following five empirical chapters (Chapters 6–10) stand, again in a similar manner to the dual purpose of the Introduction. Thereafter, some of the issues raised are considered in an internationalised context with regard to Australia, Canada and the United States (Chapters 11–13). Lastly, the conclusion (Chapter 14) seeks to bring together the contributions to this volume by considering their implications for the future of the union movement in Britain and other Anglo-Saxon countries.

A number of common themes run through the chapters in this volume. The most obvious one concerns the relationship, on the union side, between the dynamics of the social processes before and after gaining recognition. Here the main issue is how union activity, particularly in relation to its members, prior to union recognition can heavily influence post-recognition intra-union relations and thus also bargaining power. A second revolves around the influence, and interaction, of structure and agency in the struggle for the representation of workers' interests. Here the issue concerns the extent to which human agency (i.e. unions and their members) is able to resist institutional constraints on their behaviour, particularly in pursuit of their interests, or by contrast, influence institutional settings to realise more fully the attainment of their goals. Other themes comprise (a) the relationship of a union with an employer (does a closeness allow a more fruitful bargaining relationship – with attendant outcomes – and does this sustain weakness and generate incorporation?); (b) the relationship of members' expectations of their union with their commitment to, and participation in, that union in furtherance of issues of bargaining power, union renewal and mobilisation; (c) the interlinkage between democratic renewal of unions and the widening of their agendas; and (d) whether the project of union revitalisation and resurgence can be set in train by the actions of leaders in the absence of significant social turmoil to promote advances in workers' consciousness. Suffice it to say that the contributors consider these issues in different ways, sometimes more or less directly, and without settling upon a finalised view. The remaining part of this section discusses the main issues considered by the chapters.

Bryson considers contemporary union effectiveness in Britain, through the experience and perceptions of members and non-members alike, by examining a number of dimensions such as union presence, contact with unions and union bargaining power. He thus examines what unions currently achieve, assesses this and lays out an agenda for what unions should be doing in newly recognised workplaces. Emphasis is laid on neither 'organising' nor 'servicing' but upon measured partnership from a position of strength in order to satisfy a number of contending worker demands and expectations. Utilising survey data, Heery and Simms consider the influence and implications of different regulatory environments and union organising approaches on union presence, organising outcomes and bargaining power. They suggest that there exists a strong connection between the union approach and organisational outcome.

Regardless of the potential specificity of Colgan and Creegan's study of finance sector unionism, what seem to emerge are the considerable difficulties of a particular milieu of a union trying to engage with and mobilise wider internal and external constituencies within the context of deploying (a variant of) union organising. In other words, can a small cog turn a bigger one, generating forward motion? This sobering account focuses attention on the problems that existing trade unionism has and, thus, the problems unions in newly recognised workplaces either face already or will soon face. 'Strength through participation' appears to be the salient nostrum, even though significant and identifiable hurdles exist to this. Underneath the obvious specificity of their case study, Tuckman and Whittall are concerned with the inherent as well as contingent nature of union recognition and collective bargaining under capitalism. On the one hand, both union recognition and collective bargaining are heavily influenced by interests and power relations arising from property resources, ideology, accumulation and economic exchange in terms of the defining nature of capitalism. On the other hand, they are also shaped by management, labour and product markets, general economic conditions and state intervention as contextual influences. From a union orientation, this involves mobilisation, demobilisation, activity, passivity, compromises and an array of strategies and tactics on the union and worker side as well as legitimacy, resources, access and operational space from the employer and state. The foundations on which collective bargaining exist as well the process and outcomes of collective bargaining themselves are shown to be characterised by both dynamism and inertia, and their interactions.

McKay *et al.* demonstrate that ERA has had a considerable and generally deleterious influence on the nature of new recognition agreements and the process by which they have been created. This has then had implications for the outcomes of consequent collective bargaining. Where employer opposition has been significant, ERA was shown to be of little leverage in countering recalcitrance and resistance to representation and bargaining post-recognition. They suggest that a combination of greater independent union leverage through mobilisation and a legal 'duty to bargain' obligation is required to overcome restriction and resistance. Gall examines the fortunes of the National Union of Journalists in the provincial newspaper sector, concluding that the union has made only small steps towards turning *de jure* rights of recognition into de facto rights. Having conceded recognition, the newspaper employers have heavily circumscribed the operation of collective bargaining, often engaging in a blunt and concentrated form of 'surface bargaining'. Strike action has failed to break the impasse, leading to the conclusion that mobilisation per se is not sufficient and that particular types of wider mobilisation are necessary. Gollan examines two different approaches by employers to recognition, one using a non-independent collective body and the other a partnership agreement with a union. In both cases, company council forums were used. The former approach held independent unions at bay through 'exclusion', while the latter approach neutralised the union through 'inclusion'. Echoing the research questions and findings of Markowitz (2000), Simms examines the implications of the dynamics and nature of a specific organising drive for the post-recognition period, concluding that the forces of inertia, inexperience and exhaustion significantly contributed to the establishment of a particular framework for representation and bargaining. Holgate concludes in a similar vein, albeit from studying the organising process in quite different surroundings. She points to variations in vibrancy of member and activist agency and examines their implications, suggesting that the degrees of cohesiveness and collective psyche are significant variables in explaining different outcomes.

Jordan and Bruno, Rose and Griffin deploy data (for which there is no comparator in Britain) on bargaining outcomes of recognition agreements in three quite different environments. In the context of the USA, Jordan and Bruno make a strong case for recognising that it is neither the form of organising nor the form of bargaining that should command our attention but rather the degree and type of mobilisation and consequent points of leverage over the employer. They therefore also point to the relational importance of pre-recognition organising and post-recognition bargaining outcomes, albeit in a heavily contingent manner. Griffin examines the fateful dependency of trade unions in Australia on state-sponsored recognition and collective bargaining. Upon recent changes in the body politic, the importance of this method of regulation of the employment relationship has been usurped with dramatic consequences for unions' bargaining power and political influence. Broadly speaking, Griffin highlights the long-standing conundrum of unions benefiting from, but trying to avoid, dependence upon third-party regulation whilst attempting to generate independent resource. His analysis suggests that union organising is helping to revitalise and renew the union movement there but this is a slow and fragile process from a low base. In contrast, Rose shows that supportive labour law in Canada has had a marked and positive effect on bargaining outcomes. By implication, this indicates that a syndicalist, ultra-left perspective towards state regulation, detectable in the writings of some proponents of union organising in Britain and the USA, is unwarranted. But, of course, such systems of regulation have consequences for authority and power, control and accountability, and independence of interests within trade unions (as Griffin notes, too, in a different way).

Acknowledgement

My thanks are to Ed Heery for commenting on an earlier version of this chapter.

Notes

1 See Heery (2001) for a wider discussion of the value of such comparative work.
2 But, of course, pre-existing forces of tradition and practice may still exist. The moment of gaining recognition is not the moment of the creation of workplace unionism. Rather, the latter will overwhelmingly predate the former, and often by many years.
3 Whilst there has been a debate on the extent of union workplace renewal (e.g. Fairbrother 2000; Gall 1998c, 1999, 2001b; Kelly 2001), the result of this has not undermined the possibility of renewal.

2 Working with dinosaurs?

Union effectiveness in Britain

Alex Bryson

The desire of non-members for union membership, and members' satisfaction with representation by their union, are higher where the union is perceived as an effective organisation capable of delivering better terms and conditions for employees (Bryson 2003). Higher union effectiveness implies higher returns to membership net of costs (Farber and Western 2002). An increase in perceived union effectiveness will increase the individual's propensity to purchase membership (or remain a member) by shifting the individual's perceptions of the benefits relative to the costs. The relative returns to membership are not the only factor determining employees' union-joining behaviour and union membership status. Other factors include social background, parental influence, demographic characteristics, job satisfaction, employer attitudes to unionisation and the availability of other voice mechanisms, and the joining decisions of others in the same workplace. However, the role of union effectiveness has attracted less attention. The literature indicates that unions can help determine their own future through strategic choices (Boxall and Haynes 1997). Broadly speaking, there are two dimensions to the choices currently facing unions. The first concerns how unions engage with their two constituencies, namely employees and employers. The choice is usually characterised as one between 'organising' workers and 'partnership' with the employer. Although the two are not mutually exclusive, there may be a tension between the two approaches, stemming from the priority unions attach to employer objectives. The second dimension relates to the weight unions attach to servicing their current membership versus organising non-members. Most research has focused on the former, what I term, organising effectiveness. What is lacking is research on what makes unions effective in the eyes of employees. This is surprising, given that at a time of declining membership, declining union density and rising never-membership (Bryson and Gomez 2002), unions have an interest in identifying measures which can improve recruitment and retention of union members. Improving employee perceptions of union effectiveness is one such method.

This chapter distinguishes between two types of union effectiveness. The first is organisational effectiveness, a term used to encapsulate those factors that give a union the capacity to represent its members by virtue of its 'healthy' state as an organisation. A 'healthy' union is one that is open and accountable to its membership, is good at communicating with and listening to its members, and understands the business setting in which it operates. The second type of effectiveness is union bargaining effectiveness, namely unions' ability to 'deliver' for employees in improving work and working conditions. In practice, organisational effectiveness may feed through to bargaining effectiveness, while bargaining success may encourage non-members to join, providing a sound basis for improved organisational effectiveness. The data deployed to assess these issues is drawn from the British Worker Representation and Participation Survey 2001 (BWRPS), the Workplace Employee Relations Survey 1998 (WERS) and British Social Attitudes Surveys 1983–2001 (BSAS). The data cannot distinguish new from old union agreements but, judging from the coverage of new agreements in Gall (Chapter 1, this volume), the vast majority of employees would have been covered by older agreements, so this chapter provides a benchmark against which to judge the effectiveness of new agreements.

The chapter considers the meaning of union effectiveness, and identifies features of union structure and behaviour associated with employee perceptions of union organisational effectiveness as well as union features and practices associated with bargaining effectiveness. No attempt is made to identify the direction of causation. The incidence of union practices and conditions conducive to union effectiveness is discussed to establish the nature of the organisational challenge facing unions in their efforts to become more effective.

Recent evidence on union effectiveness

Declining union density since the early 1980s may reflect a downward shift in employee perceptions of union effectiveness. Certainly there is evidence of a decline in employee *desire* for unionisation. Most of the decline during the 1990s was due to declining membership within unionised workplaces. The main reason for this, cited by managerial respondents to the Workplace Employee Relations Survey, was 'a decline in employee support for their union' (Millward *et al.* 2000: 92). This trend may be unrelated to union effectiveness, reflecting instead rising costs of membership, such as stems from increased employer opposition to unionisation. However, Millward *et al.* (2000: 149–51) state that nearly all the decline 'can be attributed to a reduced propensity among employees to join trade unions, even when encouraged to do so [by management]'. In any event, declining density and bargaining coverage where unions continue to operate implies difficulties in unions remaining organisationally effective and, since research shows the importance of union density and bargaining coverage in being able to deliver benefits such as higher wages (Bryson 2002; Forth and Millward 2002), this implies a reduction in bargaining effectiveness.[1]

Difficulties arise in assessing changes in union effectiveness in delivering for employees because so many of the benefits which unionisation confers, such as procedural justice, are not easily measured. There are three measures of the benefits over time that do help gauge how effective unions have been in improving terms and conditions for employees. The first is the membership wage premium. Recent empirical evidence points to a premium that is significantly lower than the 10 per cent typical in earlier studies. However, analyses using consistent data and methods over time suggest that this may be a counter-cyclical effect, as opposed to a secular decline (Blanchflower and Bryson 2003). Furthermore, the decline began with the economic upturn in the mid-1990s, so it cannot account for declining density in the period since 1980. The second measure is the impact unions have on wage inequality. Some maintain that unions remain a 'sword of justice', tackling pay inequality, pay discrimination and low pay by altering procedures governing the contract of employment, and challenging the way employers set pay (Metcalf *et al.* 2001). However, Card *et al.* (2003) suggest that, among men, there has been a decline in the union wage differential between 1983 and 2001, resulting in a smaller union effect on wage inequality. The third measure relates to employees' evaluation of how well unions do their job. In all years since 1983, except 1995 and 1997, BSAS employee respondents in unionised workplaces have been asked: 'On the whole, do you think the union(s)/staff association(s) in your workplace do(es) their job well or not?', with the results shown in Table 2.1.

Table 2.1 shows that those saying 'yes' has remained fairly static at around six in ten employees, while the percentage saying that unions have not done their job well has fallen. It seems that where employees have the opportunity to experience unions first hand, the experience is generally positive. Among members, the figure was 63 per cent in 1983–85 and 65 per cent in 1999–2001, indicating that close to two-thirds of union members are satisfied with their union. This evidence is somewhat contradictory, with some measures pointing to declining union effectiveness, while others do not. A clearer picture about union effectiveness emerges at the end of the period when employees in unionised workplaces are asked what it would be like to work at their workplace if there was no union. Such

Table 2.1 Employee perceptions of how well unions do their job in unionised workplaces, 1983–2001

	1983–85	*1986–89*	*1990–94*	*1995–98*	*1999–2001*
% who say unions do their job well	59	60	58	61	62
% who say unions do not do their job well	37	35	36	32	31
Base	1,574	2,671	2,880	1,478	2,094

a question was asked in 1998 and 2001. In both cases, around half the employees say the workplace would be worse without a union, a proportion rising to two-thirds among members (Table 2.2). Only one in twenty (6 per cent in BWRPS and 4 per cent in BSAS) employees say things would be better in the absence of a union.

However, 37 per cent (BWRPS) and 40 per cent (BSAS) of employees say the union's removal would make no difference. The figure among union members is 29 per cent (BWRPS) and 30 per cent (BSAS). If the perceptions of employees in unionised workplaces are correct, the influence of unions at the workplace is very limited in a substantial minority of cases. Even if the perceptions are inaccurate, the low value attached to unionisation may make employees less inclined to join. So how can unions improve employees' perceptions of their effectiveness in making the workplace a better place to work?

Organisational effectiveness

Table 2.3 shows how employees rate unions on organisational effectiveness. Ratings range quite widely according to the issue addressed, with between four and six in ten tending to give unions a positive rating. Members tend

Table 2.2 Percentage employees who think the workplace would be worse without the union

	All employees	*Current members*	*Ex-members*	*Never-members*
BWRPS	55	67	41	27
BSAS	49	64	33	26

Table 2.3 Employee perceptions of union organisational effectiveness

	All	*Members*
% saying union excellent/good at communicating/ sharing information	46	53
% turning to union first for rights advice	32	47
% saying union excellent/good at being open and accountable to members	53	62
% saying union takes notice of members' problems and complaints	66	72
% agreeing union has too little power	39	43
% agreeing management take the union seriously	45	49
% saying union excellent/good at understanding employer's business	61	66

Sources: BWRPS and WERS98.

to rate unions more highly than non-members, perhaps reflecting union targeting of resources on their membership base. Whether unions should take comfort in these ratings, or treat them as a cause for concern, depends on their aspirations.

The first four items measure union effectiveness in servicing their membership. Higher ratings are correlated with union strength (density, the presence of on-site representatives, perceived power), positive employer attitudes to unionisation, bargaining coverage and locus of bargaining. This is illustrated in Table 2.4 in relation to union responsiveness to members' problems and complaints. Members' perceptions of union responsiveness to their problems and complaints improve with on-site representation and with the extent of contact members have with their representative. Union recognition is of little consequence in this regard unless the union has a representative on site. The union is more able to respond where the representative-to-employee ratio is higher. Responsiveness rises with the union's organisational strength as indicated by the perceived power of the union and union density. Bargaining structures and bargaining coverage are also important: members perceive unions as more responsive where their terms and conditions are subject to collective bargaining and where that bargaining occurs at the workplace. Employer support for unions is also associated with unions being more responsive, perhaps because supportive employers offer the facilities and time that representatives need to function effectively.

Union democracy also influences employee perceptions of union organisational effectiveness. For instance, unions are more likely to be rated 'excellent' or 'good' at being open and accountable to their members where there is an elected representative on site. Fifty-nine per cent of employees give unions this rating where the representative is elected, compared to 51 per cent where the representative is a volunteer and 41 per cent where the representative is chosen by the union leadership. 'Servicing' the membership is a necessary but not a sufficient condition for organisational effectiveness. Unions' influence in the workplace derives largely from their bargaining power, stemming from their ability to disrupt the supply of labour in pursuance of members' interests. It also comes from the union's role as the workers' representative 'voice' in resolving workplace grievances and disputes (Freeman and Medoff 1984). Both sources of influence depend on the union's credibility in claiming to represent the workforce. This has diminished since the 1980s because, even where unions are recognised for bargaining purposes, there has been a decline in union density. These trends are reflected in employees' perceptions of declining union power between 1989 and 1998. However, perhaps surprisingly, by 2001 employee perceptions of union power at the workplace had returned to their level in 1989 (Table 2.5). Employees make a conscious link between union strength and unions' ability to deliver for employees, with 70 per cent of employees in 2001 believing 'strong unions are needed to protect the working conditions and wages of employees'.

Table 2.4 Percentage members who 'agree'/'agree strongly' that the union takes notice of members' problems and complaints

Union, but not recognised	69
Union recognised, no reps	65
Union recognised, external rep only	68
Union recognised, with on-site rep	72
Union recognised, with full-time on-site rep	74
Frequent contact with union rep	87
Occasional contact with union rep	72
Never contact with union rep	57
Don't know of a rep	43
On-site rep covering ≤50 employees	74
On-site rep covering ≥51 employees	70
Power of the union:	
'about right'	85
'too little'	76
Union density:	
1–24%	66
25–49%	69
50–74%	72
75–99%	73
100%	75
Members' pay set through collective bargaining:	
yes	72
no	65
Locus of collective bargaining:	
workplace	75
organisation	74
industry	68
Employer attitude to membership:	
in favour	73
neutral	67
opposed	69
Employee perceptions of employer attitudes towards unions:	
in favour	82
neutral	66
not in favour	66

Source: WERS.

Table 2.5 Union power at the workplace, 1989–2001 (% employees)

	1989	*1998*	*2001*
Far too much	<1	<1	1
Too much	4	2	3
About right	52	45	53
Too little	32	40	33
Far too little	6	7	6
Don't know	6	5	4

Source: BSAS and BWRPS.

The seriousness with which employees think management takes the union is associated with unions' organisational strength, as indicated by recognition, the presence of on-site representation, union density and union power. Bargaining coverage is of little consequence, but the locus of bargaining makes a difference. Where bargaining occurs at industry level, unions are taken more seriously than where bargaining occurs at organisation or workplace level, perhaps because sectoral bargaining survives only in traditional union strongholds. Although there is an association between positive employer attitudes to unionisation and the seriousness with which management takes the union, a quarter of employees in unionised workplaces who think the employer opposes unionisation also think that the employer takes the union seriously. The figure is even higher (42 per cent) when characterising employer opposition using what the employer says at interview. These are likely to be workplaces where the union is particularly strong, and therefore able to demand the serious attention of management, even though management is reluctant.

Bargaining effectiveness

Which aspects of union organisational effectiveness are associated with improvements in employees' working environment? In 2001, employees in unionised workplaces were asked to say how important a set of issues should be for the unions at their workplace and how they rated the union on these (see Table 2.6). The ranking of importance and the union rating follow the same order, suggesting unions are reasonably good at identifying employees' priorities. However, the union ratings vary considerably and are not always high. Ratings of bargaining effectiveness using the full ordinal scales ranging between 'excellent' and 'fail' are highly correlated, with coefficients ranging between 0.41 and 0.59, all significant at a 99 per cent level. This suggests that unions that are good on one dimension tend to be good in others.

These assessments of union bargaining effectiveness relate to employees' work experiences. For instance, where the union is rated as 'excellent'/'good'

Table 2.6 Assessment of issue and union bargaining effectiveness among employees in unionised workplaces

	Very important (%)	*Union excellent/good (%)*
Protection against unfair dismissal	85	63
Promoting equal opportunities	68	62
Winning fair pay increases	61	40
Working with management to improve quality or productivity	58	44
Making work interesting/enjoyable	40	26

Source: BWRPS.

at winning fair pay increases, the percentage of employees who agree that workers at their workplace 'are being paid unfair wages' is half that in workplaces where the union is rated as 'fair', 'poor' or 'a failure' (12 per cent to 25 per cent). Where the union is perceived to be 'excellent'/'good' at protecting workers, the percentage citing unfair disciplining or dismissal as a problem at their workplace is 9 per cent, but rises to 17 per cent where the union is rated 'fair' to 'failure'.

Regression techniques isolate the independent associations between union organisational effectiveness and perceptions of union bargaining effectiveness having controlled for a wide range of other variables. Findings are illustrated using three dependent variables: the traditional core objective of collective bargaining, namely winning fair pay increases and bonuses; an index capturing bargaining effectiveness on non-pecuniary matters; and managerial responsiveness to employees. The importance that employees attach to pay relative, say, to job protection varies with the business cycle (Bryson and McKay 1997:37), but in 2001, 61 per cent of employees in unionised workplaces thought 'setting pay, bonuses or perks' was a 'very important' priority for unions, and another 31 per cent considered it 'important'. Union members attach higher priority to it than non-members, with 69 per cent viewing it as 'very important'. Asked to evaluate unions' performance in 'winning fair pay increases and bonuses', 40 per cent of employees in unionised workplaces rate them as 'excellent' or 'good', as do union members in those workplaces.

Table 2.7 presents three models showing the percentage change in the probability of a union being rated 'excellent' or 'good' at winning fair pay increases and bonuses with changes in union characteristics and behaviour, controlling for personal, job and workplace characteristics. Model 1 shows that this probability increases by 22 per cent where the union is recognised for pay bargaining. The presence of an on-site union representative also increases the probability. Model 2 adds employees' perceptions of union organisational effectiveness. Five of the six measures are statistically significant and the effects are large. For instance, the probability of an employee

Table 2.7 Union effectiveness in winning fair pay increases (%)

	M1	*M2*	*M3*
Union recognised (ref.: union not recognised)	22**	14	12
Type of union representation (ref.: elected representative):			
volunteer	−8	−1	2
chosen by union leadership	2	21*	22*
don't know of a representative	−16**	−5	−5
Power of the union (ref.: too much or about right): too little	–	−18**	−14**
Union–employer relationship (ref.: disagree or neither agree/disagree): management/union work together	–	10*	9
Union excellent or good understanding and knowledge of employer's business (ref.: fair to failure)	–	21**	16**
Union excellent or good at being open and accountable to members (ref.: fair to failure)	–	18**	9
Union excellent or good at sharing information about employer and workplace (ref.: fair to failure)	–	42**	35**
Who to go to first for advice about rights at work (ref.: all other sources): union	–	−6	−8
Index of bargaining effectiveness on non-pecuniary matters	–	–	22**

Source: BWRPS.

Notes
Tables 2.7, 2.8 and 2.9: N = 597. * = significance at a 95 per cent confidence level, ** = significance at a 99 per cent or above confidence level. Models control for a number of variables. See author for further notes on specification.

perceiving the union to be 'excellent'/'good' at winning fair pay is 42 per cent higher where the union is 'excellent' or 'good' at sharing information about the employer and the workplace, relative to a 'like' employee with a union perceived to be less than good at sharing information. Employees do not think that union effectiveness at winning fair pay increases comes at the expense of good relations with management. Indeed, employees view good relations with management as conducive to pay bargaining effectiveness. Where there is a cooperative relationship in which unions and employers work together, the union is perceived by employees to be more effective in winning pay increases. Unions that understand the employer's business are also better negotiators. However, the union can only collaborate with the employer from a position of strength: where the union has 'too little power' the probability of being 'excellent' or 'good' at winning fair pay increases drops by 18 per cent. Union recognition is not significant once these variables are added, suggesting that part of the recognition effect is the result of organisational effectiveness. Model 3 shows that bargaining effectiveness on non-pecuniary issues is associated with effectiveness in pay bargaining too.

The findings are similar when it comes to bargaining effectiveness on non-pecuniary matters (Table 2.8). These indicate the nature of the challenge facing unions: effectiveness at bargaining on pay and non-pay issues is related to fostering relations with the employer, getting to know the employer's business, cultivating relations with employees, ensuring openness and accessibility, having representative structures in place on the ground, and operating from a position of relative power. Shortcomings on any of these fronts can compromise their ability to deliver fair pay increases.

Increasing managerial responsiveness to employees

WERS98 asks employees to rate their workplace managers on managerial responsiveness to employees by 'Keeping people up to date about proposed changes', 'Providing everyone with the chance to comment on proposed changes', 'Responding to suggestions from employees', 'Dealing with work problems you or others may have' and 'Treating employees fairly'. The five-point scales ranging from 'very good' to 'very poor' were rescaled and combined to produce a single index of managerial responsiveness running from −10 ('very poor') to +10 ('very good'). Half the employees working in unionised workplaces score 1 or more on this scale. Table 2.9 identifies aspects of unionisation associated with being in the top half of this distribution (scoring between 1 and 10).

Employees in unionised workplaces view management as most responsive to their needs when they think the union is having an impact on the employer, either because they think the employer takes the union seriously or they think the employer is favourable towards the union. Where employees think the union is not taken seriously by management, or management is perceived not to favour the union, management is viewed as less responsive.

Table 2.8 Union bargaining effectiveness on non-pecuniary matters (%)

	M1	*M2*	*M3*
Union recognised (ref.: union not recognised)	34**	13	11
Type of union representation (ref.: elected representative):			
volunteer	−23**	−9	−10
chosen by union leadership	−25**	−6	−10
don't know of a representative	−22**	0	0
Power of the union (ref.: too much or about right): too little	–	−21**	−18**
Union–employer relationship (ref: disagree or neither agree/disagree): management/union work together	–	12*	10**
Union excellent or good understanding and knowledge of employer's business (ref.: fair to failure)	–	24**	20**
Union excellent or good at being open and accountable to members (ref.: fair to failure)	–	43**	40**
Union excellent or good at sharing information about employer and workplace (ref.: fair to failure)	–	44**	34**
Who to go to first for advice about rights at work (ref.: all other sources): union	–	7	−8
Index of bargaining effectiveness on non-pecuniary matters	–	–	27**

Source: BWRPS.

Note
N = 597.

Table 2.9 Union effectiveness in increasing managerial responsiveness (%)

Arrangements for union membership (ref.: union recognised, no management recommendation or closed shop):	
management strongly recommends union membership	+8**
closed shop	+3
Employee perceptions of management attitudes to unions (ref.: neutral):	
in favour	+20**
not in favour	–28**
Employer attitudes to union membership (ref.: neutral):	
in favour	+1
not in favour	+6
not an issue	+6
Employer would rather consult directly with employees than with unions (ref.: neither agree nor disagree):	
strongly agree	+4
agree	–2
disagree	–3
strongly disagree	–2
Union is 'taken seriously by management' (ref.: neither agree nor disagree):	
strongly agree	+30**
agree	+23**
disagree	–22**
strongly disagree	–41**
Union 'takes notice of members' problems and complaints' (ref.: neither agree nor disagree):	
strongly agree	+18**
agree	+10**
disagree	–19**
strongly disagree	–36**

Source: WERS.

However, the situation is not so clear cut if managers' attitudes to unionisation are taken into account. Managers' support or opposition to unions at the workplace, and their preferences for direct consultation over consultation through unions, had little impact on employee perceptions of managerial responsiveness. What matters is whether the employer actively encourages membership by recommending it to employees. It is this active support of membership, rather than underlying support or opposition, which influences employees' perceptions of managerial responsiveness. The union's organisational effectiveness is also important, as indicated by the sizeable impact of union responsiveness to members' problems and complaints.

Incidence of 'effective' union practices and structures

Table 2.10 shows the incidence of union practices and structures conducive to organisational and bargaining effectiveness. A high percentage of employees remain untouched by the union, either because they are not members or because their terms and conditions are not set by collective bargaining. Where bargaining does occur, it is often above workplace level. In nearly half unionised workplaces (covering 20 per cent of employees in unionised workplaces) there is no on-site lay union representative, suggesting weak workplace organisation. One-third of employees in unionised workplaces say that there is no union on site, and one-quarter say they have never been in contact with a union representative. Unionised employers rarely admit to overt opposition to unions but high percentages are non-committal about unions, and over half prefer direct consultation to working with the union. Only half agree that unions help improve workplace performance, something that substantially improves employers' attitudes to unions (Bryson *et al.* 2004b). Only 2 per cent of employees in unionised workplaces work for an employer who admits to not being in favour of unions, but many more (17 per cent) employees in those workplaces believe that their employer opposes unions. One-third think that the employer does not take the union seriously. Across all these measures, features of unionisation in the private sector indicate that they are less likely to be effective than public sector unions.

Table 2.11 shows similar information taken from the BWRPS 2001. A third of respondents believe unions have too little power at the workplace, despite 78 per cent saying that the union has a representative. In practice, however, only a fifth of employees in unionised workplaces report frequent contact with their representative.

Conclusions

Three major points emerge from the analysis. First, employees are able to discriminate across different dimensions of union effectiveness, with employees rating their union differently according to the issue addressed. That said, aspects of union effectiveness are strongly associated. A broad distinction can be made between organisational effectiveness, concerning the internal workings of the union, and union bargaining effectiveness in delivering better terms and conditions for members. Second, union organisational effectiveness matters in delivering outcomes that are valued by employees. Third, there is room for unions to improve their effectiveness on all fronts, especially in reaching non-members and engaging with employers. Unions cannot do this alone. Employer support for unionisation has an independent, significant effect in raising union effectiveness. Unions, therefore, need the active support of management, something that is often lacking. There are benefits in this for management since, if employees are right, unions are

Table 2.10 Practices and structures influencing union effectiveness in recognised workplaces, 1998 (%)

	Private sector	*Public sector*	*All*
Worker representatives:			
recognition, no representatives	37 (12)	33 (15)	35 (14)
recognition, external rep only	12 (5)	13 (6)	13 (6)
recognition, on-site part-time rep	49 (65)	50 (61)	50 (63)
recognition, on-site full-time rep	3 (18)	4 (18)	3 (18)
Bargaining level: no coverage	30 (16)	8 (7)	18 (12)
Bargaining level: under 50% employees covered	9 (8)	20 (23)	15 (15)
50%> covered: workplace level	11 (26)	1 (4)	5 (16)
50%> covered: organisational level	30 (38)	27 (24)	28 (32)
50%> covered: industry level	19 (11)	44 (40)	33 (25)
Bargaining coverage:			
100%	29 (24)	56 (58)	44 (40)
80–99%	20 (34)	5 (8)	11 (22)
60–79%	8 (14)	8 (4)	8 (9)
40–59%	6 (5)	10 (6)	8 (6)
20–39%	2 (2)	8 (15)	5 (8)
1–19%	6 (5)	6 (4)	6 (4)
Union density:			
1–24%	33 (20)	6 (9)	17 (15)
25–49%	21 (24)	17 (24)	19 (24)
50–74%	25 (22)	31 (27)	28 (25)
75–99%	18 (31)	30 (29)	24 (30)
100%	2 (1)	14 (5)	9 (3)
Closed shop	7 (3)	1 (1)	3 (2)
Strong employer recommendation of membership	10 (6)	28 (21)	20 (13)
Union membership arrangements: neither	83 (91)	71 (78)	77 (85)
Employer response to 'Unions help find ways to improve workplace performance':			
strongly agree	3 (5)	6 (6)	5 (6)
agree	39 (47)	44 (47)	42 (47)
neither agree nor disagree	24 (20)	34 (26)	30 (23)
disagree	30 (25)	13 (18)	20 (22)
strongly disagree	3 (3)	4 (2)	4 (2)
Employer attitude to union membership:			
in favour	45 (49)	74 (75)	61 (61)
not in favour	5 (3)	1 (1)	3 (2)
neutral	50 (48)	25 (24)	36 (36)
not an issue	1 (<1)	0 (0)	0 (<1)

Table 2.10 continued

	Private sector	*Public sector*	*All*
Employer 'would rather consult direct with employees':			
strongly agree	24 (15)	13 (7)	18 (11)
agree	37 (28)	35 (25)	36 (26)
neither agree nor disagree	23 (26)	23 (27)	23 (26)
disagree	14 (28)	28 (35)	22 (31)
strongly disagree	1 (3)	2 (6)	2 (5)
Employee: employer attitude to union membership:			
in favour	(22)	(32)	(27)
neutral	(58)	(55)	(57)
not in favour	(20)	(12)	(17)
Employee: 'Union takes notice of members' issues':			
unaware of the union	(33)	(35)	(34)
strongly agree	(7)	(8)	(8)
agree	(37)	(36)	(37)
neither agree nor disagree	(17)	(16)	(17)
disagree	(4)	(4)	(4)
strongly disagree	(1)	(1)	(1)
Employee: 'Union is taken seriously by management':			
unaware of the union	(34)	(35)	(34)
strongly agree	(5)	(5)	(5)
agree	(28)	(30)	(29)
neither agree nor disagree	(22)	(21)	(21)
disagree	(10)	(7)	(8)
strongly disagree	(3)	(3)	(3)
Amount of employee contact with union/other worker rep:			
frequent	(15)	(10)	(13)
occasional	(38)	(39)	(38)
never	(24)	(29)	(26)
I am the rep	(2)	(2)	(2)
do not know of a rep	(20)	(20)	(20)
'Union makes difference to what it is like to work here':			
strongly agree/agree	(43)	(39)	(41)

Source: WERS.

Note
Figures relate to unionised workplaces with 10> employees. Figures in parentheses are the same figures expressed as a percentage of employees in those workplaces.

Table 2.11 Practices and structures influencing union effectiveness in 2001 (%)

	Private sector	*Public sector*	*All*
Recognition and representation:			
no recognition, no reps	2	1	2
no recognition, on-site reps	7	6	7
recognition, no reps	14	16	15
recognition, rep volunteered	17	16	17
recognition, rep chosen	5	4	5
recognition, rep elected	55	57	56
Employer attitude to unions:			
in favour	31	50	41
neutral	48	39	44
opposed	16	6	11
Contact with rep:			
frequent	23	18	21
occasional	46	47	46
never	29	31	30
respondent is rep	1	1	1
do not know of any rep	2	3	2
Impact on workplace if no union:			
little/lot worse	51	58	55
no different	41	34	37
little/lot better	7	6	6
Power of union at your workplace:			
far too much	1	<1	<1
too much	3	3	3
about right	47	57	52
too little	37	29	33
far too little	8	5	6
don't know	4	6	5
Agree management/unions usually work together	57	56	57
Would turn to union first for advice about rights at work	38	27	32
Union is most useful source of information about employer	4	3	4
Excellent/good at winning fair pay increases and bonuses	37	44	40
Excellent/good at understanding/knowledge of employer's business	56	66	61
Excellent/good at being open and accountable to members	51	56	53
Excellent/good at sharing information about employer	43	47	45
Excellent/good at promoting equal opportunities	56	67	62
Excellent/good at working with management to increase quality and productivity	42	45	44
Excellent/good at making work interesting and enjoyable	23	29	26
Excellent/good at protecting workers against unfair treatment	61	65	63

Source: BWRPS.

most effective in working with the employer to improve productivity where the employer is supportive. Previous research indicates that perceived employer support for unionisation is associated with greater employee trust in management, a valuable commodity for employers in its own right, and a sound basis for partnership (Bryson 2001).

What are the implications of these findings for the future of newly recognised unions? The first is that unions need to improve their bargaining effectiveness as perceived by employees. Employees' ratings of unions in delivering on what they want are pretty low. In many instances, unions are simply not effective because in a sizeable proportion of workplaces they lack effective union representation at local level and a sufficient power base on which to negotiate with employers. That power depends, in part, on the union's ability to control the labour supply and to organise workplaces where rents are available to share. However, it also stems from unions' ability to invest in on-site representational infrastructure. Newly recognised unions will face organising problems if they lack the credible on-site representation and employee support at local level to bargain effectively with the employer. Furthermore, although many unions do deliver on many fronts, they do not always gain credit for their achievements. Unions continue to deliver on a broader agenda in protecting workers from arbitrary employer actions and in effecting a better 'work–life' balance for employees, even if they have some way to go in meeting workers' wider agenda of advancement and progression in the workplace. Newly recognised unions must establish their value in employees' eyes, something that is inherently difficult when so many union benefits are public, rather than private, goods. However, there are ways in which they can promote themselves and 'privatise' the benefits of membership, helping employees make the link between a better workplace and unionisation (Bryson and Gomez 2003).

The second lesson is that unions need to think hard about how they conduct their relationship with the employer. Kaufman (2001: 526) remarked that 'workers do not join unions to help make firms more competitive, they do so to restrict the employer in various ways and gain higher wages and more secure employment'. However, unions have to be sensitive to employers and employer responses to the union to guarantee their own survival and ensure that they maximise the benefits they offer members. There are a number of reasons for this. In working 'with' management, a sensitivity to employer needs and the ability to pass information about the employer to employees are associated with greater bargaining effectiveness, and can thus deliver better terms and conditions for employees. Moreover, union survival is dependent upon careful engagement with employers. Good information about the nature of employers and the constraints under which they operate can help unions establish whether they are operating in a positive-sum environment or whether they face a zero-sum environment vis-à-vis employers' and workers' interests. If an increasingly competitive product market reduces the number of employers with surplus rents to share, new recognition agreements may be located predominantly where there is a zero-sum game. In these situations, unions need to know the employer's business in order to maximise the returns to membership without jeopardising either their institutional position or the employer's survival. Recently, concerns have been expressed about the union wage premium coming at the expense of the union's employment base, as higher wages lead to falling employment in the union sector relative to the non-union sector. Although employers may welcome the lower unit labour costs this might entail, it means that, unless unions can organise in new sectors, they may be operating from a shrinking base, putting themselves out of business. Furthermore, members and non-members alike want harmonious relations with the employer if at all possible (Diamond and Freeman 2001). Employees thus value collaboration between unions and the employer as a good in itself. This may be because they are seeking to maximise their own job satisfaction, something which is strongly associated with perceptions of the employment relations climate at the workplace.

But the danger in being too close to management is that unions can be marginalised by management or be used primarily as an agent for the pursuit of employer-initiated change. For unions to pursue their members' interests, it is vital that the employer takes the union seriously whether the employer is supportive of the union or not. This can only be achieved where the union can resort to sanctions against the employer if necessary. These sanctions require a union power base that is independent of the employer. Partnership without the 'punch' will not work. Where newly recognised unions find that a collaborative relationship with the employer is being bought at the price of low membership or restricted bargaining rights, the union is unlikely to meet members' needs. Employers are more likely to want to deal with unions where they improve financial performance but they are also more likely to favour unionisation where the union has organised a sizeable proportion of the workforce (Bryson *et al.* 2004b). Thus, it would appear, employers are not interested in engaging with weak unions unable to carry the workforce with them. The third lesson, then, is that newly established unions should be pushing the organising agenda well beyond the moment that they have gained recognition. This will not only strengthen their bargaining position, but it is also something that encourages employers to want to engage with them. Of course, this is not to say that unions and workers cannot benefit from adversarialism; they can and do. Union organising often necessitates confrontation with the employer (Kelly 1998) and, in many instances, union organising and bargaining effectiveness are built on adversarialism. In the case of the Canadian Auto Workers, it appears that it is the strategic choice to balance militancy with constructive engagement that has led to that union's bargaining successes (Eaton and Verma 2004). Thus, the 'conflict' versus 'cooperation' dichotomy is a false one. What matters is unions' ability to discern when to 'go militant' and when to engage constructively. This is partly about knowing the employer –

something that is best done through adequate training of on-site representatives – but it also means being aware of the mood of members. This brings us to the fourth lesson for newly recognised unions, namely the importance of listening, and responding, to members' needs and concerns. This brings dividends in terms of bargaining effectiveness. It is achieved by having open, democratic structures. Listening is not only a 'good thing' but, oftentimes, the majority view is the right one (Surowiecki 2004). This is a further rationale for the median voter model that is so often invoked as a guide to union behaviour. These are tough lessons for unions to learn. It seems that bargaining effectiveness requires unions to be organisationally effective on a number of varied fronts and terrain. If they can do all of this, they may at least slow the rate of union decline in Britain.

Acknowledgement

Financial assistance of the Quintin Hogg Trust Fund and TUC is acknowledged, as are the DTI, ESRC, ACAS and PSI as the originators of the 1998 WERS data, and the Data Archive at the University of Essex as the distributor of the data. The usual disclaimers apply.

Note

1 In North America, a similar interplay between unions' organisational health and their effectiveness in attaining bargaining and political goals exists (Rose and Chaison 1996).

3 Union organising under certification law in Britain

Edmund Heery and Melanie Simms

In comparative industrial relations there are two competing traditions of analysis: nomothetic and idiographic (Hyman 2001a: 209). The former seeks to identify regularities in the behaviour of industrial relations actors or in industrial relations outcomes, which correlate with, and are assumed to be caused by, institutions that are common across national cases. Thus, in this tradition, institutions like neo-corporatism, works councils or equality legislation are believed to generate determinate effects independent of context. Those effects, moreover, will vary depending on the degree to which the causal institution is present within each national case. In idiographic analysis, cases are unique and it is regarded as problematic even to identify a common object of study across national boundaries (Locke and Thelen 1995). Common institutions may thus generate diverse effects as they are bent to existing traditions and a nationally specific institutional context. Hyman (2001a: 209) has characterised this idiographic position thus: 'the interrelationship among the elements of each societal ensemble makes these inescapably context-bound, so that every national case must be analysed holistically; by implication there are no variables, only differences'.

This chapter provides a limited test of these competing positions by examining the impact of a recent institutional innovation in Britain on the behaviour of employers and unions and industrial relations outcomes. Since the passage of the ERA, Britain has been covered by a variant of North American certification legislation, under which unions can secure statutory recognition from employers by demonstrating majority employee support. Similar provisions, albeit with significant variations, exist in the USA and in Canada, where they lie at the heart of national systems of collective employment law (Wood and Godard 1999). The analysis here is concerned to establish whether unions' and employers' behaviour in Britain has begun to approximate to that of their North American counterparts in response to a common institutional stimulus. It is also concerned to identify whether there is a common pattern in outcomes of recognition campaigns conducted under certification law in the three countries.

In the literature on Britain's statutory recognition procedure, competing answers have been offered to these questions. Adams (1994, 1995b, 1999) has forcefully argued that certification law does generate determinate effects, that minor variations in the form of certification law are dwarfed by shared features and that the effects of certification law are largely negative when viewed from a labour movement perspective. In Adams' view certification law 'is bad labour policy' because it promotes adversarial industrial relations and has facilitated the de-unionisation of much of the US and Canadian economies. Similar arguments have been developed in some of the investigations of ERA's impact. Gall (2004a) and Moore (2004) described the counter-mobilisation tactics of a minority of employers who have successfully frustrated attempts at unionisation precisely in the manner of their American counterparts. In an overview of membership trends, Metcalf (2004) acknowledged ERA's success in stimulating new organising, but argues that the rate of organising is insufficient to maintain density. In his view, British unions face 'perdition', not resurgence, despite the change in public policy. For Logan (2001), the new law may hasten union decline to levels currently seen in the USA as employers learn to manipulate recognition procedures to remain union-free.

Contrary assessments have been advanced by Wood and Godard (1999) and by Towers (1997: 80–1, 2003). These claim that the recognition law has the potential to generate partnership, not adversarialism, between employers and unions. Towers suggests that the tradition of accepting unions amongst British employers will lead them to react to certification law in a less conflictual manner (see also Brown *et al.* 2001: 190). Some of these themes are echoed in Gall's (2004b) analysis of union recognition since the statutory procedure's introduction. This emphasises the extent of union campaigning, the sharp increase in recognition agreements and the number of workers covered, union success in securing bargaining rights and the relatively favourable response of employers. For Gall and other writers, distinctive British norms for the conduct of industrial relations, plus the interaction of certification law with other legal initiatives stemming from Europe, or with product market changes that promote cooperative industrial relations, mean that certification law will fail to generate convergence with American practice. On this view, the new law gives an opportunity for unions to get recognition and therefore may lead to the growth of a gap between revived British unionism and a US unionism that continues to decline. Thus, a similar law has different effects in different environments.

Research objectives

Our broad objective was to identify whether the pattern of union organising in Britain has converged on North American (US and Canadian) practice since the passage of the ERA. Thus, data have been collected from unions in Britain for comparison with accounts of organising in North America contained in secondary sources. The research focused on the pattern of union responses to ERA, the response of employers to union organising activity and the outcome of organising campaigns. North American certification law has encouraged unions to develop a specialist organising function to handle the discrete task of winning recognition through legally regulated campaigns. Moreover, as union decline has continued in the USA (and has begun to occur in Canada), there has been pressure to bolster this function and allocate increasing resources to organising, with mixed results (Fiorito 2003: 194; Jarley 2002: 223; Yates 2003: 232). The first objective is to establish whether British unions have responded to the ERA in similar fashion, by restructuring their organisations to develop a discrete and expert organising function.

US unions can become engaged in 'internal organising', attempts to maintain density levels where the union shop is outlawed under 'right to work' laws (Jarley 2002: 206). The primary focus of organising in the USA and Canada, however, is to establish a certified presence at previously non-union sites (Murray 2002: 96). The second objective is to ascertain whether 'greenfield organising' of this kind is beginning to predominate in the formal organising policies and activities of British unions. Is it the case that ERA is tilting the focus of organising activity from 'internal' to 'external' organising, from 'in-fill' to 'greenfield' activity?

Union organising methods differ between Canada and the USA, reflecting differences in their respective certification laws. In the USA, unions typically run campaigns aimed at winning a ballot supervised by the National Labor Relations Board (NLRB), though there has been a recent growth of organising outside the NLRB framework (Bronfenbrenner 2003: 34–6, 47; Jordan and Bruno, this volume). In Canada, card-check is the primary method through which certification is achieved (Godard 2004: 28–9). Nevertheless, there are common features. Union organising is largely channelled through formal certification procedures and seeks to exploit the law to secure statutory recognition, and there is a stress on bottom-up organising, through the identification of grievances, which has recently been refined through using a 'union-building' approach by some unions that seek to mobilise worker support through a sophisticated campaign (Bronfenbrenner 1998, 2003; Yates 2000, 2003). Particularly where there is intense employer opposition, such kinds of campaigns may spill beyond the employing organisation and draw upon political, community, consumer and other resources to pressurise employers. The third objective is to see whether British practice matches these features. Is it the case that British unions have made extensive use of statutory procedures to win recognition and that they have adopted 'union-building' tactics, which tend to be described in terms of the 'organising model' in the British context?

In Canada and the USA, the response of employers in the private sector to union organising has been largely hostile (Godard 2004; Towers 2003). Employers have developed a range of tactics to avoid unionisation, defeat organising campaigns and minimise the impact of recognition on their business. They have also established a dedicated resource for fighting recognition, via deploying 'union-busting' consultants (Logan 2002). In examining the response of British employers to recent organising, the emphasis is on establishing the extent of opposition, the nature of opposition and the degree to which it takes the form of 'suppression' and 'substitution', and the frequency with which employers have used consultants to run counter-organising campaigns.

Adams' critique of certification rests on two claims with regard to outcomes. First, certification law has failed in its explicit purpose to promote trade unionism and collective bargaining, for it has served as a vehicle for de-unionisation as employers have learnt to manipulate the legal framework to remain union-free. Second, certification law promotes a narrow and adversarial form of collective bargaining that generates wider inefficiencies within the system of production (Adams 1995a: 174). These arguments cannot be tested fully, given the data collected. However, it is possible to examine the outcomes of recognition campaigns in Britain and assess their success on three dimensions. In the USA and Canada, certification law has generated a pattern in which a significant proportion of campaigns are defeated, where the requirement to prove majority support leads to recognition in small, tightly defined bargaining units, and where successful campaigns are often not translated into collective bargaining (Bronfenbrenner 2003; Kumar and Murray 2003). The final aim of the research is to establish if these outcomes of union organising under certification law are found in Britain: are bargaining units small-scale, are campaigns frequently defeated and do a significant proportion of successful campaigns fail to result in bargaining?

Research methods

Our research here was conducted as part of a larger study of union organising in Britain, which has embraced qualitative and quantitative work and comprised observing policy meetings, conferences and organising activity, interviewing TUC and national union policy makers and organisers, and surveying unions, specialist organisers and union paid officers.[1] While the chapter is informed by all of these, it rests primarily on the survey of union officers conducted in mid-2002. This gathered information on the level of recruitment and recognition activity, the methods used and the nature of the targeted workforce, employer responses to organising and the outcomes of campaigns.

Nearly 600 union officers, employed by nineteen unions responded to the survey (see Table 3.1). It is broadly representative of union officers with a negotiating or recruiting function employed by British unions, though the failure of Amicus, NASUWT and the NUT to respond, and the TGWU's low response rate, should be noted. The vast majority of respondents were generalist officers with a broad responsibility for organising, bargaining and representing workers in company procedures and before tribunals. Most were locally based, though a small percentage (8 per cent) consisted of national officers with a wider remit. A further 13 per cent was made up of

Table 3.1 Union participation and responses to the union officer survey, 2002

Trade union	*Membership 2001*	*Number of officers*	*Number of responses*	*Response rate (%)*
AUT	42,709	10	6	60
BECTU	25,799	30	12	40
Connect	17,616	20	7	35
CSP	32,576	13	7	54
CWU	284,422	32	11	34
Equity	35,246	24	10	42
GMB*	692,147	111	62	56
GPMU	200,676	94	44	47
KFAT	20,650	7	6	86
NATFHE	65,031	43	23	53
NUJ	22,930	9	5	56
PCS	267,644	90	37	41
Prospect	103,942	53	29	55
TGWU	858,804	300	58	19
TSSA	31,494	18	12	67
UCATT	123,000	50	31	62
UNIFI	160,267	108	38	35
UNISON	1,272,470	283	103	36
USDAW	310,222	111	84	76
Total	4,567,645	1,406	585	42

Note

* In the GMB, the survey was restricted to four of the union's constituent regions: Northern, Wales and South West, London and Liverpool, North Wales and Northern Ireland.

specialists who concentrate on recruitment, research and other activities. In a small number of unions (CWU, PCS, UNIFI), seconded lay representatives who take on a role analogous to that of paid officers provided an additional 4 per cent of responses. Responding officers were largely male (76 per cent), overwhelmingly white (98 per cent), and were experienced, with five or more years' service (80 per cent). Just over a third had been educated to degree level. The majority had previously served as workplace representatives (86 per cent) and as union branch officers (75 per cent). Paid union officers have played a central part in developing the union response to ERA (Gall 2004b: 259) and they constitute a group of expert informants on the nature of recent union organising. The survey has provided a unique record of organising in the first three years of the statutory procedure.

Specialisation

Since 1998, a specialist organising function has developed within the TUC and several of its affiliates (Heery *et al.* 2003: 67). An Organising Academy has been established, which has trained some 200 organisers, the majority of whom have been retained in organising positions within the unions. Unions such as GPMU, ISTC, Connect, Prospect, NATFHE, AUT, TSSA and UNISON have invested in employing specialist organisers, and in several cases have created specialist organising units. This represents a major change in internal organisation for some: for GMB London region, ISTC, Connect, Prospect, TSSA, GPMU and UNIFI, organisers now form a substantial component of staff. On this dimension, therefore, there is convergence with North American practice but the degree of specialisation to date has been limited. Across the survey of union officers, only 8 per cent reported that they filled a specialised recruitment or organising position and half of these were concentrated in just two unions (GMB, GPMU). There were no responses from specialist organisers from seven of the nineteen unions. This may reflect survey distribution problems: both USDAW and TGWU have invested in specialist organising staff in recent years but recorded a nil response. Even if there is some underreporting, it remains that dedicated organisers constitute a fairly small minority within unions' paid staff.

A more common response to the new institutional environment, however, may be encouraging generalist officers to spend more time on recruitment and organising. Previous research has tended to play down this aspect of their work and emphasise the barriers to their involvement, particularly in systematic organising activity (Kelly and Heery 1994: 103; Snape 1994, 1995; Watson 1988: 122). The survey suggests that this work may have become more central to the paid officer role. Three-quarters of generalist officers responded that 'recruiting workers into the union [was one of the] most important parts of the job'; more than half reported the same for 'identifying sites for union recruitment', as did 41 and 46 per cent respectively for 'identifying sites where union recognition might be achieved' and 'negotiating new recognition agreements'. Moreover, there was evidence that pressure to engage in organising work was being exerted through internal union management systems. Seventy per cent of generalist officers reported that they set and reviewed 'recruitment/organising objectives', while two-thirds reported that they had received training in recruitment techniques, and 62 per cent reported training in the 'organising model'.

Other research (Gall 2004b: 259) has indicated that the primary responsibility for negotiating new recognition agreements under ERA has fallen on generalist union officers. Our findings reinforce this view. The 436 locally based generalist officer respondents reported involvement in 1,515 recognition campaigns over the previous three years, an average of 3.47 cases per officer. In comparison, the forty-nine specialist organisers reported involvement in 288 campaigns, with a mean campaign score of 5.88. The higher mean for specialists may point to the benefit of functional differentiation: unencumbered by other duties, specialists can concentrate on organising work. Generalist officers cannot do so and those reporting heavy involvement in recruitment and recognition were more likely than other officers to report heavy involvement in collective bargaining and were just as likely to report involvement in member representation. It seems that the response of unions to the organising opportunity presented by ERA has been to intensify the work of existing generalist officers by adding responsibility for recruitment and the seeking of recognition to their duties. The risk here is that saturation will be reached: officer workloads may become excessive, particularly as newly organised workers are likely to be more demanding, and the capacity to continue launching new recognition campaigns will be limited.

While the main burden of response to ERA has fallen on generalist paid officers as a group, this responsibility has not been shared evenly: 29 per cent reported no involvement in recognition campaigns in the previous three years, while 20 per cent reported involvement in ten or more. Heavy involvement in organising, and the number of recognition campaigns in the previous three years, were found to be correlated with several factors. Officers who had been trained and set objectives who reported they had a high level of discretion and who claimed personal commitment to securing recognition were more likely to report involvement in organising work. Union management systems seemed to be effective in directing officers towards organising, supporting the views of what can be called the 'articulation school', that is, writing on unions that stresses the importance of integrating front-line union work with policy development through systems of performance management (Colling and Claydon 2000; Heery 1996; Waddington and Kerr 2000).

Another important factor was the characteristics of the officer's allocation. Greater involvement in organising and recognition was particularly a feature of officers with manufacturing and construction membership responsibility, composed either of operatives or craft and related workers (see also Moore *et al.* 2004: 31). Those reporting less involvement tended to have memberships in public administration with a preponderance of managerial, administrative, professional or clerical workers. It was also the case that officers with responsibility for mainly female memberships reported less organising. Directing generalist paid officers towards organising, not developing a new specialist function, emerges from the research as the primary union response to the new institutional environment created by ERA, but this is particularly evident in the more traditional private sector economy, dominated by male, manual employment.

Targeting

Research indicates a growth of 'greenfield' organising activity by unions in Britain, at least partly in response to the stimulus of ERA (Gall 2003d; Moore *et al.* 2004; Wood *et al.* 2003). Unions have shifted resources into this type of work, as indicated by the figures above on the involvement of officers in recognition campaigns. To further map the pattern of recruitment and organising activity, officers were asked whether a series of groups in the workforce had been chosen as priority targets. The results (see Table 3.2) show the degree to which recruitment by union officers has been directed at 'internal' or 'external' organising under ERA. The main finding is that non-union workers in unionised workplaces continue to be the main target of union recruitment activity. Notwithstanding ERA, in-fill recruitment is the primary focus, for there is considerable scope for recruitment because of low density at many unionised workplaces, unions can rely on lay recruiters and the problems of restricted access and employer opposition are less likely to be encountered where recognition already exists (Bach and Givan 2004: 106; Heery and Simms 2003: 4). The framework of legislation also promotes internal organising. The post-entry closed shop has long been outlawed in Britain, which means that unions have continually to recruit to maintain strength and the emphasis on demonstrating majority support with ERA has arguably reinforced this pressure. Certification law in Britain operates in the context of an 'open shop' and consequently internal organising continues to dominate union recruitment activity.

Table 3.2 also shows that there is a considerable proportion of union officers who accord priority to recruitment at non-union sites. The primary emphasis here is on recruiting workers doing the same jobs as existing union members, what Kelly and Heery (1989: 198) termed 'close expansion'. But a fifth of officers report that it is important to recruit at greenfield sites outside their union's existing job territory, namely 'distant expansion' (Kelly and Heery 1989: 198). The GPMU, for instance, requires all its organisers to have at least one organising target outside of its core paper, packaging and printing territory. The ISTC has embarked on a similarly ambitious attempt to recruit in light manufacturing beyond the metals industries, while TSSA, CWU and Connect have targeted call centre and other workers in the burgeoning ICT and service sectors (see also Findlay and McKinlay

Table 3.2 Recruitment priorities of paid union officers (%)

Employee group	*High*	*Moderate*	*Low*	*None*
Employees in unionised workplaces (in-fill recruitment)	81	14	4	1
Employees of subcontractors or suppliers to unionised workplaces	22	25	32	22
Employees doing the *same* work as existing members but for *non-union employers*	41	26	20	13
Employees doing *different* work from union members for *non-union employers*	21	21	29	29

Note
N = 574–7.

2003b; Taylor and Bain 2003; Wills 2003). These developments often preceded ERA and have been driven by the decline of traditional job territories (Heery *et al.* 2003: 60). But they have been reinforced by ERA, stimulating some convergence with North American organising practice. Targeting workers at non-union sites has become more feasible and undoubtedly more common under the new legislative framework.

Table 3.2 indicates that attempts to expand union membership under ERA have not been uniform across unions. Union officers who prioritised expansion tended to be found in the private sector and to be responsible for male workers in manufacturing, construction and manual employment, particularly skilled manual workers. They were also more likely to report receiving training in recruitment and organising and to describe their job as containing a substantial organising component. It is in the traditional economy and where unions have developed proactive recruitment policies and reshaped officer roles that organising practice has converged most closely with the North American pattern.

Methods

Unions in Britain continue to attach importance to voluntarism, by virtue of a preference for dealing with employers outside the bounds of legal procedure. Of 377 officers who provided details on their latest recognition campaign, only fifty-seven (15 per cent) reported using the CAC. A higher percentage (30 per cent) had involved ACAS in campaigns and just over a quarter (27 per cent) had made use of a balloting procedure to demonstrate member support. It remains, though, that in most cases union officers seeking recognition have sought a voluntary deal and have not resorted to direct legal pressure. In the first years of ERA there has been only limited convergence with the North American pattern of channelling organising through statutory certification procedures (see also Oxenbridge *et al.* 2003: 324; Wood *et al.* 2003: 140). Although direct use of the statutory procedure has been limited, it has provided an important context, encouraging unions to invest in organising, knowing that legal pressure can be exerted if needed. Table 3.3 shows the varying frequency of union officers using different recruitment and organising techniques. About half have used the statutory recognition procedure at least occasionally to try to secure recognition and promote recruitment. Another component of ERA, the accompaniment provisions in serious disciplinary cases, has been used to gain access for recruitment by about 40 per cent of officers (see also Oxenbridge *et al.* 2003: 321). Unions may retain a preference for voluntarism but, clearly, recent organising activity has developed in the shadow of the law.

Table 3.3 also shows the frequency of usage of using 'union-building' techniques including mapping the workplace, relying on activists to engage in direct recruitment, building membership around rank-and-file organising committees and using frictional issues current in the workplace to attract

Table 3.3 Recruitment methods of paid union officers (%)

Recruitment and organising method	*Used frequently*	*Used occasionally*	*Used rarely or not at all*
Use of statutory recognition procedure to secure voluntary recognition	22	27	51
Use of statutory recognition procedure to encourage recruitment	21	30	49
Use of accompaniment provisions of ERA to gain access for recruitment	17	24	59
Rating of potential members in terms of likelihood of joining the union (mapping)	37	34	29
Person-to-person recruitment at the workplace	74	17	9
Reliance on principle of 'like recruits like' in recruitment activity	34	39	27
House calls to non-members' homes	1	5	95
Direct recruitment by activists at their place of work	88	10	2
Direct recruitment by activists at other workplaces	32	37	31
Setting up an 'organising committee' within targeted workplaces	39	36	25
Identification of grievances as a basis for organising	44	40	16
Link-up with community organisations (e.g. ethnic, religious, local associations)	3	14	83
Corporate campaigning (e.g. contacting shareholders to encourage recognition)	2	7	91
Union presence at employee induction	52	31	17
Employer encouragement of union joining	30	40	30
Use of 'partnership' agreements with employers to help recruitment	26	33	41
Offer of 'partnership' to employers to gain recognition	22	27	51

Note
N = 572–5.

workers. In cases where there is significant employer opposition, union-building may also embrace use of house-calling and attempts to build support amongst community groups and other stakeholders. The findings indicate fairly widespread but uneven take-up of these methods. The involvement of activists in recruitment activity is very common but heavy reliance on organising committees, workplace mapping and issue-based organising is reported by 34 to 40 per cent of officers. The other elements of union-building, which extend organising beyond the workplace, such as house calls, community coalitions and corporate campaigning, are reported by only small minorities. There is evidence of quite widespread experimenting with an 'organising model' in Britain therefore, but it is far from ubiquitous, and concentrated on those techniques that are most easily integrated with the existing tradition of workplace unionism. Moreover, use of these methods represents a deliberate attempt to learn from North American (and Australian) unions as much as a direct consequence of ERA (Heery *et al*. 2000c: 1002–3).

Table 3.3 also points to fairly widespread use of employer-supported recruitment. It is common for officers to recruit at employee induction and not unusual for employers to recommend membership. Moreover, a quarter of officers have frequently used an existing partnership agreement with an employer to help recruitment, and a fifth have offered a partnership in order to gain recognition. Thus, no one method has dominated union practice since the ERA. There is evidence of unions using a variety of techniques, with reliance on employers being strongly present alongside use of the law and more adversarial union-building. Experiments with labour–management partnership are not unknown in North America (Frost 2001b) and it is quite common for unions there to seek 'neutrality agreements', which oblige employers to refrain from opposition when the union seeks to extend organisation to new sites (Fiorito 2003: 202). Nevertheless, the relatively high incidence of employer-supported or 'collaborative' organising seen in Britain is probably distinctive when viewed from North America. Once again, there is only limited evidence of convergence, with union organisers in Britain making use of multiple methods, and experiments with 'partnership' lying alongside those with the 'organising model' and use of statutory procedures (Heery *et al*. 2003: 66).

To analyse variation in the pattern in Table 3.3, statistically reliable scales were created from the clusters of items describing officers' use of statutory procedures, organising methods and employer support. A familiar pattern emerged. Officers reporting frequent use of all three types of technique were more likely to report training and working towards set organising objectives. Those using organising methods and statutory procedures tended to have a membership concentrated amongst skilled manual workers in manufacturing. Those using partnership, in contrast, tended to have a membership in retail or public administration. Officers responsible for other parts of the public sector and for a managerial and professional membership were distinctive in their relative lack of use of any of these methods of recruitment. Public service officers, in particular, were significantly less likely to report use of statutory procedures to recruit or seek recognition. The final significant feature of variation was that there was a positive association between all of the three composite measures of organising: those officers reporting frequent use of union-building techniques were more likely to report use of employer-supported recruitment and statutory procedures, the latter association being particularly marked. This points to the pragmatism (or opportunism) of recruitment and organising practice in British unions (Heery *et al.* 2003: 66) and underlines the fact that no single approach has emerged as dominant under ERA.

Employer responses

Table 3.4 shows the pattern of employer responses to the latest attempts to secure recognition in which union officers had been involved. The most frequently reported responses were positive: in two-thirds of campaigns, employers provided access to recruit, and in 44 per cent facilities, to the union, with employers allowing a union presence at induction in about a

Table 3.4 Employer responses to recognition campaigns

Employer response	*Percentage of campaigns*
Supportive responses	
Provision of employee list to help recruitment	24
Allowing union organisers access to the workplace	63
Encouraging employees to join the union	23
Permitting union presence at induction	26
Offering facilities for union recruitment	44
Negative responses	
Denying union organisers access to the workplace	29
Discouraging employees from joining the union	35
Distributing anti-union literature	17
Using managers to brief against the union	34
Seeking to delay submission to CAC, e.g. contesting bargaining unit	20
Threatening closure or relocation	18
Victimisation of activists (short of dismissal)	19
Dismissal of union activists	10
Resolving employee grievances to reduce demand for union	26
Improving pay and conditions to reduce demand for membership	15
Setting up/strengthening alternative channels of worker participation to substitute for union	38
Use of a management consultant to advise on avoiding recognition	21
Inviting another union to recruit or seek recognition	16

quarter of cases, recommending that workers join, and providing lists of employees. This pattern of reported employer response diverges sharply from that of employers in North America (Godard 2004). While not all North American employers are hostile to organising and some lend assistance (Safford and Locke 2001: 13), the British pattern appears distinctive and provides support for those who have argued that the experience of British certification law may not converge on the North American pattern because of the more favourable orientation of employers towards unions (Towers 1997).

Nonetheless, not all reported employer responses were positive and Table 3.4 shows that there has been resistance to organising. In about a third of campaigns, the employer was reported to have discouraged joining, held anti-union briefings and denied access to the workforce. More vehement attempts at suppression, equivalent to the use of unfair labour practices in North America, and involving threats of closure, sackings and victimisation, were less common, though still featured in between 10 and 20 per cent of campaigns. A more frequent response was substitution, particularly by resolving grievances, reported in a quarter of cases, and setting up or strengthening alternative channels of participation, reported in more than a third of cases. In a fifth of cases the employer was reported to have hired a consultant for advice on union avoidance. In some campaigns this service has been provided by US union-busters, either acting independently or in concert with UK-based law firms (see also Logan 2001: 95–7). In a similar percentage of cases, the employer had resorted to delaying tactics, designed to frustrate a submission under the statutory procedure (cf. Moore 2004). The final response of employers, seen in 16 per cent of campaigns, was to invite another, rival union to seek recognition. There has been intense competition between unions to secure recognition at some companies (Oxenbridge *et al.* 2003: 323) and this has allowed managers to play unions off against each other and select the recognition partner that is most cooperative. This response can be viewed as an attempt by the employer to determine the character of the recognised union where recognition itself cannot be avoided (Gall 2004a: 37).

In a proportion of recent recognition campaigns, therefore, the employer had acted in a manner that is reported as typical in North America. The central finding, however, is that hostile employer tactics are encountered less frequently in Britain. Bronfenbrenner and Juravich's (1998: 22–3) analysis of employer tactics in 165 NLRB elections in 1994 provides a point of comparison (see also Rundle 1998). They found that in 87 per cent of elections an outside consultant was used, in 76 per cent there were supervisor briefings, in two-thirds there were five or more captive audience meetings, in 28 per cent there were discharges for union activity and in 24 per cent there were wage increases. The only tactic for which there is broadly equivalent data and which was used more frequently in Britain was use of a non-union channel of participation. An institution of this kind existed or had been created by the employer in 34 per cent of USA cases, compared with 38 per cent in Britain. This comparison suggests that British employers are significantly less likely than their American counterparts to campaign against union recognition and that when they do they are more likely to adopt a strategy of substitution.

Table 3.5 shows how the pattern of employer response has varied across campaigns. It shows the standardised mean positive and negative responses of employers for the entire sample and for different sectors, occupations and union tactics. The data underlines that positive responses have been more frequent than negative but show considerable variation. A strong negative response has been a feature of manufacturing and construction and campaigns directed at craft workers and machine operatives. Employers have been most robust, and have used a greater number of oppositional tactics, in the traditional, private sector economy. A strong positive response, in contrast, has been seen in the voluntary and public sectors and in business services, many of which are provided to public sector organisations and employ an outsourced public service workforce. They are also a feature of non-manual employment and of campaigns where the main target group are personal and protective service workers. The evidence demonstrates that the

Table 3.5 Variation in employer responses to organising

Campaigns	*Number of cases*	*Mean positive response*	*Mean negative response*
All campaigns	378, 373	0.36	0.23
Sector			
Manufacturing	122	0.28	0.34
Construction	19	0.40	0.31
Media	18, 17	0.20	0.24
Financial services	22	0.27	0.23
Healthcare	43	0.39	0.16
Voluntary sector	18, 16	0.48	0.14
Business services	18	0.54	0.12
Public administration	27	0.47	0.10
Occupation			
Craft workers	37	0.27	0.38
Machine operatives	96	0.34	0.30
Drivers & warehouse	42	0.40	0.19
Personal service workers	54, 52	0.41	0.17
Clerical workers	47, 45	0.37	0.15
Managerial & professional	47	0.41	0.10
Union methods			
High use of union-building	119, 117	0.32	0.32
High use of legal procedure	107, 105	0.30	0.31
High use of partnership	106, 105	0.49	0.18

public sector continues to provide a more favourable environment for unions, which echoes the US pattern (Juravich and Bronfenbrenner 1998: 266). It demonstrates, too, that the public sector casts a positive shadow that influences the behaviour of other employers who come within its ambit.

Table 3.5 also shows an association between union tactics and employer responses. Whilst this data refers to the methods that are used frequently by the union officer, not to a specific campaign, the findings are instructive and suggest that employer opposition is associated with use of union-building techniques and with use of legal procedures. A more positive employer response, in contrast, is associated with collaborative methods. It is not possible, however, to say whether the employer or the union plays the major part in initiating this association. In some cases employers may react adversely to an aggressive organising campaign, while in others unions may opt for aggressive tactics or threaten resort to the statutory procedure where the employer is resistant. Most likely there is an interaction, with the tactics of the union and the employer feeding off one another, generating an adversarial campaign in some cases but a more collaborative one in others.

Campaign outcomes

The pattern of organising outcomes that is typical of the USA is for certification to be achieved in narrowly defined, relatively small bargaining units and for many campaigns (more than 50 per cent) to result either in an election defeat or in a failure to establish collective bargaining even when there is majority worker support (Bronfenbrenner and Juravich 1998: 22; Logan 2001: 66). The situation is not quite so grim in Canada, where a more favourable legal certification framework raises union success rates, but even here a significant number of campaigns are defeated by employers (Godard 2004). An additional feature of union organising under certification law claimed by some commentators (Markowitz 2000; Jordan and Bruno this volume) is a relatively shallow form of workplace organisation: the focus on winning majority support as quickly as possible can make it difficult to develop lay activists, with the result that, post-certification, the union loses its effectiveness.

To what extent is this pattern being reproduced in Britain under ERA? The average size of the bargaining group in the 361 campaigns for which union officers provided information was 417, substantially higher than that recorded for NLRB elections in the USA, which by the end of the 1990s was well below 100 workers (Logan 2001: 66). However, the British data are affected by a small number of very large campaigns: 8 per cent were targeted at bargaining groups of 1,000 or more workers. Just under half (47 per cent) were targeted at 100 workers or fewer, and three-quarters were targeted at 300 workers or fewer. Most recognition campaigns in Britain, therefore, are directed at relatively small groups of workers, typically concentrated in a single enterprise or at a single worksite, though this pattern is complicated by a small number of very large campaigns (see also Gall 2004b: 260).

Other campaign outcomes are summarised in Table 3.6, which provides separate assessments for campaigns that officers regarded as complete and those that were still continuing at the time of the survey. The level of recorded success seems relatively high, particularly in relation to USA evidence. Officers claimed that nine out of ten completed campaigns had resulted in recognition and that, in 70 per cent of these, majority membership had been achieved in the bargaining unit (see also Moore *et al.* 2004: 28). Even in the continuing campaigns, a fifth had resulted in recognition, and in just under half there was majority membership. But not all the evidence is positive: in more than a third of campaigns no workplace branch or equivalent structure had been created, suggesting that recognition rests on a relatively shallow foundation in many cases. In more than half the completed campaigns, moreover, it was reported that a collective agreement on pay and conditions had not been negotiated. The negotiation of such agreements may be pending in some cases: officers were asked to provide information on the most recent recognition campaign in which they had been involved. Nevertheless, the evidence provides prima facie evidence for a relatively weak form of recognition in a significant proportion of recent campaigns. It is probable that the data do not reflect continuing employer resistance and a failure to negotiate a first contract, as is often the case in the USA. It is more likely in the British context that recognition has been restricted in a significant proportion of cases to consultation and has not embraced collective bargaining, at least in a strong form. Such a conclusion would fit with evidence that a significant recent trend in British industrial relations is the displacement of bargaining by consultation in mature unionised environments (Oxenbridge *et al.* 2003: 328–40; cf. Moore *et al.* 2004).

Table 3.6 Outcomes of recognition campaigns (%)

Campaign outcome	*Continuing campaigns* N = *129–33*	*Completed campaigns* N = *240–4*	*All campaigns* N = *370–8*
Recognition was not achieved and the campaign was abandoned	7	9	8
A workplace union branch or equivalent was set up	54	61	59
Membership of more than 50 per cent of the target workforce was achieved	45	70	61
The employer granted recognition	21	89	65
A first agreement on pay and conditions has been signed	19	48	38

Table 3.7 shows the pattern of variation in organising outcomes for completed campaigns, providing information on the rate of recognition and whether or not a strong or weak form of recognition has been achieved, the former defined by the existence of recognition plus majority membership and the negotiation of a first agreement, and the latter by the absence of these other two conditions. Table 3.7 also shows the frequency with which campaigns have been abandoned without recognition having been achieved.

Table 3.7 Variation in organising outcomes (%)

	Number of cases	*Union recognised*	*Strong recognition*	*Weak recognition*	*Campaign abandoned*
All completed campaigns	214–44	89	40	16	9
Sector					
Manufacturing	68–76	90	51	12	8
Construction	11–15	80	54	0	20
Media	11–13	92	33	9	0
Financial services	10–16	63	6	50	25
Business services	15	100	53	7	0
Public administration	17	100	41	18	0
Healthcare	22–26	85	15	23	0
Voluntary sector	12	100	17	33	0
Occupation					
Professionals & managers	29–30	97	27	24	0
Clerical workers	27–29	93	38	19	7
Craft workers	23–25	96	61	0	8
Operatives	55–66	83	52	13	11
Personal & protective service workers	32–38	90	22	13	11
Drivers & warehouse	26–28	93	50	19	7
Union methods					
High use of union-building	46–63	96	49	17	5
High use of legal procedure	59–66	89	47	14	3
High use of partnership	62–71	88	42	18	7
Employer methods					
Strong positive response	64–65	99	55	19	1
Strong negative response	27–49	69	42	7	25
Third-party involvement					
ACAS mediation	63–70	91	49	6	6
CAC procedure	28–37	76	44	7	8

Note
Strong recognition means that the union has been recognised, membership of more than 50 per cent has been attained and a first agreement has been negotiated. Where there is weak recognition the membership and bargaining outcomes have not been attained.

With regard to sector, there is a notable difference in the pattern of recognition between the public and voluntary sectors and the private sector. In public administration, healthcare and not-for-profit sectors, the rate of recognition is high and there are no cases of abandonment, but there is a higher proportion of cases with weak recognition. In the private sector, manufacturing and business services stand out for their record of strong recognition, while construction and financial services have the highest rates of abandonment, which has led to lower-than-average rates of recognition. There are also notable differences between occupational groups. Strong recognition agreements are a feature of manual employment, and particularly craft work, while personal service and white-collar workers tend to have weaker recognition arrangements.

Table 3.7 also gives some indication of the factors that lie beneath these sectoral and occupational patterns. It seems that union tactics have a rather modest effect on outcomes, although again the weakness of the measures used must be emphasised. The involvement of third parties also seems to have a limited effect, though it is notable that the rate of recognition is significantly lower where cases are taken to the CAC, underlining the fact that this can be a tactic of last resort for the union (Wood *et al.* 2003: 140). What stands out as the most significant influence on recognition outcomes is employer behaviour. Where employers are supportive of the campaign, the success rate is higher, there are virtually no abandoned cases and there is a higher-than-average number of strong recognition arrangements. However, there is also a substantial number of weak recognition cases, suggesting that employer support allows unions to be established where they lack membership and exert relatively limited influence over employer behaviour. In a proportion of cases, it seems that employers have cooperated with the recognition of relatively weak, and perhaps compliant, unions (cf. Heery *et al.* 2004). Employer resistance can also have a marked effect, though again in complex fashion. The rate of recognition is reduced and the rate of abandonment increased where the employer uses five or more anti-union tactics in the course of a campaign. Where recognition is attained in the face of opposition, however, it tends to be relatively robust, with few cases of weak recognition. The evidence here is arguably encouraging for unions. Employer counter-mobilisation can frustrate attempts to organise workers but it is not an absolutely determining factor and successful union recognition can be established even when the initial response of employers is hostile (cf. Bronfenbrenner 1998).

Conclusions

This chapter sought to gauge whether the pattern of union organising in Britain is converging on that seen in North America under the shadow of the ERA. The results are complex and point to limited convergence alongside continuing British peculiarities. British unions have created specialist organising units, experimented with US organising techniques and become more focused on greenfield campaigning. A proportion of employers has reacted so as to counter union efforts and turned to management consultants to help them do so. A North American pattern of small bargaining units and a failure to convert recognition into bargaining is also apparent. These are minority trends, however. The bulk of organising in Britain is carried out through the established hierarchy of officers and lay representatives, is directed at maintaining and increasing density at established sites, uses a variety, not a particular method and avoids legal entanglement. Where greenfield campaigns are attempted, employers are often receptive and most campaigns reach a successful conclusion. Moreover, the pattern of union response, employer reaction and resulting outcomes has been variable across sectors and occupations. Despite a common framework of collective employment law, union organising in Britain is variable and has failed to converge on a common format. It is in the traditional, private sector economy, characterised by male, manual employment that organising practice most closely resembles the stereotypical certification pattern. What conclusions can be drawn from this?

First, supporting the arguments of the idiographic school, certification law in Britain has interacted with other features of the institutional framework. The pattern of union activity reflects the fact that certification law in Britain exists alongside the open shop, leading unions to prioritise in-fill recruitment, and the receptiveness of employers may reflect its interaction with EU law on worker participation. Given the pressures emanating from the latter to establish a system of collective consultation, it may be efficient for employers to recognise unions when they become active (Oxenbridge *et al.* 2003: 328). Even the nature of union avoidance in Britain, with its emphasis on substitution, may derive partly from the European legal framework. Second, the pattern also reflects the force of tradition: the relatively positive employer response is surely path-dependent in the manner suggested by Towers (1997). Other features of organising in Britain are also probably path-dependent, whether it is the relatively adversarial interaction between unions and employers in manufacturing and construction or the more collaborative relationship visible in retail, public service and the voluntary sector. Unions and employers have brought their established modes of behaviour to the new law. They have not simply adapted to its requirements.

Third, differences are to be expected because certification in North America is mature, but in Britain it is infantile. Kochan (2003: 174) argued that the pattern of union organising apparent in Britain today has strong parallels with that seen in the USA in the immediate aftermath of the passage of the NLRA, including employer receptiveness and voluntary recognition. What this suggests is that British organising practice may grow to resemble that in North America as employers learn to use the framework of certification law to frustrate attempts at unionisation. There are already some signs of this, including an increase in the proportion of recognition cases being taken to the CAC. However, we believe that while there may be some greater convergence over time, this is unlikely to be complete and distinctive features of organising in Britain will remain for the reasons already given: the interaction of certification with other features of the environment and indigenous tradition. Fourth, even when organising has converged with American practice this may not be a result of the unmediated influence of the law. British unions have attempted to learn from their US counterparts and apply union-building techniques to recognition campaigns. For their part, some employers have looked to American counter-organising, with US consultants acting as a conduit for US union-busting techniques (Heery and Simms 2003). To use the language of organisational theory, isomorphism in union organising may reflect mimetic as much as coercive pressures (DiMaggio and Powell 1983).

Finally, while certification law in Britain has not reproduced a North American pattern of behaviour and outcomes, there is also some evidence of convergence alongside distinctiveness. On this basis we believe a purely idiographic account of certification law in Britain is invalid. Certification law comprises a class that exhibits 'bounded variability' (Rose 1991: 447). It displays common features and generates some common effects in the countries where it operates: unions in Britain, Canada and the USA have adapted their organisations and developed tactics to exploit the opportunities in the law. But certification law varies both in content and in terms of the context in which it operates. As a consequence there is a range of practice and outcomes where it applies. In Britain, we believe, the content of certification law is more favourable to unions than it is in the USA (Wood and Godard 1999), while the context in which it operates is more favourable to unions than in Canada. As a consequence, it is a system of law that may prove more beneficial to British unions than to unions elsewhere, albeit that the scale of the positive effect is modest and insufficient to reverse union decline. What this suggests is that comparative industrial relations should combine elements of the nomothetic and idiographic traditions, using the former to identify the boundaries of particular classes and the latter to describe and account for variability within those bounds. Thus, 'In the process we may attain a deeper and more sensitive understanding of difference in similarity and similarity in difference' (Hyman 2001a: 210).

Note

1 The research was funded primarily by Cardiff University, which was later supplemented by a small TUC grant. The 2002 survey was funded by the ESRC (Award No. L212252023). We are grateful to these providers and to the union personnel who supplied us with information. Any errors of fact or interpretation are our responsibility alone.

4 Organising and diversity in banking and insurance

Reflections on the approach of UNIFI

Fiona Colgan and Chris Creegan

Following UNIFI's creation in 1999, a considerable emphasis has been placed on organising within the new union's agenda. Faced with declining membership, including lower density in the major banks, UNIFI urgently sought to recruit members in non-traditional areas, and committed itself to organising 'in order to build the democratic structure of the union and more effectively combine its twin resources, lay and paid, into the growth and development of the union' (UNIFI 2000a). Whilst UNIFI's creation brought opportunities for reflection and innovation about growth and sustainability in the context of membership losses, the effects of business reorganisation and globalisation created imperatives to develop and implement a strategy for renewal. This turbulent context, and UNIFI's attempt to marry both 'organising' and 'partnership' approaches, provides an interesting case study given recent debate on union renewal in Britain (see, for example, Ackers and Payne 1998; Heery 2002; Kelly 1999; Wills 2004a). This chapter examines the implementation of organising in UNIFI during 2000–2, first at national level and second at the workplace level, where the latter include, in UNIFI's view, the 'new' fastest-growing banking workplaces, namely contact (call) centres. However, we focus in particular on the extent to which UNIFI has sought to integrate a diversity perspective into its approach to organising, and the efficacy of doing so, for previous studies on mobilisation and organising principles have largely neglected the diversity perspective (Mantsios 1998; Wajcman 2000; cf. Holgate 2004b). Whilst Kelly (1998) has questioned whether so-called 'new' movements and identities will strengthen or reinforce trade unionism, Colgan and Ledwith (2002a) emphasised their significance in the search for new union democracies and union renewal, and Heery *et al.* (2000c) have suggested there may be evidence that the organising and equality agendas are developing in tandem either because underrepresented groups promote organising and/or because unions bolster their equality agendas to attract 'non-traditional' members.

UNIFI and the finance sector

UNIFI, formed from the merging of the Banking Insurance and Finance Union (BIFU), UNIFI (Barclays Staff Association) and the NatWest Staff Association, was born out of their recognition of the logic of ending 'divided recognition' and the need to 'widen representation' and improve membership support and services in a finance sector undergoing considerable change (UNIFI 1999a; Morris *et al.* 2001).[1] Gall (1997) saw the merger and membership growth as evidence that finance workers, particularly bank workers, were becoming more 'unionate'. However, he cautioned against arguments that they were becoming 'militant', recognising that there remained an uneven propensity towards trade unionism and collective action amongst finance workers. UNIFI's structure operated principally at four levels: national, regional, company and branch. At national level, the principal body was the National Executive Committee, comprised of a mix of regional, company and equality representatives in addition to the union's principal FTOs. There were eight regional councils which met four times annually and were attended primarily by branch representatives. There were fourteen national company committees, some responsible for single companies and others for groups of companies. There were 236 branches and these were a mix of institutional (trade group/company) and geographic (general). The union also had provision for the establishment of 'workplace committees', though these were not explicitly referred to in the rulebook.

The combined effects of economic recession, financial deregulation and the spread of new technology and telephone banking since the 1980s have, under a highly employer-determined regime, led to significant cost cutting, organisational restructuring, a harsher employee relations climate and job losses in the finance industry. In 1990, employment in 'financial intermediation' (banking, building societies, life insurance and other insurance activities) was 1.055 million, falling to a low point of 0.971 million in 1996, before rising again to 0.996 million in 2000 (UNIFI 2001a). Women made up just over half the workforce (50.7 per cent) in the sector (UNIFI 2001b) and UNIFI (2001c) estimated that as many as a third of employees might be under the age of thirty. In 2001, 80 per cent of UNIFI's members worked in the four major banks: HSBC, Royal Group, Lloyds TSB and Barclays. UNIFI recognised that it needed to deepen its membership within recognised workplaces as well as organising 'greenfield' sites (Colgan and Creegan 2002), identifying contact centres as the fastest-growing area of the finance sector and, thus, one of its target areas for organising (UNIFI 2000b). However, by 2000 the threat of the global shift of financial services work, particularly contact centre jobs, was of concern to the union (UNIFI 2004b; DTI 2004).

Research methods

The research methods comprised document collection, participant observation at key events and conferences, workplace surveys and focus groups and interviews. A particular focus was on organising at national and workplace levels. We carried out semi-structured interviews with seventy-six respondents between 2000 and 2002, including the joint general secretaries, FTOs, lay representatives, members and non-members. We also carried out four workplace case studies in 2001–2, comprising a questionnaire survey to 1,401 employees in four contact centres from three of the four major banks. All employees, both members and non-members, were surveyed at each centre, generating a total of 410 responses (29 per cent response rate). This approach recognised the need to examine the specific strategies and tactics of the organising process and its application at workplace level. We included lay representatives involved in UNIFI's equality structures in our interview sample and included gender, race, sexuality, disability and age questions in our survey. In doing so, we took a comprehensive view of diversity, recognising the need to reclaim the term diversity as a 'neutral descriptor of variation within a workplace' (Noon and Ogbunna 2001) and to respond to the challenge to integrate a gender and diversity analysis into industrial relations research (Colgan and Ledwith 2002b; Wajcman 2000). In 2004, we conducted a further ten semi-structured interviews with FTOs and lay representatives in order to examine progress in organising in each of the four contact centres and explore the relationship between organising and bargaining outcomes.

Organising

UNIFI's approach to 'organising' was built on the recruitment strategies of its forerunners, most notably BIFU. In 2000, it sought to forge its identity in an environment characterised by the shift from branch banking to telephone and online banking, and from the high street branches to out-of-town contact centres. In that year, UNIFI (2001d) recruited some 12,000 new members, but lost a greater number, so that there was an overall decline. The move to 'organising' was strongly associated with a debate about the respective roles, and interrelationship, of servicing and organising, where neither was seen as necessarily mutually exclusive of the other. Indeed, organising was not necessarily viewed in opposition to partnership, as UNIFI sought to marry a commitment to both, in order to help it develop a local profile and ensure representation and access to members and potential members where appropriate (Earls 2002; Wills 2004a). Despite some dissatisfaction from ex-BIFU members at its inaugural conference, the union advocated a pragmatic position (UNIFI 1999b).

Within the new union, the development of organising was essentially a top-down process and led by FTOs, rather than lay members. The union's principles and practices in relation to the adoption of an 'organising model' were neither clearly documented nor appeared to be singularly understood by FTOs and lay activists. Consistent with this top-down approach, a key tool for implementation was the introduction of project management for FTOs, as it had been in a number of other unions (Heery *et al.* 2000c). UNIFI national leadership regarded project working and project management skills as crucial in delivering a more 'systematic' way of dealing with recruitment and getting the union to orientate on an organising approach. Project working was adopted at the annual staff conferences following UNIFI's formation, where staff, working in multidisciplinary teams, were galvanised by senior FTOs to take responsibility for devising and implementing organising projects. At the first conference, entitled 'Changing minds, changing work' in 2000, the keynote presentations by the general, and deputy general, secretaries stressed the new union's potential as well as its financial and membership problems (see Sweeney 2000). Officials, organisers and attendant administrative staff were split up into twelve groups and asked to develop organising projects in relation to predetermined themes: communicating with members, organising in the branch network, organising recognised and unrecognised 'greenfield' sites, organising large sites, organising HSBC managers, organising in partnerships, negotiating in an organising union, organising in merging employers, ending divided staff representation, merger with small finance unions/associations and measuring success.

Prior to their deliberations, staff were briefed about project management techniques. A group, G12, which included the senior management team, was given the task of overseeing and evaluating the other projects. Reports and evaluation of project outcomes were given by project coordinators at meetings of G12 as well as the second staff conference in 2001 (UNIFI 2001e). This considered UNIFI's strategic objectives, and project management was again emphasised as the 'way forward' on organising because it provided 'the opportunity for everyone to be involved in the actual management of UNIFI'. The breadth of focus taken at these conferences underlined the scale of challenges facing UNIFI, and emphasised that even for a single union based in one sector, organising is a far from homogeneous activity (Charlwood 2004). Projects focused on both recognised and unrecognised 'greenfield' sites were, therefore, both expansionary and consolidatory (Kelly and Heery 1989). Though the approach of some teams was to foster a collaboration with lay representatives, this was neither prescribed nor universal and the union leadership appeared more focused on motivating FTOs to deliver organising than on mobilising active members.

A further element of the mode of delivery was the creation of the role of national development officer, which sought to develop organisation within specific institutions, 'embracing' organising and focusing on 'the training and development of representative systems in co-ordination with the company based and regional structures'. Just as project working was multidisciplinary, these various teams and roles cut across traditional intra-union boundaries such as the distinction between national negotiators and regional organisers. Thus, rather than creating a separate organising function (see Heery 2002), their creation sought to connect organising and bargaining, underlining the view that organising drives bargaining and not vice versa, and that successful outcomes in bargaining were dependent on effective organising. At workplace level, organisers played a pivotal role in delivering organising centred on 'coaching and advising' workplace reps and stimulating workplace activity by developing workplace committees and fostering effective communication with members. However, whilst this suggested that their role should be as 'strategists', putting systems in place and organising training, often their time and energy was diverted to servicing and to individual casework.

Diversity

In late 2001, UNIFI (2001f) had 155,057 members, of whom 62 per cent were women and 45 per cent worked part time. Approximately a quarter of members were aged thirty or under (UNIFI 2001c). The union estimated that 97 per cent of members were white. At its creation, it expressed its commitment to equal opportunities and by 2001 had mostly achieved gender parity on NEC and national company committees but was aware that this was not so for its regional council and branch structures. Moreover, the national company committees had a poor record in terms of the representation of ethnic minorities, disabled and younger members (UNIFI 2002a) and conference activists were not representative of members (Jefferys 2003). In 2001, UNIFI had a number of different national equality structures. At a formal level it had an equality committee, which was an NEC subcommittee and a disablement advisory committee. At a less formal level, it had lesbian and gay and youth networks, while its 2001 annual conference passed a resolution to establish a race relations committee. Following a restructuring in 2001, the equality committee structure included a reserved seat for a black member, disablement advisory committee member, lesbian and gay network member and youth network member, unless a member from each of these constituencies had already been elected to the committee. With the exception of equality subcommittees within four of the national company committees, formal equality or self-organised structures below national level were undeveloped. By 2001, UNIFI (2001f) employed 165 staff; 63 per cent were women, though 70 per cent of these were clerical staff, and black and ethnic minority staff accounted for 4 per cent of the complement, of which nearly all were clerical. Of the 165 staff, thirty were regional organisers (37 per cent were women), twenty-one support staff based in regions and twenty-seven national negotiating staff. Since 2000, six national development officers with a specific focus on organising were appointed.

UNIFI's organising strategy

In order to assess the efficacy of organising tactics and mobilising within the workplace, we first consider the national dimensions of the organising strategy and mobilising leadership, how they were understood in theory and practice and the extent to which it acknowledged diversity within the workforce. We then examine the way in which organising was implemented in four case study workplaces and how far it was sustained.

There was no single definition of what organising meant in UNIFI: it was understood and defined differently by and between FTOs and lay activists (cf. Carter 2000 on MSF). Moreover, although a range of measures had been put in place to deliver organising, there was a perception that the strategy lacked clarity and coherence and that understanding of organising principles remained superficial. Levels of understanding were also perceived to vary, between full-time organisers (employed within regions), full-time negotiators (employed at national level) and lay representatives. For example, one FTO commented: 'The organisers do [understand it] because their role is more organising than the rest of us. I'm not sure that national negotiators do fully. I'm absolutely convinced that the lay activists by and large don't.' Although workshops on organising were run at each of UNIFI's national conferences between 2000 and 2002, many lay representatives remained unaware of the shift to organising. Amongst those who were aware, it was believed that the organising model was like a 'virus' to be resisted. They were used to officers carrying responsibility for representing members and wanted temporary recruiters back to carry out most recruitment. Nonetheless, these groups were not homogeneous, so for example some national negotiators embraced the shift to organising, whilst some regional organisers were resistant to it.

For those who embraced the new approach, terms like 'ownership', 'participation', 'empowerment' and 'self-organisation' were used. According to one FTO, the consequent aim was to 'set up little cells of self-recruiting, self-organising sets of people who will raise issues in the workplace and take up the union profile in their workplaces themselves'. This suggested a lower profile for FTOs in the workplace, with members owning a significant proportion of the servicing of other members. In contrast, concerns existed regarding whether this was something that members wanted, and whether organising might be less suited to the finance sector than elsewhere: 'I think, yes, it's good to move towards organising but I think if you go too far that way you scare off a lot of the traditional bank workers . . . the more proactive you get as a union the more your traditional type bank worker will not want to know' (lay representative).

Most UNIFI members belonged to geographic branches spanning workplaces and institutions. However, with some 30 per cent of members working in workplaces of 150 or more employees in 2001, up from 22 per cent in 1999, many FTOs recognised the utility of shifting the organisational and democratic focus towards the workplace. Lack of membership identity with geographic branches was cited as underlying poor participation because members lacked confidence in their efficacy, particularly in relation to enhancing their terms and conditions. In turn, this arguably led to a narrowed participation in the regional and company committee structures. In contrast, workplace committees were considered more suited to delivering organising and a democratic base by being more accessible, visible and relevant to members, better able to deliver on local issues without necessarily having to rely on FTO support as well as to encourage involvement of a broader range of members at all levels of the union structures. However, their suitability to small and non-recognised workplaces was questioned, and concerns were expressed about whether a sufficient activist base existed or could be encouraged to sustain this development.

Workplace representatives were seen as particularly effective because their day-to-day presence and local credibility enabled them to gain members' trust. But a note of caution was sounded that most members would not want to be 'activists' and some would continue to view the union as a service provider, even an insurance policy. It was also recognised that enhancing workplace representatives' role had implications for the way in which they were selected, elected, trained and supported. Lay representatives underlined this, and for some the move to an organising culture required extra work from them, whilst not sufficiently acknowledging the importance of supporting them, leaving them feeling isolated.

The differences between organising within a partnership agreement and a more traditional agreement appeared marginal. Though UNIFI's approach to marrying organising and partnership appeared to be segmented (see Heery 2002), this appeared based on circumstances and developments within individual institutions rather than on strategic choices or ideological preferences. Respondents primarily took pragmatic and non-ideological approaches and partnership was not necessarily seen as either helping or hindering organising. Whilst concern was expressed that partnership could involve diluting the union's objectives to make them acceptable, FTOs working in both partnership and traditional arenas acknowledged that members' perceptions could be of an 'ineffectual' union, 'hand in glove with the bank', regardless of the formal agreement with employers. However, for most of the FTOs and lay representatives working within a partnership arena, partnership working was thought to provide a more constructive negotiating relationship, which some FTOs and lay representatives working under more traditional agreements, particularly with hostile employers, perceived as beneficial. One argued: 'That kind of arrangement can help to make the union more present in the workplace. And that can breed members and make us a less faceless organisation, more real. In a lot of respects the [partnership] type agreement would be great' (lay representative).

The tradition of joint accreditation of union representatives (JAOR) and seconded representatives in the banking industry was not perceived by respondents as a threat to the union's autonomy or an obstacle to organising. Rather, it was thought to ensure that the employers were more likely to formalise and respect arrangements and provide training and facilities for union representatives, so enabling them to fulfil their role. Any attempt to veto accreditation by employers would be seen as an 'acid test' of partnership that would have to be challenged by UNIFI. The potential for involvement of workplace union representatives in bargaining was reliant on the willingness of national company committees and national negotiators to consult with them and their membership on issues, given that most collective bargaining between UNIFI and companies in the financial sector was carried out centrally at a national company level.

Diversity

Diversity was defined differently by respondents and a greater awareness of gender was combined with a perception that the union had a stronger record in responding to the needs of women than those of other diverse groups. However, the sector's changing nature, particularly the move from bank branches to large sites such as processing and call centres, was seen as creating an imperative to respond to the challenge of a diverse workforce. The extent to which UNIFI was believed to be doing so was subject to debate. An optimistic view was that equality issues were seamlessly woven into recruitment, organising and bargaining, whilst a more common view was that the union's track record had been somewhat uneven, particularly with respect to the recruitment of black and ethnic minority workers. The most pessimistic view was that, despite a formal commitment, in practice the union tended to pay lip service to equality issues.

In spite of a strongly espoused commitment to equal opportunities, the organising strategy lacked an explicit equalities dimension, for project and teams largely failed to address diversity beyond its relevance to mapping workplaces, even though some organising teams were aware of the need for a gender balance amongst representatives. Their plans fell short of the aspiration expressed by one lay representative who considered that the issue of equalities was central to organising:

> equality issues are about how we attract new members, so it's all part of that organising agenda in my view. And to give it its proper priority, it goes slap bang right in the middle of organising and is to do with how we publicise what we do, what policies we can take forward and obviously the policies that we take forward are relevant to our members.

Thus, though it was suggested that the union's ambition should be to mainstream equalities issues and make equalities and organising 'indivisible', they remained largely invisible.

The absence of an equalities dimension to the union's strategy related to a number of structural weaknesses. First, the engagement of the 'mainstream' with the activities of the equalities committee and networks was limited and there was a lack of connection between the equalities committee and company, regional and branch structures. Second, there was no black and ethnic minority network and the voices of those involved in youth and lesbian and gay networks and the disablement advisory committee were cut off from the recruitment and involvement of members in the wider union.[2] Third, it was recognised that the influence of the equalities structures would be improved if its representation were underpinned by greater participation of diverse groups within a full range of union structures. One FTO argued:

> You'll never organise black workers in banking unless you set up a network ... We did that with women, there was never anything that was successfully organized unless women actually kick up about it and organise against it and organise for it. And that's not encouraged, it's still very stratified, committees referred this, committees referred that.

Despite some evidence that organising had resulted in increased numbers of women and black and ethnic minority representatives, more needed to be done to diversify the activist base, according to a lay representative:

> If you look at the democratic structures and look for different types of faces in conferences and on all the committees, there aren't the people there you would expect. So I think, that's something we have quite a lot of work to do on.

In a similar vein, some FTOs questioned whether the union's workforce was sufficiently reflective of its membership. One commented: 'We haven't got enough women, we've certainly not got enough black officers predominantly because we're still reflecting [the] old industry, white lower middle class male and it's still reflected.'

Implementation

Between 2000 and 2001, UNIFI ran organising initiatives in the four case study workplaces. Three (Workplaces A, B and C) were stimulated by the staff conference in 2000, and the fourth (Workplace D) emerged from a project to build and support a bank representative network initiated by one of the two national development officers appointed in 2000. Table 4.1 provides some essential details of the four contact centre workplaces in 2001. Workplaces A and B were in the same bank, and in common with Workplace D, there was a traditional recognition agreement in place. Workplace C was in a bank with a partnership agreement. When employees in these workplaces (both members and non-members) were asked about the employer's attitude to UNIFI, the union's perceived workplace influence and

Table 4.1 Attitudes to UNIFI in case study workplaces in 2001

Workplace	*A*	*B*	*C*	*D*
Number of employees	478	244	158	521
Jointly accredited representatives	0	1	1	1
Other representatives	4	3	4	3
Employer positive to union (% agree)	56	72	62	64
UNIFI has too little power or influence in my workplace (% agree)	71	50	57	69
UNIFI is well organised in my workplace (% agree)	38	57	46	43

effectiveness of workplace organisation, agreement type did not appear to be an influential factor. With the exception of Workplace B, the majority of employees did not perceive the union as well organised and the influence of the union was felt to be lacking by 50 per cent or more employees in all four workplaces.

Table 4.2 describes the effect of the organising initiatives in each workplace. Following the initiatives, density increased in all four and also resulted in members coming forward to be representatives or to assist with recruitment. As all save one of the existing representatives were white men, women organisers in particular were sensitive to the need to encourage women, young and black members to take on more active roles. However, the immediate consolidation of the initiatives was patchy.

In Workplace A, after the project team had distributed leaflets and an issue-based questionnaire and held lunchtime surgeries, officers ran a 'winning the organised workplace' (WOW) course attended by six members, including one of the existing representatives. Six months after the initiative, neither the two existing male representatives nor the two new women representatives had received the accreditation training and so continued to rely on FTO assistance. A similar path was followed at Workplace B, but six months later a WOW course had not been run and the male JAOR was experiencing difficulty getting time off for the new women representatives,

Table 4.2 Effect of organising initiatives in case study workplaces, 2001

	A	*B*	*C*	*D*
Membership density increased	47% to 51 %	13% to 23%	55% to 75%	50% to 60%
New reps came forward	Yes	Yes	Yes	Yes
Training provided	Yes	No	Yes	No
New reps accredited	No	No	Yes	Yes
Workplace committee established	No	No	Yes	No
Workplace meetings organised	No	No	Yes	No
Surgery days organised	No	No	No	Yes

so that they could attend training and meetings and take on their role. The union was also struggling with the need to provide training in a format sympathetic to the women reps' childcare responsibilities. Representatives within both workplaces were under pressure to meet sales targets and found it difficult to leave their desks to undertake union work. Communication between representatives was limited and follow-up recruitment and organising activities were minimal.

In Workplace C, the situation was better. After recruitment visits by the project team, a WOW course was run, a workplace committee that reflected diversity at the workplace was established and met regularly after work. One of the initiative's strengths was that the FTO involved in the original initiative continued to work with the representatives in order to develop an organising approach. Arguably, another was management support for the organising initiative, whereby the HR director (a UNIFI member) allowed the organising officer free access to the workplace and supported the establishment of the workplace committee, including attending it regularly. At Workplace D, the initiative resulted in two members undertaking training to become JAORs, and another was being trained to become a learner representative. Their intention was to start 'trying to meet once a month' either during work time or outside working hours. One of those encouraged to come forward did so because she wished to ensure representation for the diverse workforce, saying, 'If people like me [female, Asian, qualified bank employees] don't get involved, then who is going to make the break?'

Although each workplace had UNIFI notice boards identifying the JAOR representatives and displaying UNIFI information and publicity, including equality networks, there was little evidence of a local focus. With the exception of Workplace C, there appeared to be no regular UNIFI workplace meetings, though even here they were held outside the workplace and were not well attended. Members complained about the lack of union communication. One member commented, 'Apart from the odd leaflet here and there, you don't really hear that much about it. If you need to get an opinion there's someone there, but you don't really hear that much about it. . . . Yes, I'd like something a bit more involved than they are now.' Awareness of organising amongst union representatives and members appeared to be limited, with those who did speak about organising seeing it largely as a 'more proactive approach to recruitment'.

The extent to which employees were discontented varied by workplace. While a majority of both members and non-members thought that their jobs were secure, interesting, enjoyable and well managed and that they had a say in how they worked, a majority also thought their jobs were stressful, and the percentage was higher for union members than non-members (Table 4.3). Similarly, whilst the majority of respondents also thought that their jobs were secure, union members were less confident of this than non-members. The most important collective bargaining issues were broadly similar for union members and non-members, with the top three being pay

Table 4.3 Attitudes to work in case study workplaces in 2001

	Members	*Non-members*
My job is interesting and enjoyable (% agree)	68	73
My work is well managed (% agree)	79	82
My job is stressful (% agree)	72	62
My job is secure (% agree)	54	69
I have a say in how I work (% agree)	68	65

and conditions, job security and working conditions. However non-members, particularly women, black and ethnic minority workers, also cited equal opportunities among their top three issues.

Table 4.4 summarises the most important reasons cited by UNIFI members for being a union member. There were slight variations by gender, race and age. The findings contrast with Waddington's (1999) research in other unions where, on average, the three most important reasons cited were support with problems at work (68 per cent), improved pay and conditions (40 per cent) and a belief in trade unionism (37 per cent). Only 24 per cent of the UNIFI respondents cited a 'belief in trade unionism', suggesting a limited pool of members who might be encouraged to become active. Despite recent organising drives in these workplaces, 62 per cent of non-members cited not knowing what the union had to offer, 56 per cent that they saw no advantage in membership and 40 per cent that nobody had approached them to join as reasons for non-membership. Table 4.5 shows the most important factors which non-members said would encourage them to join UNIFI. Support with problems at work and improved pay and conditions are in the top two. Interestingly, 59 per cent of non-members cited the union having more influence as a factor that would encourage them to join. For women, black and ethnic minority non-members, working towards equal opportunities was also cited as a key factor. Although 12 per cent said that they did not believe in trade unionism, none said they were 'opposed' to UNIFI and only 13 per cent said that they were not interested in it.

Amongst members there was little evidence of engagement or involvement in the union. Only 5 per cent described themselves as 'active', whereas 19 per cent said they took an interest and 76 per cent said they were 'just a member'. However, men (39 per cent) were nearly twice as likely as women (19 per cent) to say that they were active or took an interest. Just over a quarter of black and ethnic minority members (28 per cent) and 38 per cent of young members described themselves as active or taking an interest. When asked what might encourage them to be active, the existence of problems in the workplace was the major trigger for all members (87 per cent), regardless of gender, race or age. However, for women, the provision of training and greater encouragement from existing representatives was more

Table 4.4 Principal reasons for being a UNIFI member

	All N = *190*	*Men: 30 years and under* N = *19*	*Women: 30 years and under* N = *41*	*White men* N = *41*	*Black men* N = *5*	*White women* N = *125*	*Black women* N = *16*
Support with problems at work	1 94%	1 95%	1 95%	1 95%	1 = 100%	1 94%	2 = 88%
To achieve better pay and conditions	2 81%	2 90%	2 76%	2 81%	1 = 100%	2 78%	1 94%
Members' services	3 57%	3 = 58%	4 49%	3 = 51%	3 60%	4 54%	2 = 88%
To work towards equal opportunities	4 54%	3 = 58%	3 54%	3 = 51%	6 = 20%	3 55%	4 63%
Financial services	5 27%	6 32%	5 39%	6 22%	– –	5 30%	7 = 19%
I believe in trade unionism	6 24%	7 = 11%	7 = 17%	5 24%	4 = 40%	6 23%	5 = 25%
Most people at work are members	7 17%	5 37%	6 27%	7 20%	6 = 20%	7 17%	9 13%
Union training and education	8 12%	7 = 11%	7 = 17%	8 10%	4 = 40%	8 10%	5 = 25%

Note
A dash (–) indicates that there was no choice of this option. Respondents were given a choice of ten options, although the table reports on only the first eight options.

Table 4.5 Main factors which would encourage non-members to join UNIFI

	All N = *145*	*Men: 30 years and under* N = *34*	*Women: 30 years and under* N = *67*	*White men* N = *33*	*Black men* N = *9*	*White women* N = *86*	*Black women* N = *16*
Support with problems at work	1 90%	1 88%	1 90%	1 88%	1 100%	1 92%	3 75%
To achieve better pay/conditions	2 74%	2 82%	2 76%	2 79%	2 100%	2 66%	1 88%
If the union had more influence	3 59%	3 56%	3 55%	3 60%	6 44%	3 55%	2 81%
To work towards equal opportunities	4 37%	6 = 27%	4 43%	7 = 21%	4 57%	4 = 35%	4 69%
Members' services	5 36%	6 = 27%	5 37%	5 33%	7 33%	4 = 35%	5 50%
Financial services	6 34%	4 47%	6 31%	4 39%	3 67%	6 30%	6 = 25%
If more colleagues were involved	7 26%	6 = 27%	7 28%	6 27%	9 11%	7 26%	6 = 25%
Union training and education	8 22%	5 29%	8 24%	7 = 21%	5 44%	8 20%	6 = 25%

Note
Respondents were given a choice of ten options, although the table reports on only the first eight options.

important than for men. Young, black and ethnic minority women in particular cited the provision of training as a factor and the opportunity to work on equal opportunities. Thirty-four per cent of members said that they would become active if they knew what activities they could join in. However, without a workplace committee or meetings, there was no clear focus for collective activity at workplace level and it fell to individual members to approach the JAOR, to contact one of the equality networks or answer one of the advertisements for JAOR/learner representatives in UNIFI newsletters/website if they wished to become more active.

Pressurised work environments driven by quantitative imperatives (Taylor *et al.* 2002), whether in the form of targets or call volumes, in addition to a lack of workplace union activities, was widely cited by employees as an obstacle to engagement and involvement. Facility time was key if representatives were to take on a more proactive role. However, not all members wished to take on a formal role: 22 per cent of members said that they would like to help but without taking on a formal role. Moreover, not all representatives wanted to go through what they saw as an onerous process to become jointly accredited. However, at the two workplaces where WOW courses had been run, there was evidence of increased understanding of, and enthusiasm for, an organising approach, though there was some resistance from long-standing (male) representatives.

Sustainability

Three years after the original organising initiatives, there was little evidence that the initial limited progress had been sustained or consolidated. Whilst density had increased in Workplace B, it had remained constant or fallen in the others. None of the original representatives remained in place, all having either left or been promoted, and whilst the situation had improved in Workplace B, activity had fallen away elsewhere. Although one new representative had been accredited for workplaces A, B and C, there were no representatives at Workplace D. The workplace committee at Workplace C had withered away when the key representative there left. According to a FTO, 'It was [the key representative] and I that pulled it together. I think once she disappeared, I think some of them were quite glad to leave. . . . Once she disappeared, they all didn't really want to know. They all had enough. They had done their two years.' No workplace committees had been established in the other three workplaces and none of the representatives organised workplace meetings or indicated evidence of membership mobilisation.

Whilst some of the reasons for poor sustainability can be located in the organising initiatives (e.g. lack of training, communication and member involvement), other factors were related both to the nature of the workplace environment (e.g. staff turnover, shifts and targets) and the banks' corporate activities (e.g. takeovers and outsourcing). For example, at Workplace A, where staff turnover was cited as a key factor, the FTO conceded, 'In organising terms our aspirations [here] are relatively modest. It would be good to have a workplace committee, but not easily achieved in practice. Getting four or five reps here at any one time will be difficult.' This was compounded by the pressures placed on the one remaining representative as a result of the targets culture in the workplace: 'I do enjoy it, but it's very difficult with the pressure of my job. I'd love to have more time to devote to it. But I do the bare essentials because I don't have much time. If I didn't have targets that were unobtainable, I would do more.'

At Workplace D, where the absence of workplace representatives was cited as making a 'big difference' to perceptions of union effectiveness, membership concerns about the union's allegedly complicit response to the outsourcing globalisation agenda had also taken their toll, though not by galvanising local collective activity. One lay representative stated, 'The union does get blamed for problems with the bank. Members kick up a lot and get very vocal. But . . . that doesn't necessarily mean they'll do anything. . . . They are frightened by change and the union is seen as letting change happen.' Similarly at Workplace C, it was recognised that the outsourcing of jobs was often a lose–lose situation for the union, particularly given the time taken to negotiate the best deal available, whereby 'Staff will still blame you for the fact they even had to transfer in the first place because they would have preferred to stay with the bank' (FTO). The membership appeared resigned to the inevitability of management drives for these changes. At best, the workplace representative had found that union opposition to outsourcing and the protection it offered in these cases had enabled her to 'sell' the benefits of membership and had helped to retain members.

Common to all, a further key factor was a lack of local bargaining and, therefore, of a collective focus for workplace organisation. Thus, despite the view expressed by one negotiating official that organising and bargaining were 'inextricably linked' and that bargaining could not 'sit separately from organising', in practice organising and bargaining can be 'disconnected' and 'separated' rather than 'intimately related' (Gall 2003f). The absence of local bargaining has been argued to result largely from the hierarchical and centralised nature of the banks as institutions, giving managers little discretion to bargain within an individual centre (Gall 2005a). Hence, workplace bargaining and collective bargaining over business issues within local centres remained almost exclusively in the hands of national FTOs. As a result, even the most active workplace representatives focused almost exclusively on resolving individual grievances and disciplinaries and struggled to find time for recruitment. Their relationship with local managers was confined to these activities, providing reps with very few opportunities to relate the efficacy of (limited) workplace organisation to collective bargaining outcomes in the eyes of employees at a local level. This was compounded by the reluctance of members to engage in collective action:

> The problem is because ultimately the only power that the union has is in its individual members, and because the individual members aren't militant enough to stand up and be counted, aren't willing to do anything themselves, it's extremely hard to turn round and show them a victory (lay representative).

Conclusions

This chapter offers evidence of a substantial shift in thinking within UNIFI towards integrating recruitment, organising and bargaining. However, despite the development of innovative organising practice, UNIFI (2000) found it difficult to translate this into achieving its goals, to 'build the democratic structure of the union' and 'more effectively combine its twin resources, lay and paid, into the growth and development of the union'. The prevailing culture remained that of recruiting to service, as opposed to recruiting to organise with a 'narrow vision' of local activity, on the part of both FTOs and senior lay activists, focused primarily on servicing individual members. Workplace structures remain underdeveloped, and local union activity has been little changed and is still primarily restricted to the recruitment and servicing of members, many of whom still see the union as an 'insurance organisation' rather than an organising union (Wills 2004a).

The four workplaces discussed suggest that establishing a culture of workplace unionism remains an aspiration rather than a reality. Workplace representatives are barely involved in membership organising and mobilisation, and opportunities for them to take decisions that directly concern the work environment and local employment relations are constrained by both union and employer. Bargaining, even in relation to developments within contact centres, is driven nationally by management and the union. Whilst national negotiating officials bargain with reference to organisers and, where possible, local representatives, attempts to engage and consult members are limited and sporadic. Moreover, though FTOs and senior lay activists (seconded representatives and company council members) communicate regularly with workplace representatives, there is little evidence that this filters down to members, for whom UNIFI newsletters and its website are the main day-to-day sources of information. Bargaining thus takes place outside the workplace and will remain effectively disconnected from it without a concerted emphasis on membership participation and on representing members both collectively and individually (Gall 2003f).

By conceptually applying the conditions necessary for unions to mobilise workers in collective action developed by Kelly (1998), we can identify some possible explanations for this malaise. In the workplaces, despite some indicators of job satisfaction, there was a sense of grievance and injustice on the part of workers and attribution of this to the employer. However, despite the implementation of top-down organising initiatives, effective workplace organisation remained elusive and the culture of workplace unionism fragile.

Workplace representatives appeared isolated and members appeared to be at best unconvinced and at worst ignorant of the potential of collective organisation and action as a route to addressing the issues most fundamental to their discontent. This configuration has arisen as a result of several factors.

The first factor concerns the nature of UNIFI's membership. In addition to problems created by high staff turnover, our survey confirmed Waddington's (1999) findings that despite emphasis placed by finance workers upon problems at work and pay and conditions as determinants (or potential determinants) of membership, a belief in trade unionism was less likely to be a key reason for workers to join the union than elsewhere. Thus, they may aspire to individual rather than collective modes of redress and may have limited interest in active participation resulting in a scarcity of activists with a commitment to collective mobilisation. The second issue is that of employer strategy. One of the key sources of discontent, namely targets and bonuses, remained firmly outside the collective bargaining arena and local managers had limited discretion to negotiate. Third is the topic of national union limitations, whereby there existed an insufficient focus on building effective grassroots workplace organisation, the absence of workplace democratic accountability and a reluctance, albeit in part based on the perceived best interests of members, to devolve bargaining to local workplaces. Fourth comes the issue of the union–employer relationship. Both the process of the operation of recognition agreements and content and terrain of bargaining were determined primarily by the employer's values and agenda, and superior resources, despite UNIFI's attempts to retain ideological and organisational autonomy and influence outcomes.

This poses the question of whether a mobilising leadership could articulate a distinct union agenda and, with this, generate collective action. In UNIFI's case, the evidence is mixed, indicating a top-down approach characterised by attempts to motivate FTOs to recruit and organise within constraints determined by the employer, rather than attempts to work with lay representatives to organise and where necessary mobilise members against the employer. The fate of the organising initiatives explored here suggests that the causes of 'mobilisation dissipation' (Taylor and Bain 2003) are diffuse. Finally, we examined whether UNIFI's commitment to equality resulted in the integration of a diversity perspective into its organising approach. Research suggests that a combination of mainstream union mobilisation for equality, together with activists' work representing the interests of the diverse constituencies whom unions wish to recruit and mobilise, is crucial to union renewal (Colgan and Ledwith 2002b). Colling and Dickens (1989) argue that an 'equality bargaining' approach within unions is dependent upon equality provisions within collective agreements, awareness of an equality dimension to bargaining amongst negotiators and an equality dimension to the structure and content of bargaining. If translated to organising, and considered in UNIFI's case, there are doubts over the extent of each. For example, the organising strategy lacked specific equality outcomes, and despite some awareness of an equality dimension to organising, diversity was understood and defined differently. Meanwhile, an equality dimension to the structure of organising was limited by UNIFI's 'self-organised' equality structures being insufficiently developed to underpin its national equality structures and assist the union to organise and mobilise across its diverse membership.

Acknowledgement

Our thanks are to UNIFI lay members and FTOs who participated in the research and, in particular, to Pam Monk, UNIFI joint-head of the Research Department for her assistance during the research and for providing valuable comments on this chapter, and to Gregor Gall for comments on an earlier draft.

Notes

1 In 2004, UNIFI merged with Amicus in order to create a union where 'two thirds of all trade union members in the finance industry would come together for the first time in order to represent members' interests much more forcefully' (UNIFI 2004c).
2 Some of these weaknesses were addressed in 2002 by the establishment of a Race Relations Committee and the relaunch of UNIFI's work with young members through 'UNIFI Active'. Both initiatives sought to encourage the recruitment and participation of black, ethnic minority and young members through annual seminars, networks, targeted courses, newsletters and websites. Both have met with some success (UNIFI 2002b, 2004c).

5 As a phoenix arisen?

Union organisation, Rover cars and the British motor industry

Alan Tuckman and Michael Whittall

Decried as a symbol of all that was wrong with British industrial relations, the motor industry, or at least the rump which had been taken into public control in the 1970s, has since the 1990s appeared in the vanguard of 'social partnership' (Employment Committee 1994). For Rover – or more so its precursors – worker mobilisation was associated with walkouts and mass meetings at the factory gate. After decades of turbulent relations, shop stewards and management there now appear in a rapprochement. The most recent public demonstration by Longbridge workers through Birmingham's streets was to promote the buy-out by Phoenix, a consortium established by Rover's ex-management after owner BMW announced the sale of this element of what had become known as its 'English Patient' (Chinn and Dyson 2000). This is in marked contrast to 1979, when management pioneered the 'symbolic defeat' (Hyman 2001c: 105) of unions with the sacking of the AEUW convenor at Longbridge (Claydon 2000). Derek Robinson's unceremonious removal, coinciding with the first Thatcher government, represented the beginning of a major shift in the climate of British industrial relations. It was a direct attack on the heartland of 'militant unionism' with an emergent 'managers' right to manage' (Edwardes 1983) and proved to be the first attack in an escalating assault on unions (Kelly 1998; see also Smith and Morton 1993). Such developments, perhaps the demobilisation of the 'symbolic mass worker' towards the end of the twentieth century (Hyman 2001c: 31), pose an important case for assessing fluctuations in employer–employee relations in the last quarter of the twentieth century.

Despite the symbolism of British Leyland (BL), the unions never directly faced derecognition nor became dependent on the ERA for recognition. This did not mean that shop stewards experienced neither periods of exclusion nor experiments with novel forms of representation. Although the 1980s were certainly a period of marginalisation for workplace unionism at BL, the 1990s not only saw the 'Rover Tomorrow' agreement but also, under BMW, unions drawn into new forms of representation at both established and greenfield sites. Struggles for union recognition and the right to organise set the context of employment relations in the motor industry in Britain, as they have in the USA (Fine 1969). Industrial relations at Rover and its ancestors, though punctuated by various armistices, remained embedded in mistrust, if not out-and-out conflict, between management and labour. Management attempts either to impose or negotiate their right to rule resulted in a fluctuation between employee and union inclusion and exclusion. Employers paid high rates to avoid unionisation, a feasible strategy in the boom years of the 1920s but, by the 1930s, faced by a downturn in markets and increase in production through speed-up, workers staged strikes in an attempt to extend union recognition (Whiting 1983).

This chapter presents a narrative relating the last quarter-century to discuss the shift and fluctuations which management, unions and shop stewards negotiated in BL/Rover. In doing this, we explore Kelly's theory of mobilisation, in which stewards and union organisers constitute the leadership of purposeful behaviour in which 'discontent is translated into collective action' (Kelly 1998: 100). We argue that workers' interests are far from homogeneous, with fractures appearing in collectivities, alliances emerging between sections of management and workers, and manifestations of conflict arising. We explore the context for the political construction of how these interests are formed and articulated where interpretation and action around a changing context were already highly politicised. Ultimately, however, the 1970s and 1980s saw continued and precipitating crisis, marked by overproduction in the global motor industry (*The Economist*, 4 September 2004) with relatively low composition of capital in old established manufacturing centres like Longbridge and Cowley, helping augment an already attenuated alliance between labour and local agents of capital. As the crisis developed over the future of Rover under BMW, Ford and Vauxhall were also rationalising production at Dagenham and Luton respectively. Thus, while suspicions and (usually) tacit antagonisms remained at the centre of relations between owners, management and workers, this often remained submerged in the survival project for these particular fractions of capital.

Based on a longitudinal study of employment relations at Rover cars, the chapter traces developments in industrial relations from state holding, through privatisation and sale to BMW and then its fragmentation with the rump of MG Rover retrenched to Longbridge but with – at least at corporate level – global ambition. While making no claims to replicate the 'intellectual high-water mark' of workplace studies of the 1970s (Kelly 1998: 7), our approach – sympathetic to these studies – attempts to grasp activists' construction of their changing reality of employment relations, particularly in emergent relations with their German counterparts. Between 1998 and 2003, some seventy-five interviews were conducted with members of BMW and Rover management, FTOs and lay officers of the relevant unions in Austria, Britain and Germany, and from the European Trade Union Confederation, the European Metal Workers Federation and the European Commission.[1]

'Trench warfare' in the British automobile industry

In relating developments at Rover, we adopt the chronology used by our informants and their tendency to arrange industrial relations into three periods prior to the BMW takeover: around the Ryder Commission, the management offensive under Michael Edwardes, and the 'social partnership' initiative of the 'Rover Tomorrow' years. It is these periods that we will now consider. In 1974, the Labour government established the National Enterprise Board (NEB) to manage state industrial interests. One of its actions was to set up a commission, chaired by Lord Ryder, to examine ways of revitalising the British motor industry. The Ryder Report (1975) proposed a ninety-five per cent government equity stake and an extension of employee participation. As many writers have noted (e.g. Whisler 1999; Wilks 1984; Williams *et al.* 1994), the proposals did not address, or resolve, BL's underlying problems of overcapacity, design and marketing. These issues became more fundamental when the Labour government's early economic and industrial interventionist strategy was replaced by cutbacks in state spending, prompted by conditions imposed by the IMF's loan (Healey 1989; Leys 1983). The arrival of new chairman, Michael Edwardes, a member of the NEB, marked a major change in BL's strategy. In 1979, following cash-flow problems incurred by the previous year's losses, Edwardes initiated a plan for the 'Coordination of Resources' (CORE). CORE was designed to deal with the interrelated issues of low productivity and the continued problem of industrial action – in short, to win back control of the shop floor, reduce overcapacity and introduce new capital-intensive process methods.

Ultimately, the plan led to plant closures and the concentration of volume production at Longbridge, Cowley and the old Rover factory in Solihull. The Shop Stewards Combine Committee produced a pamphlet in condemnation of the Edwardes plan (LCTUC 1979), being as much a criticism of the lack of negotiation or consultation as it was of the proposed closures. Derek Robinson, chair of the Combine Committee, refused to withdraw his name from the pamphlet and was subsequently suspended and then dismissed. Management took the proposals straight to a ballot of the workforce, thus by-passing unions and formal bargaining procedures (Edwardes 1983). This represented a low point for trade unionism within the company. One senior steward noted,

> it was certainly true that there was a very low ebb after the dismissal of Derek Robinson . . . it was certainly difficult in the early 80s because [management] were telling people . . . coming in 'you do not have to join a union and we would prefer that you did not'.

As well as union marginalisation, another element of Edwardes' strategy involved forging a production alliance with Honda. Apart from the economic advantages gained through this joint venture, Longbridge becoming the assembly plant for the Honda Concerto, British management closely analysed Japanese manufacturing methods. A better understanding of Total Quality Management, teamworking and 'lean production' helped lay the foundation for what eventually became 'Rover Tomorrow'.

When the company was returned to private ownership in 1988 and controversially bought by British Aerospace, management realised, following Edwardes' departure, that advantages gained through plant closures and employee exclusion were now ending (Whisler 1999). Prompted by the influence and apparent success of the Japanese model – which became known as 'lean production' (Womack *et al.* 1990) – management reversed almost a decade of union marginalisation by trying to obtain their support for promoting change. The unions, when approached, felt that management would go ahead with plans for change with or without their involvement, believing that challenging the introduction of increased flexibility would only further marginalise them in workplace relations. After months of intensive negotiations, a deal was eventually struck in 1992 and endorsed by a narrow margin in a ballot of workers. Management improved conditions, in particular agreeing to no lay-offs and forced redundancies. This – the feature which has become the defining feature of 'partnership agreements' – seemed to reverse a tradition whereby workers would periodically be laid off. This had been one of the fundamental causes of conflict in periods of downturn. In return, the workforce accepted a fifteen-point plan for working practice and employment relations change (IRS 1992; Scarbrough and Terry 1996; Whittall 2003). Essentially, management, in the context of heightened competition, had co-opted unions into the promotion of new working practices and flexibility.

Although 'Rover Tomorrow' is often depicted as a watershed for British industrial relations (Taylor 1994; Employment Committee 1994), unions continued to feel excluded from important decision-making processes (see e.g. Rover worker 1998 in References). One informant observed that:

> The whole basis of partnership . . . even in Rover, to me is dishonest and dishonourable. . . . My view on that is that it was an agreement with the very best of intentions, but it was brought on . . . by crisis. . . . And whilst it slightly changed the way in which we did business together . . . that they were preaching partnership but still practising deceit and discrimination. There has been no involvement, no real involvement right through to shop floor level.

'Rover Tomorrow', therefore, represented a truce in a 'war of manoeuvre' in which long-standing controversies around flexibility were agreed, rather than the settlement of fundamental conflict. Considerable reservations remained amongst both shop floor workers and union officials, even when they were conspicuously promoting such deals. Only two years after the 'Rover Tomorrow' agreement, British Aerospace sold their stake to BMW. Unions, shop stewards and employees in general were to encounter a very different approach, one which seemed to go even further in the direction of employee involvement associated with German co-determination. It also became increasingly clear that there were differences within BMW management concerning the purpose of the Rover takeover within their broader strategy. These divisions concerned whether the acquisition represented a shift towards BMW moving into the realm of mass production companies or simply the gaining of Mini and Range Rover, constituting a consolidation of their status as a premier niche producer within the industry.

Co-determination at BMW

BMW was founded in 1916, initially to produce aero-engines, only moving to automobile production in the 1930s. By 1959, it manufactured one large model along with the Isetta bubble car and was facing closure. After unsuccessfully approaching a number of potential suitors, including Lord Nuffield, who owned the Austin plant at Longbridge, management supported a takeover bid by Daimler-Benz. The Deutsche Bank's representative on BMW's supervisory board, Herbert Quandt, initially backed the Benz offer. However, impressed by the concern voiced at a shareholder meeting in December 1959 by workforce representatives and a small group of shareholders that BMW would become a satellite component plant, Quandt drew up an alternative plan. Although Quandt's own wealth was an important element of the salvation strategy, it was the alliance between the German industrialist and Kurt Golda, the Munich works council chair and deputy chair of the supervisory board, that proved to be a defining factor in retaining BMW as an independent car producer. Mönnich (1991: 552–3) points to the central importance and lasting implication of this relationship:

> 'Quandt knew very well how much the inner peace within a company depended upon enhancing industrial relations.... Therefore, Quandt sought dialogue, as did Golda. Both men conducted it not in the spirit of from 'keeper to keeper', but more like neighbours at the fence, sometimes like friends, especially when it was socially and politically awkward.'

BMW's history in this period can almost be seen as a metaphor for the founding of a new Germany, involving compromise between capital and labour. The objective of the system, in almost a pluralistic sense, was to achieve compromise around corporate interest (Streeck 1995). This story of BMW's salvation has entered into corporate mythology as the key to understanding the essence of employment relations in the company, whereby it was the works council and not management that had historically worked for the benefit of the company.

The relationship between owners and worker representatives at BMW reflects the close cooperation between capital and labour interests procured by '*Modell Deutschland*', statutory co-determination forcing worker representatives to play an active role in furthering corporate interests. While the relationship is alien to the traditions in the British motor industry, such alliances are far from unknown when it appears to be a precondition for employment security. Although works council representatives operate in terms of delegated responsibility, taking decisions on behalf of constituent workers, with Rover stewards functioning within a system of direct democracy, Rover unions were willing to override such traditions – or at least modify them – when they felt that jobs might be under threat.

The first test of the new environment came with BMW's review of engine production. Around 3,000 jobs in power-train at the Longbridge and Solihull plants were under threat if a new engine plant was not attracted to the area. One senior steward observed that 'if we were to maintain any semblance of engine production we needed a plant'. It was also the case that the location of a plant engaged in mid-range engine production would integrate Rover into BMW's global operations, ending much insecurity. After five possible locations were explored, Hams Hall in Birmingham was chosen. Although the workforce was to be moved from other Rover sites, there was a suspicion amongst shop stewards that this might see an attempt by management to transfer 'greenfield' terms and conditions throughout the group. They were conscious of BMW's production site in South Carolina in the USA, where unions were not recognised. A negotiating team drawn from Rover unions ultimately gained a recognition agreement that took on many aspects of *Modell Deutschland*. Plant workers were represented through an employee council, with members elected from work-area-based constituencies formally resembling German works councils, although without the legal framework. While there was no requirement for members to be union members, officials agreed that they should have shop steward status and perform that role. Although the form of recognition and employee representation was agreed without much controversy – especially notable given the departure from tradition – substantive issues caused problems. Negotiations broke down for eight months over the establishment of working-time patterns. Concerns existed that shift premiums, payment for working unsocial hours, were being undermined as a result of BMW's introduction of working time accounts, in which overtime or undertime would be accrued in a system of debit and credit, rather than plus-payment.

Learning from BMW: the experience of co-determination from a distance

Within months of BMW's takeover of Rover, a process was initiated to establish an EWC to cover plants in Austria, Germany and England. The EWC's foundation in 1996 not only represented an opportunity for Rover shop stewards to develop transnational union positions with BMW colleagues, but was also a chance to review their own employee representative practices. Though at the outset British respondents were poorly informed about *Modell Deutschland*, they soon became conscious of the differences when interacting with their German counterparts. The character of *Modell Deutschland*, particularly the guidelines imposed by the German co-determination law and relationship between plant- and industry-level relations, conflicted with the heritage of Rover shop stewards. These differences became only too apparent when Rover shop stewards undertook discussions with BMW colleagues on the founding of the EWC. From the outset, differences in representative practices were glaring. Activists found themselves attempting to locate key aspects of their own system within that of their counterparts. This should not be a surprise, considering the parochialism of employee organisation. The comment from a Rover shop steward, typical at the time, draws explicit comparison between the UK and German systems: 'there is a group of people on the works council that are responsible for the day-to-day running of the plant. I can only associate that with the things that we might do [at Rover] and things the company might seek to change.'

These cultural differences became most pronounced once the formalities were addressed of locating who the key negotiation parties were and consideration turned to the contentious issue of seat allocation (Whittall 2000, 2004). The main obstacle concerned the presence and role of FTOs within the respective countries. In contrast to the German situation, the absence of any substantial industry-wide collective bargaining or legally defined corporate role for organised labour has meant that the power base of FTOs is traditionally located within the workplace. At Rover, officers headed up negotiations; this appearing anomalous for BMW respondents used to an environment in which the 1952 Works Constitution Act bans FTOs from participating in shop floor organisation (Markowitz 1986). It was also beyond the comprehension of our BMW interviewees that Rover convenors, individuals who deal with day-to-day issues of their plant, were not entrusted with a more substantive position in decision-making processes. Although all BMW works council chairs were active IG Metal members, they viewed works council independence, enshrined in the 1952 Act (Kittner 1997; Thelen 1991), as sacrosanct. It soon became clear that deep-seated differences regarding industrial relations practices lay behind difficult discussions over EWC seat allocation. The German system of co-determination, 'orientated towards cooperation and . . . therefore incompatible with any form of confrontational ideology' (Streeck 1998: 7), remained a mystery for most Rover trade unionists.

The majority of Rover respondents had a high degree of suspicion of the 'cooperative unionism' (Fürstenberg 1998) practised by their BMW counterparts. BMW works council members, dressed in smart suits, sitting in plush and well-equipped offices, driving company cars, and excluding FTOs from plant affairs, were viewed as quasi-personnel managers. As one convenor put it, the Rover negotiators 'had this attitude that we were the genuine trade unionists and . . . [German works council members] were sort of playing at it, sort of management lackeys'. However, BMW respondents could have been forgiven for pointing a critical finger at their Rover counterparts. Although the institutional settings clearly differed, the emphasis placed on job security and positive terms and conditions for the 'immediate' workforce have traditionally been a concern of both Rover and German respondents. But deregulation of industrial relations at Rover at the time made the notion of the 'immediate' a far more pressing concern in Britain than in Germany.

Problems of accountability and confidentiality

An aspect of co-determination of which Rover shop stewards interviewed were highly critical, irrespective of union affiliation, was the perceived lack of accountability and the emphasis placed on confidentiality within works councils and supervisory board meetings. The following position was common to most of the Rover shop stewards:

> I think the thing we look at is the actual distance between the works councils and the people on the shopfloor . . . any of my members can kick the door in and get me by the throat and say: 'What are you doing about this?' and I would not have it any different . . . it has to be explained to the members. I don't have the luxury of, if you like of being a works council member [saying]: 'That is the decision we have made whether you bloody well like it or not' (shop steward).

Forms of accountability, a distinction between 'direct' and 'representative' democracy (Arblaster 1994; Kahn-Freund 1979), mark the difference between British and German employee representation. With the former attuned to the British shop steward experience and the latter practised in Germany, it became a major topic of discussion amongst Rover and BMW employee representatives. For Rover stewards, the fact that works council members took soundings from the shop floor before negotiating a deal, and an unacceptable decision could lead to deselection, did not alleviate their criticism of such a decision-making process. For Rover stewards, changes in working practices should not be implemented without being put to the vote of the workforce. That German company law prohibits supervisory board members from sharing information deemed sensitive with individuals outside this institutional setting was viewed with great suspicion:

> It would have been difficult for us to find some lay member to sit [on the supervisory board] in Munich [and] behave like [employee members on the supervisory board] because that is not our tradition. If I received information I would have to impart that information to my immediate union colleagues. [BMW employee representatives] don't see it necessarily that way.
>
> (Rover shop steward)

Not being able to confide in the workforce, what had arisen in discussions with management, never mind failing to ballot on issues relating to employment changes, was inconceivable for Rover respondents prior to 1998. While factory-gate show of hands may now be a thing of the past, following employment legislation, mass involvement of members is still a central part of employee representation. Until 1998, it remained heresy that any decisions affecting employment at Rover should be taken in the confines of a body that excluded wider employee involvement. Events in 1998, however, represented a major challenge to traditional labour relations at Rover.

Appropriating co-determination

Rover activists' reservations regarding *Modell Deutschland* became only too apparent in 1998, when they were called upon to consider changes in the labour process and employee representation. With Rover reportedly losing £2m a day, management approached senior FTOs about cost-cutting measures outside the realms of the JNC. Consisting of thirty delegates, the JNC was considered too cumbersome an employee forum, and inappropriate to deal with highly sensitive information. An FTO argued, '[Management] were not willing to impart information to thirty-odd people. . . . What we decided to do was set up the Involvement Group.' A shop steward commented,

> BMW were prepared to relate lots of information but not to this full body because it would get out, it would be misused. But they said: 'If you have got a small body of nine then we are prepared to take the chance' because the people who will be on there are convenors and can handle that information.

Central to management demands was the introduction of a working-time account (WTA). Already in place at BMW since 1996, the process of fixing working time to fluctuations in market and model demands was seen as central to achieving necessary savings.

The attempt to convince the JNC of the necessity of establishing an Involvement Group (IG) to discuss changes in working practice proved a fraught affair. A number of reservations came into play, being rooted in activists' heritage. There was the suspicion that this would displace the JNC as the main employee negotiating body linked directly to the shopfloor, replacing with a body which was unaccountable to broader constituents. It was also feared that the IG would lead to company unionism, with its members simply rubber-stamping management decisions, and thus according with the perception of many JNC members of how the supervisory board worked at BMW. Confidentiality most troubled respondents:

> I always looked at it . . . as a secret sect, because they had this confidentiality clause and you just could not repeat what was said there because it was so business-oriented . . . it was the sub-committee of the JNC that could not report back to the JNC until they came with a proposal.
>
> (Rover shop steward)

A number of factors helped to alleviate the JNC's reservations towards the IG. First, the severity of Rover's economic situation. The signals emanating from BMW indicated that failure to reach a compromise would lead Munich to reassess its long-term commitment to the Rover Group. The structure also helped to ease respondents' doubts. The employees' representation, six altogether, would have a strong lay officer presence as well as FTOs from all the main unions. Finally, the EWC made a positive contribution. Since the end of 1997, relations within the EWC had noticeably improved, with various workshops contributing to this change. BMW delegates to the EWC helped to convince Rover sceptics of the potential strengths of such a body. Not only was it argued that the IG would allow trade unionists to be included in governing change, but concession bargaining need not simply be about job security. In fact, the eventual agreement confirmed these views, with Rover employees obtaining a staggered reduction in working time to a thirty-five-hour week.

By the end of 1998, it was quite noticeable that shop stewards were committed to this new path, one that involved them challenging parochial pressures and expressing fewer reservations concerning *Modell Deutschland*:

> I think it is reality, we have to change, I am not saying I like doing the business, but I have to do it at times. But there is an alternative, I can say no to change, but I know we have not got the wherewithal to compete on that basis.
>
> (Rover shop steward)

It is commonly believed that change is never easy, especially when it involves taking on board alien influences. For Rover employee representatives, it not only entailed participating in areas traditionally viewed as management's domain, overseeing initiatives which would enhance the company's competitiveness, but also moving from a reactive to a proactive position with regard to company strategic decisions. Prior to 1998, this had not been the case. A major criticism by BMW employee representatives of their British counterparts concerned the fact that shop stewards took an active role in proposing potential working-time patterns only after management prompting. Nevertheless, the active participation of British trade unionists in drawing up the WTA in late 1998 helped to bring about a realisation that values of co-determination involved a substantial change. According to one Rover shop steward, 'Because along with that involvement comes responsibility, you can't just have the good bits and not get involved in the bad bits.'

Breaking up Rover

The turnaround still proved too slow for some BMW managers, and in early 1999 at an extraordinary meeting of the supervisory board, the company chairman was forced to resign. But, conscious that his heir apparent was in favour of closing Longbridge, the employee representatives on the supervisory board opposed his appointment in favour of Joachim Milburg (Whittall 2000). Following the acceptance of the recovery plan for Longbridge, there was apparent optimism for the future that heightened the surprise of the announcement the following year. In early 2000, after continual speculation, the BMW supervisory board announced it would make a decision on the future of its 'English Patient'. A delegation of Rover shop stewards and FTOs again flew to Munich and sat in an adjoining room while colleagues from the EWC, as German employee members of the board, made decisions on the future of the UK plants. Moreover, Quandt's children, who sat on the supervisory board, were reported to be less attached to BMW than their father (*Sunday Times* 9 April 2000). Having seen the value of their shareholding decline and the company become vulnerable to takeover, they favoured a new strategy.

The decision taken was to retain the Cowley plant, where Mini production was to be relocated, accept 'memoranda of understanding' from Ford for the Land Rover plant in Solihull and from Alchemy – a venture capital firm with plans for small-scale niche production – for the Longbridge plant. Each was given six weeks to establish a bid. Despite increased contact with their British colleagues through the EWC and the Longbridge recovery plan, as well as other activities, the employee representatives on the board feared that Rover could threaten the independent future of BMW. The importance of the 'memorandum' with Alchemy for the BMW employee representatives was that, instead of the closure of Longbridge with the loss of all jobs there, it held out the promise of salvaging jobs from the wreckage. With the resignation of three members of the management board, however, it is clear that not even all management were happy with the decision.

The sale to Alchemy was also challenged locally. It was seen as an attempt at asset stripping, and an opposition campaign took shape. While focusing on the maintenance of local jobs along the supplier chain for mass production (Batchelor 2001), in some ways it was reminiscent of the events surrounding BMW in 1959. An alliance was established around both the Longbridge unions and management, the latter associated with 'Rover Tomorrow' and who had departed under BMW ownership. While the unions distanced themselves from some of the more nationalistic manifestations of the campaign, it was very much presented as a campaign to save local jobs. There was a rushed shift in production of the new Rover 75 from Cowley (renamed BMW Oxford) to Longbridge, which it swapped for Mini production. This move, more than the issue of Rover shares to the workforce, facilitated a sense of cooperation between management and workforce.

At Longbridge, employee relations were reconstructed almost as they had been prior to the BMW takeover. Early on, the relationship between unions and Phoenix, the eventual 'winner' in the bid to take over from BMW, meant a period of truce, with any concession bargaining – where the new management might seek to challenge the established levels of pay and conditions – restricted to the first year. Opposition grew to WTAs that were seen by many of the workforce as part of an unfulfilled agreement with BMW. The workforce had agreed to WTA in exchange for BMW's continued support. The annual pay round saw regular threats of withdrawal from WTA, especially since regular shutdowns began to be implemented by management to reduce production over an extended Christmas period, prompted by continued decline in demand for Rover cars. This enforced leave meant that the workers accumulated time debt to the company and had echoes for some of the lay-offs experienced in earlier periods. All agreed that a strike over pay would appear self-destructive when the company was struggling for survival, with continued decline in market share and overall sales (*Financial Times* 16 March 2002).

While presenting an air of defending local jobs, the new company also established a global focus in part justified by the need to establish both new markets and, perhaps even more, a new model range. Initially there was an abortive attempt at alliance with China Brilliance (*Financial Times* 27 December 2002, 22 July 2003), then a distribution deal with Tata in India, and then speculation concerning a Daewo plant in Poland (*The Times* 19 February 2004), as well as a potential agreement with the Malaysian company Proton. There emerged a dual strategy that sought to solve both production and sales problems through moves towards strategic partnerships. On the one side, the main production at Longbridge was the midrange 25 and 45 series that dated back to the Honda alliance and, although much modified, were produced on dated lines and needed replacement. On the other, there was a need to attempt to maintain market share through both importation of rebadged cars and expanding into new markets, of which booming China was seen as a favourite target (*Guardian* 24 April 2004). However, this moved corporate emphasis away from the local production facilities in Longbridge towards global licensing deals, seemingly chasing cheaper labour costs. The distancing from production appeared to be further reinforced by the corporate structure set up under Phoenix, a holding company which ring-fenced Rover's profitable parts while the car business continued to lose money and sales (*Guardian* 31 March 2004).

Reflections on mobilisation and recognition at Rover

This chapter has explored the turbulent employment relations at Rover, which through the 1960s and 1970s became symbolic of union militancy and perhaps a model for the mobilisation of workers in the workplace. Archive footage of Derek Robinson, craft union convener at Longbridge, addressing a mass meeting at the factory gate remains a common illustration of industrial relations reports in the period. Shop floor organisation at Rover remained intact but importantly neither unscathed nor unmarginalised. This process began under a Labour government's strategy for the motor industry and pre-empted that of the Thatcher government. Union exclusion under the Edwardes Plan may have robbed the plan of some wider legitimacy. This was certainly the motive of management in canvassing union involvement in 'Rover Tomorrow', the 'partnership' agreement which principally promoted the introduction of new working arrangements a decade later. It must also indicate how unions had retained some force in the period.

The sacking of Derek Robinson was as much the failure of worker mobilisation in support of the sacked convenor as it was the emergence of 'macho-management'. The events surrounding the Edwardes Plan, and to an extent its predecessor the Ryder Report, represented an escalating sense of crisis for the company, a situation in which job security not surprisingly topped the union agenda. In addition, this insecurity was not alleviated by the withdrawal of government support for a domestic motor industry, representing a general shift away from state interventionism. This background even helped shape the relationship with BMW and embedded the essential strategy of MG Rover under Phoenix ownership. This sense permeated the strategy of shop stewards and unions as much as management, who often allied together to attempt to secure this salvation, most publicly in the Phoenix rescue.

We can observe a move towards a cooperative strategy by unions, where their priorities are focused on the survival of jobs in a period marked by economic downturn. There are, though, competing tensions at play. While partnership may represent a new approach towards management, the following have to be considered. First, unions needed to maintain the support of a shop floor membership potentially concerned with keeping to a traditional agenda, i.e. improving pay and conditions as well as challenging what might be perceived as injustices (Oxenbridge *et al.* 2003). Next, and with production increasingly diversified and plants engaged in assembling different models, there was also a sense of variable subjection to crisis across different locations. There was a stronger sense of security at Cowley, for example, than at Longbridge, while ultimately German employee representatives sacrificed most of their British colleagues, believing it would save jobs in Munich. So union organisation was not a straightforward representation of shop floor opinion since it had to transcend often different interests. A strong sense of parochialism permeated the consciousness of employees across different sites – let alone across different countries – many feeling defensive about their own locale.

By the 1980s, organisational radicalism seemed to be tamed, the result of a forced alliance with management embodied in the 'Rover Tomorrow' pioneering partnership deal. Although militancy was affected by counter-mobilisation measures instituted in the early 1980s, other factors need to be considered. A sense of demobilisation pervaded union organisation within Rover, understood essentially as part of changing internal relationships and the construction of alliances between differing factions. But this reflects the complex role that unions established for recognition and collective bargaining. Not only were these the forums for establishing pay and conditions but they also became the main channels for informing and consulting the workforce. However, this situation was not without problems. There was some dependence on management's general willingness to communicate with, and involve, shop stewards and FTOs in corporate decision-making. In turn, this was dependent upon management style as well as the context of such decision-making. And in this there was almost certainly some relationship with the economic context as well as a 'cycle' of involvement (Ramsay 1977), possibly also linked with 'long-wave' cycles in the economy as Kelly (1998) suggests. Finally, there was the restriction of this involvement vis-à-vis the potential sensitivity of information that might be communicated.

But in the encounter with *Modell Deutschland*, the Rover union reps were all too conscious of the duality of consultation and involvement. Not only were they acclimatised to a tradition which favoured direct democracy rather than the delegation exercised by the works council officers, they initially saw their German counterparts as much as representatives of management than of employees. This was not just in their demeanour and resources available, but their very position within German labour relations. Distanced from collective bargaining, which normally occurs between management organisation and trade unions at regional and national level, pluralism is inherent in the works council constitution, where works council delegates are required to articulate a common interest with the company. The essence of *Modell Deutschland*, the basis of the establishment of the dual system of unions and collective bargaining formally separated from the works council, is the demobilisation of the shop floor. However, despite initial reservations concerning the air of managerialism that permeated the employee representatives within *Modell Deutschland*, Rover union officials noted how German employee representatives had access to the heights of corporate power and decision-making. What they also encountered was a very different relationship between workers and their representatives, where the managerialism of works councils was rooted in confidentiality and forms of representative democracy alien to traditions of British shop stewards.

In the context of crisis and decline, as well as of a direct Europeanisation through BMW ownership, the unions were willing to challenge British traditional practices and experiment with new forms of representation and involvement. But there was more to collective bargaining than mere institutional arrangements. Although union recognition struggles were experienced only by our most long-serving informants, the past still pervaded current activists' thinking. Irrespective of age, there was acceptance that gains in pay and conditions won since the 1950s had been hard fought for. In the process of achieving and defending these gains, plant organisation had become the very symbol of militant trade unionism. It had, through collective bargaining, also established a complex system of regulation over the employment relationship that not only measured their gains or position against management but also acted as a means of defending workers' interest within the workplace. These rules had often been considered sacrosanct by some Rover workers even more than by stewards, at times to the extent of 'pig-headedness'. Stewards were not immune from images of their own past, though. Stoppages of work had been called because of some minor contravention. But the inference was that such occurrences were now in the past. Although the rules of the game were far more flexible on their side – as with WTAs – there was resentment when management appeared to have contravened its side of the bargain. But, while employee representatives had been instrumental in mobilising for partnership with management, more than they had been party to the Phoenix buy-out, this did not put labour and capital on a joint path, however much they might strive for a more secure future. In part, it is potentially a very different future for which they strive. But it is not a continuance of 'trench warfare', with the mobilisation of class warriors in regular skirmish and periodic battle. Although class struggle may have ceased, this in no way signals the end of hostilities. Rather, an unsteady truce exists, based on employee pragmatism rather than an unconditional surrender to management rule.[2]

Acknowledgement

Our thanks are due to Gregor Gall for helping revise the chapter.

Notes

1 While we have attempted to maintain the confidentiality of our interviewees, given their role within employment relations and the broader stage of these events, we directly recognise the support of Manfred Schoch, chair of the EWC and deputy chair of the BMW Supervisory Board, and Tony Woodley, TGWU general secretary and formerly TGWU national officer for the automobile industry.

2 This chapter was written over a year in advance of the bankruptcy of Rover in mid-2005.

6 The nature of collective bargaining achieved through the statutory procedure

Sonia McKay, Sian Moore and Hannah Wood

The Employment Relations Act 1999 marks a departure in British industrial relations: for the first time, the law is beginning to shape the formal content of collective bargaining, despite the government's declared intention to create conditions that encourage the conclusion of voluntary recognition agreements. First, under the legislation, if the parties cannot come to an agreement over a bargaining procedure, the CAC may impose a legally enforceable method, setting out strictly defined procedural arrangements. Second, the statutory award of recognition sets a minimal model for bargaining over pay, hours and holidays only. This statutory minimum is considered by unions to be restrictive in its scope (TUC 2003). Although the parties may agree to broaden the content of the agreement, the existence of the statutory model may influence the scope of any agreements the parties conclude following a statutory award.

This chapter explores the outcome of the statutory recognition procedure in terms of the conclusion of procedural agreements for collective bargaining. It looks at those cases where the parties have not been able to come to an agreement and examines the effectiveness of the statutory process in facilitating meaningful collective bargaining. Following this, it examines the content of recognition agreements emerging from the statutory process (see also Gall 2003f, 2004b, 2004c) and explores how far agreements reflect the statutory procedure in terms of the scope of bargaining, bargaining process and termination provisions. Finally, the chapter considers whether agreements concluded after the parties have resorted to the law are restrictive beyond the limits of the statutory procedure, for example, by limiting industrial action or providing for dual channels of employee representation which may undermine union representation. The contention is that since these agreements are likely to be the outcome of recognition claims where employers have contested unionisation, the scope and depth of bargaining will be narrower and the nature of the relationship more restrictive than where agreements are concluded voluntarily, outside the procedure. Statutory or semi-voluntary agreements may reflect the statutory model, either because this is all the employer is prepared to concede or because it has been imposed by the CAC. Thus, although the existence of a statutory model of recognition has encouraged a proliferation of voluntary arrangements in its shadow (see Gall 2004b; Wood *et al.* 2002, 2003), at the same time it brings the law into the heart of collective relationships.

We begin by outlining the research methods used, and by providing a background to the statutory procedure, focusing upon the method of bargaining. Then we explore the outcomes of statutory recognition to date and CAC imposition of a bargaining method. The following section analyses the nature of the recognition agreements emerging from the statutory procedure. Finally, we offer some conclusions, where we argue that the law is shaping and limiting collective bargaining, at least as far as formal agreements are concerned. However, the statutory procedure cannot guarantee meaningful bargaining in the face of employer opposition: ultimately this has to come from union organisation in the workplace (see Gall 2004a; Moore 2004).

Research methods

A textual analysis of seventy-two recognition agreements emerging from the statutory process was conducted. This sample included agreements which have been imposed by the CAC because the parties had been unable to come to an agreement following a statutory award of recognition, agreements negotiated by the parties following a statutory award of recognition, and 'semi-voluntary' agreements where an application has been made to the CAC but later withdrawn by the union, resulting in a recognition agreement concluded outside the procedure. These procedural agreements were collected as part of a survey of all CAC cases where there had been an outcome between 6 June 2000 and 31 May 2004. The survey took the form of a postal questionnaire to the union officer responsible for CAC applications, in some cases followed up by a telephone or face-to-face interview. Where the case had resulted in recognition, the union officer was asked to supply a copy of the agreement. The survey population for this analysis is 145 cases known to have resulted in a recognition agreement, submitted by twenty different unions. In another two known cases a collective bargaining agreement had not resulted, because the workplace closed following recognition. Of these 145, eighty-five (59 per cent) were agreements concluded following a statutory award and sixty (41 per cent) were semi-voluntary agreements. Sixty-six copies of recognition agreements were returned (including two where the method of bargaining had been imposed). These, along with six cases where recognition was imposed and where the text of the bargaining method was available on the CAC website, represent seventy-two agreements – a response rate of 50 per cent. Of these, forty-three (60 per cent) were agreements concluded following a statutory award and twenty-nine (40 per cent) were semi-voluntary agreements. The agreements were concluded by sixteen different unions, including one that was not TUC-affiliated. These seventy-two agreements cover over 19,000 workers. We refer to this survey throughout the chapter as 'the survey of statutory and semi-voluntary agreements'.

For the purposes of comparison, we also draw upon our Department of Trade and Industry research (Moore *et al.* 2004), referred to as 'the DTI survey'. This analysis of the content and coverage of voluntary recognition agreements was based upon a statistically representative sample of 213 recognition agreements, drawn from the TUC/LRD surveys of new recognitions conducted between 1998 and 2002. The sample included a small proportion of semi-voluntary agreements (3 per cent), but overwhelmingly represents entirely voluntary agreements. Overall, these procedural agreements were concluded by twenty-six different unions and (since the data came from the TUC/LRD survey) all were TUC-affiliated. The DTI survey did, however, exclude one large manufacturing union which was represented in our survey of statutory and semi-voluntary agreements. However, excluding this union from our survey made very little difference to the proportion restricting bargaining to core issues.

In terms of industrial classification, there was broad similarity between our survey of statutory and semi-voluntary agreements and the DTI survey of voluntary agreements. In both, new recognition agreements were largely found in manufacturing and transport sectors, with printing and publishing, and food, beverages and tobacco subsectors featuring strongly. Manual workers were much more likely than other occupational groups to be covered by recognition agreements, whether statutory, semi-voluntary or voluntary. Around two-thirds of agreements in both surveys were based on single sites. In both, and in the vast majority of cases, the union was granted sole recognition for the bargaining unit. One difficulty in analysing the content of new recognition agreements is the absence of any previous historical study of union recognition agreements against which to make comparisons. Thus, although we highlight a number of features of new statutory and semi-voluntary agreements, it is not possible to state conclusively how far these are a departure from traditional collective bargaining.

Statutory specified method

Schedule A of ERA sets out the process by which unions can apply for statutory recognition. Statutory awards may be made either if a membership check ordered by the CAC confirms both that a majority of the workforce in the bargaining unit are union members and that a majority is likely to support recognition for collective bargaining, or if the CAC orders a ballot of the bargaining unit and if a simple majority, representing 40 per cent of those eligible to vote, favour recognition for collective bargaining. Schedule A1 of the Trade Union and Labour Relations (Consolidated) Act 1992, into which the Schedule A of ERA was inserted, includes provision for what should happen where a declaration of recognition is made, but where the parties are then unable to agree a bargaining method. It is fundamental to the legislation that recognition should have an outcome, in terms of a bargaining procedure, although there is no obligation on the parties to negotiate if both do not wish to do so. However, the assumption is that the union will wish to conclude an agreement over the bargaining method.

The parties have a period of thirty working days (the 'negotiation period') from the day on which they are notified of the declaration of recognition (or longer by agreement) 'with a view to agreeing a method by which they will conduct collective bargaining' (para. 30). If they enter into negotiations but fail to reach an agreement, either or both parties can make an application for assistance to the CAC. It must try to help the parties to reach, within the 'agreement period' (twenty working days after the day on which the CAC receives the application), an agreed method. If no agreement emerges, the CAC must specify the bargaining method. The parties can apply jointly to the CAC to have this process terminated at any stage prior to the specification of the method.

One important difference between voluntary agreement on the bargaining method and the imposition of a statutory specified method is that under the latter the bargaining method is 'to have effect as if it were contained in a legally enforceable contract made by the parties' (Article 2, Preamble, The Trade Union Recognition (Method of Collective Bargaining) Order Statutory Instrument 2000/1300). The only circumstance where this would not happen is where the parties agree in writing that the agreement shall not have legal effect. However, the agreement not to make the bargaining method legally enforceable itself becomes a legally enforceable contract. Once an agreement is legally enforceable, the parties have a legal remedy (specific performance) for breach of any matter specified in it. An order for specific performance obliges the party against whom the order has been sought to comply with the agreement. A refusal to do so exposes that party to a contempt of court action in which the High Court could impose unlimited fines or imprisonment. Of course, in practice, it will be rare for the court to do so and the criticism of the legislation is precisely its failure to promote effective sanctions. An order to impose a specified method of bargaining does not affect the rights of individual workers either under statute or contract.

The Trade Union Recognition (Method of Collective Bargaining) Order sets out the 'specified method' of collective bargaining. It is intended to apply in rare cases, the assumption being that most parties would want to agree their own bargaining method since 'most voluntary agreements are not legally binding and are usually concluded in a climate of trust and co-operation' (preamble to the Order). Thus, it was assumed that the sting in the tail of the legislation, the fact that what it imposed was a legally binding agreement, would be sufficient to encourage the parties to reach a voluntary agreement. This has proven generally to be correct (see below). The Order also states that the specified method 'is not designed to be applied as a model for voluntary procedural agreements'. However, where the CAC is exercising its powers to impose a method of collective bargaining, it must take the specified method into account, although it may depart from the method 'to such extent as it thinks appropriate in the circumstances of individual cases' (para. 168(2)(b) Schedule A1). This is surprising, since other aspects of recognition law offer the CAC limited room for manoeuvre once the statutory tests are met. The Order specifies how the parties are to bargain. They must appoint a Joint Negotiating Body (JNB) to discuss and negotiate pay, hours and holidays on an annual basis. A detailed six-step procedure sets down strict time limits, while guidance is offered on who the JNB officers are and how its chair and secretary should function. Other issues specified include facilities and time-off arrangements, disclosure of information, and a requirement that collective agreements be set down in writing.

Outcomes of statutory recognition

By 31 May 2004, the CAC had granted recognition in ninety-six of the 372 applications made to it: thirty-nine cases without a ballot and fifty-seven cases after unions had won recognition ballots. In the majority of these (N = 60), the parties had themselves agreed a method of bargaining following the declaration of recognition. In twenty-eight cases, the method of bargaining had yet to be determined. In eight cases the parties had not been able to reach agreement and as a result the CAC had to impose a bargaining method.

Of the 372 applications, ninety-eight were withdrawn before a decision on acceptance could be made. It is probable that most of these were withdrawn for technical reasons (and in some cases resubmitted), although a small number may have resulted in a recognition agreement (see Gall 2004b). In a further sixty-two cases the application had been withdrawn following acceptance or after the bargaining unit had been agreed or determined and, although the CAC has no comprehensive data on this, it is likely that a proportion of these resulted in 'semi-voluntary' agreements (see Gall 2004b). In semi-voluntary cases, provided the employer employs at least twenty-one workers and the union has a certificate of independence, the CAC can impose a bargaining method.

Imposition of the statutory method of bargaining

Once recognition has been awarded or agreed, our survey of statutory and semi-voluntary agreements suggests that securing a procedural (method of bargaining) agreement may prove difficult, even where the employer has not appeared to put significant resources into contesting recognition itself. In one such case, an FTO stated, 'nailing blancmange to the ceiling would have been marginally easier'. On the basis of the eight cases, it seems likely that the CAC will impose the statutory specified model with little or no amendment. In half, the method was imposed almost intact. For example, in the case of Amicus–Spraymasters (case number TUR/294), the method imposed was identical to the statutory specified method, other than removing references to a specific gender, by inserting the term 'chair' instead of 'Chairman'.

There appears to be little relationship between employers' attitude to recognition in the course of the CAC application and a subsequent inability to agree a bargaining method. In six imposed-methods cases, the employers had not raised major objections while the recognition claim was going through the CAC. At Spraymasters, for example, the employer had not even pressed for a ballot before recognition was awarded. Similarly in the case of UNIFI–Union Bank of Nigeria (TUR/16), both sides agreed that, as the majority in the bargaining unit were members, none of the three qualifying conditions for the holding of a ballot applied and the CAC issued a declaration of recognition. Unable to reach agreement on the bargaining method, the parties sought CAC assistance. The stumbling block was whether the obligation to negotiate on pay included an obligation to negotiate on matters relating to pensions. This was the first time the definition of 'pay' had been considered by the CAC. The union claimed that pensions were deferred pay, citing a number of other collective agreements within the industry where pensions were negotiated. The bank argued that parliamentary intention in introducing the statutory procedure had been to give 'pay' a minimalist definition.

In coming to its decision, the CAC acknowledged that its role was interpretative and not innovative. However, from the CAC panel's industrial experience, it took the view that pensions were increasingly included as a negotiating item. The CAC therefore ruled that 'the obligation to negotiate on "pay" includes all matters relating to the levels or amount of employer's pension contributions'. It then imposed a bargaining method. This was very similar to the statutory specified model, with some minor changes regarding time limits and the size of the JNB. The union reported that, since recognition, relations between the parties have been 'very congenial' and non-conflictual, with three 'amicable' pay settlements. The bargaining method had been adhered to in each pay round and the fact that it was imposed by the CAC 'had a significant influence on the conduct of negotiations'. Pensions had not been the subject of negotiations, as no specific negotiating issues had emerged.

In the GMB–A.J. Cheetham case (TUR/159), the union asked the CAC to impose a procedure agreement that would include a right to paid time off for union members attending workforce meetings, even though the statutory specified model stated: 'the employer is under no obligation to pay individuals for the time off'. The CAC panel decided not to rule either way on this issue. The method imposed is silent on whether or not there should be a right to paid time off for meetings. The panel said it would encourage the parties to 'jointly negotiate an amicable and workable arrangement'. The GMB–Ifor Williams Trailers case (TUR/182), involving a family-owned business, has been more conflictual. The union viewed the owner-manager as hostile to unions and resentful of legal interference in workplace relations, questioning the level of membership and claiming the majority of workers neither wanted, nor would benefit from, recognition. He pushed for a ballot and recognition was granted when 79 per cent of the bargaining unit voted in favour. Unable to get agreement on a bargaining method, the union applied to the CAC for assistance and it imposed the specified method. The first round of wage negotiations was acrimonious, with the union calling industrial action over the employer's refusal to make a pay award to union members. In the second round of pay negotiations, the bargaining method was adhered to and a settlement was concluded.

In the UNIFI–Persia International Bank (originally the Tejarat Bank) case (TUR/144), the bank's management pointed out that the organisation would shortly cease to exist in its current form and that any recognition award would thus have 'no practical implementation'. The CAC, applying the statutory tests regarding membership levels and workplace support, awarded recognition. No agreement was reached on the bargaining method. Indeed, seventeen days after its creation, the new bank applied to have the union derecognised on the basis that the bargaining unit no longer existed. The CAC panel decided that the legislation did not permit this on the basis that, as no procedure had been agreed, there were no bargaining arrangements in place that could be terminated. Thus, the fact that the bank had been unwilling or unable to conclude a method of bargaining deprived it of the right to have the union derecognised. This was the first time the CAC had examined the implications of this part of the legislation, but its ruling makes it clear that, for the purposes of the derecognition of statutory recognition cases, the parties must first have a method of bargaining in place. The CAC then imposed the specified method.

Imposing a legally binding agreement does not guarantee that a working bargaining relationship will be established. The design of the statutory procedure means that although the penalties for non-compliance appear stringent, in practice, an employer determined to ignore them can do so with relative impunity. At Persia International, the imposition of the specified method had not resulted in any collective bargaining and there had been no pay settlement since. According to the union, the bank refused to negotiate. In these circumstances a union has limited scope for action. It can go to court to get an order for specific performance. It can even press for contempt of court proceedings against the employer, but it cannot make the employer negotiate. Legal advice obtained by the union was that going to law would be costly, unlikely to result in constructive collective bargaining and could set an unwelcome precedent for other claims, should a decision go against the union. This reveals a fundamental flaw in the statutory procedure and explains why, by 31 May 2004, no union had taken an employer to court for specific performance, despite a number of recorded cases where the employer had refused to comply with, at the very least, the spirit of the legislation.

In the GPMU–John Brown case (TUR/115), also the subject of a specified method, there had been no subsequent pay settlement. Although meetings were held between the parties, no constructive outcome was forthcoming. The GPMU perceived this as a fault of the CAC procedure. Although it had an agreement that looked good on paper, it could not translate this into a meaningful bargaining relationship where the employer refused to cooperate. Furthermore, the union had been advised that there would be little to gain from legal action. Surprisingly, given that the companies were associated, the post-recognition picture at Derry Print (also the subject of a recognition award contemporaneous with that at John Brown) was more positive. There the union reported that there had been a pay settlement involving a substantial wage increase, together with changes to shift patterns and grading structures. The union was in negotiations to extend the bargaining unit. Thus, although a failure to agree a bargaining method does not necessarily reflect employer hostility to recognition, where an employer does resist bargaining, the statutory procedures appear to offer unions no effective remedy.

Coverage and content of statutory and semi-voluntary recognition agreements

In the majority of cases emerging from the statutory process the CAC did not have to impose a method of bargaining. However, although the statutory Order makes it clear that the method should not be used as a model, our survey of statutory and semi-voluntary agreements suggests that the statutory provisions have shaped the content of these new agreements and that the method of bargaining has been guided by the specified model.

Scope of bargaining

Table 6.1 shows that in 61 per cent of the statutory and semi-voluntary agreements, the scope of collective bargaining mirrored the minimum that

Table 6.1 Bargaining coverage in statutory and semi-voluntary agreements

Scope	*Statutory awards*	*Semi-voluntary agreements*	*Total*
Bargaining restricted to pay, hours and holidays only	33 (76.7%)	11 (37.9%)	44 (61.1%)
Bargaining defined as covering 'terms and conditions'	4 (9.3%)	12 (41.4%)	16 (22.2%)
Bargaining defined as including core and non-core issues	6 (14.0%)	5 (17.2%)	11 (15.3%)
Bargaining issues unspecified	0 (0.0%)	1 (3.4%)	1 (1.4%)
Total agreements in the survey	43 (59.7%)	29 (40.3%)	72 (100%)

the employer is obliged to offer, that is pay, hours and holidays only. If those eight agreements where recognition was imposed are removed, the figure is 56 per cent (thirty-six of the remaining sixty-four agreements). For example, in one agreement, 'the employer recognises the union as the trade union with which it will consult and negotiate on the following contractual terms and conditions of staff in the bargaining unit being: hours of work, pay, [and] annual leave'. Some agreements further defined these core issues, for example one national agreement included 'changes on general salary review, to basic annual salary i.e. the percentage change to be applied nationally; change to the standard working week; changes to the standard annual holiday entitlement or public holiday entitlement'. In another case pay was defined in broad terms: 'The company agrees to negotiate with the union on all matters relating to pay, hours of work and holidays. For the avoidance of doubt pay includes basic pay, overtime, shift allowances, holiday pay, productivity or any other contractual bonus and redundancy pay.'

In 22 per cent of agreements, bargaining was defined in much more general terms as over 'pay and conditions' or 'terms and conditions'. For example, in one agreement in the print sector, the company and union 'will negotiate terms and conditions of employment on an annual basis or when otherwise mutually agreed'. In 15 per cent of agreements, bargaining was defined as including the core issues of pay, hours and holidays, plus a number of other specified non-core issues which was not an exhaustive list. For example, in one agreement covering a bank, negotiations 'may include but will not be limited to: pay, hours of work, holidays, training, pension entitlements and any other matters which may be agreed from time to time'. In some of these cases, the subjects stated as being included did not go far beyond pay, hours and holidays: one agreement covered only 'conditions of employment i.e. pay, hours, holidays and sickness rights'. Other agreements were more expansive:

> the company recognises the right of the union to represent its members with regard to terms and conditions of employment including pay, hours, holidays, sickness and pension rights; individual and collective issues arising from the disciplinary [and] grievance procedures; security of employment matters including any redundancies, short time working, redeployment and/or retraining; equal opportunities, family friendly policies, health and safety and other subjects agreed as a topic for consultation and negotiation.

Pay

Pay emerges as a fundamental element in new recognition agreements. In 85 per cent of cases pay was specified in the agreements as the subject of negotiation, and in a further 14 per cent, bargaining was defined as covering terms and conditions in general and it is likely that pay was included. Pay and hours were not specifically excluded from bargaining in any agreement in the survey. In one agreement, holidays appeared to be excluded, since it was stated that 'negotiations on wage rates and hours of work will be conducted by the negotiating body'.

Personal contracts

Paragraph 19 of the statutory method of bargaining states that employers' obligation to discuss any variation in the contractual terms affecting pay, hours and holidays does not apply to terms in the contract of an individual worker 'where that worker has agreed that the terms may be altered only by direct negotiation between the worker and the employer'. In four agreements, this provision for personal contracts was emphasised. One stated, 'inclusion in the bargaining unit shall not prevent individuals from voluntarily agreeing to the establishing of their terms and conditions through individual contracts'. In another, 'those employees who have elected to negotiate their terms and conditions individually are not covered by this agreement'. In a further case, of a regional newspaper, a situation had also arisen whereby a number of journalists were on personal contracts and thus removed from collective bargaining. This meant that the union had no information on the distribution of pay and pay increases within the bargaining unit for those covered by collective bargaining compared to those 'opted out', and in particular whether those that had 'opted out' had received a higher percentage increase than those covered by collective bargaining. This led the union to return to the CAC and, under the terms of a subsequent CAC agreement, the company agreed to provide the percentage budgeted pay increase for the payroll as a whole across the company, the number of individuals who had opted in and out of collective bargaining, the budgeted cost of salary increases to the bargaining unit and to the opted-in members of the bargaining unit.

Pensions

Despite the CAC's decision in the Bank of Nigeria case, the government's review of the ERA proposed to clarify that pensions should not be regarded as 'pay' for the specific purposes of the procedure. Clause 20 of the Employment Relations Act 2004 inserts a definition of pay into Schedule A1, which specifically excludes pensions, although it gives the secretary of state the power to make an order to add pensions to the three core topics at some future date. Pensions were specifically included in the scope of bargaining in 11 per cent of agreements. Following the CAC ruling that pensions should be defined as pay for the purposes of bargaining, UNIFI ensured that pensions were specified in three semi-voluntary agreements included in this survey. However, pensions were specifically excluded from bargaining in 64 per cent of agreements. In one of these, 'the union undertook that it will never advance any claim for representation on any pension matter'. It is not possible to identify from textual analysis of the agreements alone whether pensions would be included for bargaining under agreements defined in general terms as covering terms and conditions. Bargaining on pensions has been constrained by the status of pension schemes as separate legal entities generally run by a board of trustees, which may or may not include union representation. Case studies in the DTI research suggest that pensions are often excluded from the negotiations, sometimes on the basis that the pension scheme was under the control of a parent company, but also because of the closure of final salary schemes and their replacement by money purchase or stakeholder schemes.

Comparison between coverage in statutory, semi-voluntary and voluntary agreements

Table 6.1 shows that agreements resulting from a statutory award were more likely to restrict bargaining than semi-voluntary agreements. Seventy-seven per cent did so, compared to over 38 per cent of semi-voluntary agreements. Semi-voluntary agreements were far more likely to define bargaining in general terms (41 per cent) than those resulting from a statutory award (9 per cent).

The DTI survey provides data for the comparison of voluntary agreements with the survey of semi-voluntary and statutory recognition agreements. If the small number of semi-voluntary agreements in the DTI survey were excluded, 21 per cent of agreements were restricted to one or more of pay, hours and holiday. In contrast, the proportion of statutory and semi-voluntary agreements restricted to pay, hours and holidays was 61 per cent. In the DTI survey, a far greater proportion (57 per cent) of agreements were more generally defined as covering pay and conditions or terms and conditions. Thus, as expected, the scope of bargaining is wider in voluntary agreements and more confined in statutory, and to a lesser extent, semi-voluntary agreements. This may reflect the more constructive nature of industrial relations between the parties in cases where recognition has been concluded outside the statutory procedure and/or the incentive provided by voluntary agreement for greater flexibility over bargaining.

In the survey of statutory and semi-voluntary agreements, a number of union officers expressed frustration at the restriction of bargaining by virtue of the ERA. One stated that despite winning a ballot of the workforce, 'the company absolutely refused to go beyond this [i.e. pay, hours and holidays]'. In another case where the union had also won a ballot, the union officer complained that, 'having achieved recognition this could be limited to the statutory procedure, pay, hours and holidays. There is apparently no way a comprehensive recognition agreement can be enforced unless the employer agrees it. This appears to me to defeat the purpose of seeking full bargaining rights.' In this case, the company had been taken over shortly after recognition and the workplace closed. Despite restriction of bargaining in the agreement, the union negotiated a severance package for those made redundant. In another national agreement, where the scope of bargaining reflected the statutory model, the employer resisted attempts by the union to broaden national discussions to sick pay and tried to prevent issues being discussed locally. Union strength in workplaces covered by the agreement meant this had not always been possible: when there had been redundancies at one workplace, the union negotiated the transfer of workers to another workplace. Nationally, there had been two pay settlements since recognition and the harmonisation of service-related holidays, resulting in an increase for some workers.

In some cases a commitment to bargain in good faith was written into the recognition agreement. In one, the employer 'undertakes to enter into meaningful collective bargaining with the union for the review of pay, hours and holidays'. Here, the union considered that substantial progress had been made since recognition, with the negotiation of the first pay increase for nine years, a cut in hours, an increase in holidays and improvements to bank holiday working. In another agreement, the union reported that there was now 'a progressive relationship': there had been two pay settlements, workers' contracts had been reissued and improved and the union had been invited into other sites to recruit, with the likelihood that recognition would be extended.

Bargaining procedures and machinery

In 68 per cent of the statutory and semi-voluntary agreements analysed, a bargaining procedure was contained, whilst 76 per cent made reference to a JNB and 60 per cent had both. Five per cent adopted the statutory specified bargaining procedure, even though this had not been imposed, and a further 9 per cent a variation on it. Half adopted a bargaining procedure which was not based on the statutory model and 34 per cent made no reference to how bargaining would be conducted. Although the statutory model establishes a JNB, it only requires the parties to meet to negotiate annual pay bargaining, rather than facilitating any regular bargaining relationship. This was considered a limitation in one case, where the parties were unable to come to an agreement on the method of bargaining because the FTO wanted the agreement to specify four meetings a year, along with the opportunity to call meetings as and when issues arose. The employer wanted a maximum of two. The FTO reluctantly agreed to this after he discovered that the statutory model specified only one meeting for the purpose of pay bargaining.

In one agreement, it was stated that 'collective bargaining will not take place outside of the annual review period'. In another, the union was 'entitled to conduct collective bargaining in respect of pay, hours and holidays. [However], in the event that the company seeks to make changes to such terms and conditions at times other than during the annual pay review period, they will consult the union.' In this case, continued employer hostility and absence of strong union workplace representation meant there was no bargaining relationship outside annual pay negotiations. In contrast, another agreement stated, 'negotiations between the two sides shall be conducted with a committee to be known as the Joint Negotiating Committee. Meetings of the committee shall be held as and when requested by either side with the proviso that there will be at least four meetings in each calendar year.'

Comparison with the DTI research suggests that voluntary agreements were less likely to provide for the establishment of any bargaining machinery. Of the DTI sample, 55 per cent did so, compared to eight out of ten statutory or semi-voluntary agreements. Since the procedure was deemed to be highly prescriptive, this may suggest that voluntary agreement provided the incentive for more flexibility. The adoption of the statutory method of bargaining may reflect an intention by the employer to restrict bargaining to the annual pay review. And one outcome of the statutory recognition procedure appears to be a focus on annual pay bargaining.

Mechanisms for termination of the agreement

The statutory procedure contains provisions which permit derecognition in a number of specified circumstances. Analysis of the statutory and semi-voluntary agreements showed that thirteen reflected aspects of the statutory provisions, most usually triggered when union membership falls below a specified level. In one, it was stated that the agreement would terminate 'if union membership falls below 15 per cent'. In another, 'if union membership within the bargaining unit falls below the number required by the relevant legislation at the time to retain union recognition then the company will discuss the situation with the union and seek the opinion of the bargaining group via a ballot as to whether this agreement and union recognition for collective bargaining purposes should continue or not'. Another specified that, 'in the event that membership of the Union falls below 40 per cent of the bargaining unit, the Company and the Union agree that there should be a membership ballot on the subject of continued recognition at the Company'. In effect, the union had to match the statutory requirement for the whole of the period of recognition, but unlike the statutory procedure, it did not allow the union at least three years of recognition before a challenge could be made on the basis of falling membership. In one national agreement, the union could have local representation only in workplaces where it could be shown that at least 50 per cent of the employees in the bargaining unit were members. Other agreements effectively committed the parties to renegotiate recognition after a period of time, most often reflecting the statutory period of three years. Two agreements concluded in 2003 protected the agreement until 2006, with one stating that thereafter the employer might apply to the CAC for derecognition. These provisions suggest that employer opposition to unionisation may not have been entirely overcome by the process of recognition.

No-strike clauses and binding arbitration

Of the seventy cases in the survey where a bargaining method had been agreed, 16 per cent contained provision for binding arbitration, with four essentially no-strike agreements. Another 13 per cent allowed for non-binding arbitration. One semi-voluntary agreement indicated the restraints that the parties could impose upon themselves, namely, pendulum arbitration resolved through ACAS. The agreement noted, 'this decision will be binding on both parties, so providing a non-strike agreement'. Since then there had been two pay settlements resulting in improvements above those achieved prior to recognition: a reduction in the working week and a commitment to introduce a bonus scheme. However, union members had indicated that they wanted the no-strike clause removed. Another agreement stated, 'there will be no industrial action or any disruption to the continuity of the Company's operations whilst this Agreement is in place'. Instead, both parties agreed that they would 'be bound by the decisions of an independent arbitrator'. Arbitration was not pendulum, so there was no obligation on the arbitrator to decide in favour of one party over the other. This agreement represented an important breakthrough for the union in a company that had been resolutely non-union. The acceptance of the no-strike clause may been seen as a concession to achieve recognition. The first post-recognition pay settlement was imposed by the employer. The next two were determined by binding arbitration, the first in the union's favour, the second not. The union officer reported that an agreement on restricting compulsory overtime had not been implemented and the employer had consistently frustrated the development of collective bargaining: 'the workforce feel isolated and undervalued as their collective voice goes unheard'. He felt, however, that the no-strike agreement was not a factor in this, since union membership was not strong enough to sustain industrial action.

One semi-voluntary agreement contained a clause which committed the union to do 'everything in its power to return members to normal working practices' in the case of unofficial action. The agreement stated that 'should that unofficial industrial action be a wildcat strike, then the Union will immediately issue repudiation notices to the individuals involved and encourage all other employees to work within the spirit and letter of their contracts of employment'. Additionally, even in cases of official industrial action, the agreement stated that the union 'will not interfere with any working employee'. This could be interpreted to mean that the union would be honour-bound, for example, not to mount picket lines even where it authorised industrial action, if the effect might be to interfere with the right of employees to attend for work.

Two other agreements, the outcome of statutory awards, contained arbitration clauses. In one there was provision for binding arbitration, obliging the parties to abide by the arbitrator's decision. The other did not stipulate the nature of the arbitration but that, where there were conflicts of interest, 'the agreed procedures will be put into practice and while in operation there will be no industrial action whatsoever. There will be complete continuity of normal production and business operation between the commencement of the resolution of conflicts of interests and after acceptance of any arbitration decision.' There is no evidence that provision for no-strike agreements or binding arbitration was more common in statutory or semi-voluntary agreements than in new or traditional voluntary collective bargaining agreements. The examples do, however, suggest that part of employer opposition to unionisation may be based upon fear of industrial action.

Dual channels of representation

The survey of statutory and semi-voluntary agreements showed that eleven per cent had retained or subsequently introduced separate consultative bodies alongside negotiating bodies. This suggests that in some cases recognition may lead to the emergence of dual channels of representation within organisations. The analysis of statutory and semi-voluntary agreements provided one case where representation for union and non-union members was entirely separate. The agreement stated, 'the company agrees to recognise the union as the sole body representing those employees of the company who are at the time fully paid up members of the union. The company recognises the staff council's right to exist and negotiate on behalf of all employees who are not union members.' Another agreement ensured that the parties were committed to the continuing existence of the company's consultative forum and that union representatives, if not themselves on the forum, would be willing to work alongside its representatives. These representatives would be consulted on terms and conditions not covered in the scope of the agreement, 'in order to secure the views of the whole of the workforce'. An additional forum was established for the company to meet union FTOs and representatives not less than twice a year.

Forty per cent of agreements established a joint negotiating and consultative body. In one, the consultative body existing prior to recognition was retained as a joint negotiating and consultative body and, instead of separate union representation, it appeared to be subsumed within the consultative body, so there was no specific union representative body. Representatives were elected from amongst the entire workforce and, where the representative of a particular constituency was not a member, the union was able to elect an additional deputy from its members in that constituency. The maintenance or encouragement of consultative bodies covering the wider workforce may be in anticipation of the Information and Consultation Regulations, but at the same time may offer opportunities for employers to undermine collective bargaining or ultimately for derecognition (see also Gall 2004a).

Conclusion

'It's like the first battle is over, we've still got to fight the war – we've not won yet' (union representative after successful recognition ballot).

The statutory recognition provisions established by the ERA simultaneously breathed life into voluntary collective bargaining whilst introducing the law into collective bargaining arrangements. This chapter has demonstrated that the law has established a model for collective bargaining. The statutory method of bargaining has shaped statutory and, to a lesser extent, semi-voluntary agreements and may have contributed to a narrower interpretation of collective bargaining, at least in so far as formal agreements are concerned. The majority of the agreements that have emerged from the statutory procedure are confined to pay, hours and holidays. Amongst voluntary agreements the scope of bargaining is wider, yet even here the procedure has cast its shadow. Our DTI research showed that one in five voluntary agreements was confined to core bargaining. Voluntary agreements signed after 6 June 2000 were significantly more likely (at the 5 per cent level) to be restricted to core bargaining than those signed between 1998 and June 2000. Voluntary agreements concluded in the printing and publishing sector were significantly more likely (at the 1 per cent level) to restrict the scope of bargaining. It is possible that in sectors where unionisation has been historically stronger and more conflictual, management has been apprehensive about re-recognition and subsequent agreements may reflect a desire to ensure that recognition is on a different, more limited, basis.

The statutory model is reflected in other aspects of new statutory and semi-voluntary recognition agreements. Our survey shows that a minority of statutory and semi-voluntary agreements are based upon a rather restrictive bargaining procedure, focused around the negotiation of the annual pay round and appearing to limit the bargaining relationship during the rest of the year. There is provision in some for personal contracts, allowing employees to opt out of the bargaining unit, thus undermining collective bargaining. A number of agreements establish mechanisms for termination. Beyond the scope of the statutory procedure, the reluctance of some employers to concede recognition may also be seen in the limitation on industrial action or on bargaining through binding arbitration, or in the provision of dual channels of employee representation, which provide the potential to undermine union representation.

However, the form and text of agreements alone cannot determine bargaining outcomes, for as we have shown these may be contested by the parties. It may be that whilst recognition has become more formalised than previously characteristic of British industrial relations, it is less able to deliver collective bargaining. Thus, what the ERA has been unable to do is to enforce bargaining in the face of determined employer opposition. On the one hand, once a procedural agreement has been finalised there is no guarantee that the employer will enter into meaningful negotiations with the union (see also Gall 2003f, 2004c). On the other hand, evidence shows that the agreements, even if formally restricted, can lead to active bargaining over a range of issues. This can be as dependent upon the presence, confidence and expertise of workplace representatives (itself often contingent upon union training) as upon the terms of the agreement. The presence and strength of union members and representatives can make it difficult for employers to sustain the formal limitation of bargaining. Statutory and semi-voluntary recognition can be conceptualised in terms of mobilisation theory (Kelly 1998) since it is generally the outcome of successful collective organisation motivated by perceived injustice in the workplace, generating a shared group identity. Mobilisation theory stresses the importance of leadership and Moore (2004) has demonstrated the key role of activists, prepared to challenge employer counter-mobilisation and the threatened costs of collective action in statutory recognition ballots. This chapter has considered the effectiveness or otherwise of unionisation following a successful campaign to secure recognition, underlining the fragility of collective organisation, since an effective mobilisation for recognition does not guarantee a subsequent meaningful bargaining relationship. Once again this would appear to be determined by the extent of employer opposition to bargaining, but also by *sustained* workplace organisation based upon the continued existence and character of activists.

For workers, the benefits of recognition are not just based upon material gains defined by the scope of collective bargaining, but also in terms of workplace 'voice' and security. As one union representative recalled, 'before there were procedures, but there was no-one to argue – it was management prerogative'. The current statutory procedure has thus provided unions with new opportunities for collective representation. Yet the procedure reflects the Labour government's ambiguity about collective bargaining as the best way of conducting industrial relations. If employers resist collective bargaining, even after a statutory award, there is seemingly no legal redress for unions. A more robust form of legislation imposing a duty to bargain would confirm union legitimacy. At the same time statutory union recognition cannot, of itself, guarantee meaningful collective bargaining, for as the Donovan Commission stated, 'collective bargaining is recognized as the best way of conducting industrial relations and as depending on strong . . . union organisation' (Donovan 1968, para. 224).

Acknowledgement

Our thanks are to those union officers and representatives who provided copies of recognition agreements and other information upon which this chapter is based. Thanks are also due to Simon Gouldstone for advice on CAC sources and to Gregor Gall and Bob Simpson for comments.

7 The National Union of Journalists and the provincial newspaper industry

From derecognition to recognition to fraught bargaining

Gregor Gall

Trade unions representing journalists and production workers in the provincial newspaper industry in England and Wales experienced the greatest extent of derecognition – in both absolute and relative terms – of any industry and for any trade union in Britain in the 1980s and 1990s. They experienced a concerted and successful employers' 'offensive' (Gall 1993; Noon 1993; Smith and Morton 1990), which allowed the newspaper companies to recast the employment relationship from one marked by some co-determination to one characterised by almost full managerial unilateralism. The outcome of this process has been the immiseration of newspaper workers' conditions of work and employment through intensification and extensification of the wage–effort bargain (Gall 1995, 1998a, 2000a, 2001a). Since derecognition, the unions, the National Union of Journalists (NUJ) and the Graphical, Paper and Media Union (GPMU), campaigned to maintain their membership base and organisational presence within these newspaper companies. On the one hand, they fought a sporadic struggle to provide representation to their memberships through individual and collective means, such as employment tribunal work and class law actions. On the other hand, both unions were the driving forces behind the crusade to achieve a statutory union recognition mechanism. Starting with the Press for Union Rights campaign in 1990, in which the NUJ and GPMU were the prime movers, the two unions were successful, through working with other unions, in winning the Trades Union Congress and Labour Party to policy positions of advocating the creation of a statutory union recognition mechanism by the mid-1990s, and seeing this through to the eventual Employment Relations Act 1999 (ERA), the provision of which for union recognition came into force on 6 June 2000.

This chapter commences by outlining the processes by which the NUJ has successfully fused the maintenance of union presence and organisation with the imminence and presence of the statutory recognition mechanism, enabling the union to regain procedural agreements with the employers, comprising rights of information, representation and collective bargaining for its chapels. Consequently, the chapter outlines the extent of this not inconsiderable achievement. This task is carried out not merely to set the scene for the post-recognition processes and outcomes, but because there exists an intimate connection between the pre- and post-recognition periods vis-à-vis employer behaviour and union prowess. Thereafter, an examination of the bargaining and organisational outcomes of the new recognition agreements, and an analysis of the social processes by which these outcomes are explicable, is presented.

The data for this chapter has been generated from fieldwork comprising some thirty periodic semi-structured interviews on employment relations in the provincial newspaper industry with NUJ lay officials (i.e. chapel and branch officials) and NUJ FTOs over the period 1998–2003. The interviews with the fourteen lay officials were telephone interviews while those with the four FTOs were conducted in person. The former covered gathering data on specific chapels, while the latter served to gain an overview of the process across the regions for which the officers were responsible. This data has been supplemented by secondary sources, such as the weekly trade magazine the *UK Press Gazette*/*Press Gazette*, NUJ documentation (press releases, circulars and the NUJ's monthly journal the *Journalist*), and coverage in the wider trade union press, such as the *Morning Star*, *Socialist Worker* and *Tribune*. The longer, contemporary context draws on previous research conducted by the author (see references).

Regaining recognition

Tables 7.1 and 7.2 outline the extent of the re-emergence of the NUJ as a potential force within the provincial newspaper industry by virtue of the recapturing of recognition agreements. Seventeen agreements were gained through winning ballots (and no ballots have been lost), while the remainder were obtained through membership audits or management intelligence confirming the NUJ's claimed density. Most (active) campaigns to regain recognition took between six and twenty-four months. Of the fifty-two agreements, only three were signed prior to 6 June 2000. This gives some indication of the extent and the depth of the employer antipathy to regranting recognition compared with employers in other industrial sectors who were, in the words of the CBI, taking the advice of 'sensible human resources directors . . . to consider negotiating recognition agreements while time is on their side and before the law imposes a statutory procedure' (*Financial Times* 9 February 1999).

Nonetheless, all but one agreement were voluntary, although that should not suggest that employers were willing. Indeed, the mildest form of employer opposition to granting recognition was simply to state that until the legal position changed, and because the newspaper companies were not acting unlawfully, the status quo would remain. Once the legal position had changed, this mild form of opposition was manifested in tardiness in meeting the NUJ to discuss the requisite membership or journalists' support thresh-

Table 7.1 Ballot results for union recognition

Newspaper centre/NUJ chapel	*Year of derecognition*	*Year of ballot*	*Ownership group at time*	*Number of journalists*	*Turnout (%)*	*Vote for union recognition (%)*
Bradford *Telegraph and Argus*	1997	2000	Newsquest	100	98	86
Oxford Mail and *Times*	1997	2000	Newsquest	100	n/a	84
News Shopper series	n/a	2000	Newsquest	30	100	90
Bolton Evening News	1992	2000	Newsquest	85	84	9
Swindon Evening Advertiser	1991	2000	Newsquest	72	98	97
North London series	n/a	2000	Newsquest	29	100	89
Dorset Echo (Weymouth)	1990	2000	Newsquest	40	100	85
Guardian Newspapers	–	2000	Newsquest	28	n/a	86
Southern Daily Echo (Southampton)	1993	2001	Newsquest	62	100	95
Bournemouth *Echo*	1993	2001	Newsquest	68	72	94
Newcastle *Chronicle* and *Journal*	1988	2001	Trinity Mirror	192	62	96
Scotsman/Evening News/Scotland on Sunday	1991	2001	European Press	200	55	99
Newsquest Kendal (*Westmorland Gazette/Lancaster Citizen*)	1990	2001	Newsquest	24	100	91
Belfast Evening Telegraph/Sunday Life/Community Telegraphs/*Ireland Saturday Night*	1994	2001	Independent News & Media	130	n/a	75
Middlesbrough *Evening Gazette*	1992	2002	Gazette Media	60	n/a	68
Eastern Daily Press/Evening News (Norwich)	1993	2003	Archant	209	90	87
Brighton *Evening Argus*	1992	2004	Newsquest	n/a	n/a	100

Source: Author's own work.

Note
n/a – not available.

Table 7.2 Recognition through membership audits

Newspaper centre/NUJ chapel	*Year of derecognition*	*Year of audit*	*Ownership group at time*	*Number of journalists*	*Membership density (%)*
Birmingham Post and *Mail*	1991	2001	Trinity Mirror	270	56
Cambridge Evening News	1994	2001	Yattendon	50	n/a
Coventry Newspapers	1991	2001	Trinity Mirror	80	66
Sheffield *Star*	1993	2001	RIM	65	n/a
Yorkshire Post/Evening Post (Leeds)	1993	2001	RIM	180	72
Halifax *Courier*	1990	2002	Johnston	50	68
Lancashire Evening Post (Preston)	1992	2002	Johnston	60	70
Newsquest Midlands South Division	n/a	2002	Newquest	40	58
Bristol Evening News/Post	1994	2002	Northcliffe	90	61
Western Mail and *Echo*, *South Wales Evening Echo*, *Wales on Sunday*, Celtic weeklies (Cardiff)	1988	2003	Trinity Mirror	200	56
Newsquest North East	n/a	2004	Newsquest	110	53
York and County Press	n/a	2004	Newsquest	60	63

Source: Author's own work.

Note
n/a – not available.

olds for recognition, methods for ascertaining these and the complexion of possible recognition agreements. The tardiness represented a strategy of obfuscation. The stronger forms of opposition comprised the standard suppressive and substitutionist tactics of anti-unionism (see Gall and McKay 2001; Gall 2004a). The former consist of victimisations and sackings, and anti-union literature and captive meetings with messages about the 'union threat' to pay, jobs and profits, and the 'evil' of parasitic and undemocratic unions. The latter comprise the establishment of non-union forms of employee voice and representation, such as company councils.

In addition, recognition has also been recaptured at another twenty-one, mainly weekly and, thus, smaller newspaper centres. In total, recognition has been regained in fifty-two provincial newspaper centres covering around 3,000 journalists (from thirty-nine cases where numbers are known) in a period of just under four years after a decade of derecognition.

Aside from the positive influence of the statutory recognition mechanism (the 'shadow' and 'demonstration' effects – see Gall 2004b), it is worth examining why the NUJ was able to regain recognition so extensively, for this relates to its ability to mobilise its membership resources after recognition. As Tables 7.1 and 7.2 indicate, the NUJ was able to maintain its membership and support base throughout the years of derecognition as well as augment these in the run-up to the arrival of the statutory mechanism. This was accomplished by adapting well to operating as an 'illegitimate' agent without bargaining or representational rights through (a) the provision of individual membership services (advice, legal representation, training), (b) being a dogged and high-profile critic of the employers, where providing voice was valued and issues of efficacy of voice were not paramount, and (c) campaigning for statutory union recognition. The FoC at the *Yorkshire Evening Post* explained,

> Management . . . expected membership to dwindle and the union to disappear. They were wrong. . . . It's been a hard slog. There were times when we felt out in the wilderness but the members always stayed solid.
> (*Press Gazette* 11 May 2001)

His counterpart at the *Birmingham Post and Mail* observed,

> The union refused to go away. With a team of activists willing to work on the chapel committee we refused to go away. And we started winning little victories . . . [like] consultation rights on the health and safety committee [and in 1999] we even negotiated an overall pay increase – despite being derecognised.
> (*Journalist* January 2001)

The contexts of these three activities were those of a determined core of long-standing and experienced activists, the widespread existence of workplace grievances amongst the journalists, and the continuing strongly held notion of the profession of journalism, with the NUJ acting as a vociferous campaigner for journalism as the 'sword of truth and justice' and as dispenser of press cards. The salience of this enforced way of organising is that, while it was an achievement in itself and consonant with the journalists' union consciousness then, it did not necessarily lay out the strongest foundations for the post-recognition period. Through counter-factualism, it can be suggested that more acute collective mobilisations like strikes to achieve re-recognition may have provided a more tested and robust form of collectivism with which subsequently to face the employers. Here, the issue of a more developed state of journalists' collective consciousness is of less importance than their ability to impose significant costs and sanctions on their employers through mobilisations at the point of production. This is not to bemoan the activities of the NUJ as they were, but rather to understand the implications of the processes it engaged in and the processes it was subject to.

After derecognition but before bargaining

In spite of variations in the intensity of employer opposition outlined above, all employers showed lethargy in the two phases prior to the commencement of collective bargaining. First, considerable time elapsed between the NUJ winning recognition through balloting or membership audit and the date on which a union recognition was agreed and signed. While some delay may be considered inevitable where the content of a recognition agreement is jointly decided upon, employers went further than this by deliberately, not expediting the process, often deploying the service of lawyers to do so. Commonly, six months elapsed and the NUJ had to involve its general secretary to command meetings with employers in order to bring matters to a positive conclusion for the union. Second, considerable time elapsed between the signing of recognition agreements and the first bargaining to produce a 'house' agreement, an agreement between chapel and employer over pay rises, pay rates and other terms and conditions of work and employment. This period of delay lasted between 6 and 12 months. Employers refused to enter into negotiations shortly after the commencement of recognition, as they might have been expected to, because they stated that negotiations could not begin until the date of the annual review of pay had been reached, i.e. the date of the annual review under derecognition. For example, the *Press Gazette* (11 May 2001) commented, 'The NUJ chapel at the *Oxford Mail* and its sister titles regained recognition last June but the company had been slow in negotiating a house agreement.'

In both instances of delay, the power relations and dynamics of the bargaining relationship dictated that the initiative lay with the employer, because the employer is a 'primary organisation' and the union a 'secondary organisation' (Offe and Wisenthal 1980). By flatly stating their position, the employers forced the NUJ into a situation of reluctantly accepting their will or undertaking a significant mobilisation of its membership resources in order to force movement. In short, the employers challenged the NUJ's willingness and ability to change their tardiness and obfuscation. Other than remonstrate, the NUJ did not in effect seek to overcome the employers' will. Moreover, it was unlikely that it could mobilise its members to do so, and do so quickly, after regaining recognition because journalists' patience had not yet been spent and a sense of fatigue from struggle was present at this point.

Outcomes of collective bargaining

The most obvious, and easiest, outcome of the post-recognition period to examine first is that of the pay and conditions bargaining settlements. Over and above the 'pounds and pence' details of the 'wage–effort bargain', this helps to inform an assessment of employer and union behaviour and the resources that both bring to bear on the bargaining relationship in the post-recognition period in order to determine its outcomes. It is first important to recognise the basis on which the bargaining took place. Tables 7.1 and 7.2 indicate that employers, setting aside any influence of the labour market, determined whether there was any uplift in pay and conditions for a long period of time (the period between derecognition and re-recognition). Indeed, the expanding supply of journalistic labour that exceeded demand in this period allowed the employers even greater discretion here. Therefore, the first bargaining took place after the stagnation of wages and conditions in real terms and relative to other comparable professional groups, meaning that the baseline on which the NUJ operated was an impoverished one.

Tables 7.3 and 7.4 provide little evidence that the NUJ chapels, judged by their submitted claims, have been successful in achieving their goals in the first rounds of bargaining after regaining recognition. Nearly all employers' first offers were not substantially different from their final offers and the actual settlements. And the level of the settlements resulted primarily from the influence of the slackness in the journalistic labour market and the willingness of employers to pay what they thought was the 'going rate' based on the rate of inflation. However, the underlying picture is a good deal more complex than this, although it does not negate what has just been stated. At the outset, it is worth noting that the initial claims represented 'wish lists' of what it would take to begin making up for the losses incurred during derecognition. In practice, these were political statements of intent for several years ahead and for the consumption of members and employers, rather than an actual bargaining agenda for a particular year. Overall, it appears that the chapels were able to obtain very minor concessions on across-the-board annual pay rises, even where striking was used. Little movement by employers can be detected on issues concerned with other working conditions and remuneration outside basic pay.

However, far greater success was recorded in raising the pay of junior staff through raising minimum rates or pay bands. For example, at the *Spalding*

Table 7.3 Annual pay and conditions bargaining involving strike action

Newspaper centre (ownership)	*Year*	*Initial offer*	*Initial demand*	*Strike action*	*Settlement*
Bradford (Newsquest)	2002	2%	7.5%	0.5 days	2.5%, some increase in minimum grade
GMWN weeklies (Scott Trust) *	2002	1.6%–2.5%	7.5%	4 days	2.5%, some increase in minimum grade rates for trainees, reconciliation bonus
Newcastle (Trinity Mirror)	2002	2%	4%	4 days	2%, 2.85% for senior reporters, subs and photographers, some increase in minimum grade rates and trainee pay (after first strike)
Rotherham (Garnett Dickson) *	2002	2.3%	10%	6 days	3%, end of Saturday working
Spalding (Johnston Press)	2002	2.5%	7%	20 days	2.5%, increase in minimum rates, group-wide union recognition
Bolton (Newsquest)	2003	1% (then 2% in talks)	7%	31 days	Two year deal: 2% 2003, inflation 2004, one-off payment, 3% increase in basic rate, some increase in long-service awards
Bradford (Newsquest)	2003	2%, £400	£2,000	47 days	2%
Cumbria (Newsquest) *	2003	1.5%	9.5%	4 days	2.5%
Sheffield (Johnston Press)	2003	2%	10%, 10% on grades	Work-time meeting	2.75%, small increases on grades
Belfast (Independent News and Media)	2004	0% then 3%	Pay rise/ higher pay rise	2 days	3%, 6–10% for lower paid, extra day's holiday
Blackpool (Johnston Press)	2004	3%	Higher pay rise	1 day	3% after withdrawal of offer, increased minimum rates for junior staff

Source: Author's own work.

Note
* denotes a chapel/centre that did not experience derecognition.

Guardian newspaper in 2002, the pay of graduate trainees was raised from £9,500 to £11,000 (16 per cent increase), while that of newly qualified seniors was raised from £12,000 to £14,000 (17 per cent). At the *News Shopper* series in 2000, the minimum rate was increased from £10,500 to £12,000 (14 per cent), while in 2002 the pay of trainees after one year was increased from £13,200 to £15,200 (15 per cent). At Bradford in 2002, the minimum starting rate increased by £1,500 (14 per cent), while rises for specific groups were: weekly reporters (3.2 per cent), evening reporters (2.9 per cent) and senior weekly reporters (7.1 per cent). This compares broadly similarly with the Greater Manchester Weekly Newspapers series, which had not been derecognised and in 2002 gained an increase in the starting rate for trainees from £10,486 to £13,060 (24 per cent). In general, the NUJ chapels were not able to secure significant increases for senior staff nor effectively to tackle the wider extent of low pay in the sector. The recognition of this has led the NUJ nationally, in the case of Newsquest Group, to submit a claim aimed to achieve a minimum of £20,000 by 2005 for seniors.

This relatively small degree of success for the NUJ needs to be set in the specific context of the provincial newspaper sector and the dynamics of its industrial relations. First, the degree of employer intransigence was considerable, whereby many employers were determined to maintain de facto derecognition. Agreeing to recognition was a tactical manoeuvre, not a strategic change of heart. For example, the FoC at the *Yorkshire Evening Post* stated,

> [We] fought long and hard to win back recognition, but this is just a start. Now we have to begin the fight to regain some of the benefits we lost during the days of derecognition. . . . The company has made it clear that it is not interested in partnership or cooperation. It has agreed to recognition because it had to. We believe it will now pursue every possible obstruction to further progress (*Journalist* June 2001),

and the NUJ (2003: 5) reported,

> At the *Bristol Evening Post*, the company is encouraging people to opt out of the bargaining unit and are not holding meaningful negotiations. In companies owned by both Johnston Press and Newsquest they have announced, and in at least one case paid, the annual pay award prior to negotiations beginning.

Elsewhere, the NUJ's Irish secretary commented on the case of the *Belfast Telegraph*'s pay freeze,

> It's hugely ironic but not surprising that having just agreed to negotiate with the union again after 15 years, the company should turn around and pull down the shutters on this year's pay talks (*Irish News* 25 June 2002),

Table 7.4 Annual pay and conditions bargaining involving non-strike action

Newspaper centre (ownership group)	*Year*	*Initial offer*	*Initial demand*	*Action*	*Settlement*
Birmingham (Trinity Mirror)	2001	–	–	None	2.5%
Liverpool Post and *Echo* (Trinity Mirror)	2001	–	–	None	2% plus individual merit money
Oxford (Newsquest)	2001	–	–	None	Increase in grade pay rates
Barrow (Cumbrian)*	2002	2.7%	4%	Strike ballot	2.75%
Bolton (Newsquest)	2002	2%	–	Strike ballot, strike threat	2.5%
Belfast (Independent News & Media)	2002	0%	–	Strike ballot, strike threat	Small grade rises, improvement in meal allowances, maternity/paternity pay
Birmingham (Trinity Mirror)	2002	2%	–	None	2% and new pay structure with rises of 3.8–10.2% for low paid
Bristol (Northcliffe)	2002	–	–	None	2.5% (3.3% for lower paid)
Cambridge (Yattendon)	2002	–	–	None	2.75%
Cardiff (Trinity Mirror)	2002	2%	–	Threatened strike ballot	2%
Edinburgh (European Press)	2002	0%	–	None	Some individual merit rises
Hertford (Yattendon)	2002	2.5%	10%	Strike ballot, strike threat	2.7%, some increase in trainee pay, other minor concessions on non-pay issues, like a healthcare scheme
Kendal (Newsquest)	2002	–	–	None	2.5%
Leeds (Trinity Mirror)	2002	–	–	None	2%, new minimum senior rate
Liverpool Post and *Echo* (Trinity Mirror)	2002	2%	–	None	2%
Liverpool Post and *Echo* weeklies (Trinity Mirror)	2002	2%	–	Strike ballot	2%, new pay structure with improvements on minimum bands
Oxford (Newsquest)	2002	–	–	None	2.5%, new pay structure with improvements on minimum bands
Preston (Newsquest)	2002	1%	5%	Strike ballot	1%

South London Press (Newsquest)	2002	–	–	None	4%
Sunderland Echo (Johnston Press)*	2002	2.5%	–	Strike ballot	2.5%, new grading structure with improvements on minimum bands
Wakefield (Johnston Press)*	2002	2.5%, lower for trainees	4.5%, increased minimum grades	Strike ballot, strike threat	2.5%, more for minimum grades and long-serving staff
Birmingham (Trinity Mirror)	2003	2.5%	–	Rejection in ballot	2.5%, improved maternity/paternity leave, premium for night working
Darlington (Newsquest)	2003	2%	–		2%
Kendal (Newsquest)	2003	1.5%	9.5%	Strike ballot, strike threat	2.5%
London/Kent (Newsquest)	2003	2%, £600 regional weighting	2.5%, £1,750 regional weighting	Strike ballot, strike threat	2.5% but with increases to bands, bringing increases of 6% in many cases
Newcastle (Trinity Mirror)	2003	2.7%	–	Threatened ballot	3%
Southampton (Newsquest)	2003	–	–	None	2.5%
Cardiff (Trinity Mirror)	2003	3.0%	–	–	3.0%
Bradford (Newsquest)	2004	–	–	None	2.85% 2004, inflation plus 0.25% 2005
Cardiff (Trinity Mirror)	2004	2.7%	–	–	2.7%, 5% for trainees
Coventry (Trinity Mirror)	2004	2.7%	–	Strike averted	2.7%, negotiations on increasing lower-paid pay rates
Leeds (Johnston Press)	2004	3%	–	None	3%, rises in minimum rates
Norwich (Archant)	2004	3%	4.75%	–	3%
Portsmouth (Johnston Press)	2004	3% or £800	–	–	3%–6% based on 3% or £800, whichever is higher
South London (Newsquest)	2004	–	–	None	3%, rises in minimum rates
Southampton (Newsquest)	2004	3%	–	–	–

Source: Author's own work.

Note
* denotes a chapel/centre that did not experience derecognition.

and of its pay offer in 2004,

> The newspaper's editorial columns have long preached the virtues of dialogue. But when it comes to its own employees, management has walked away from the table and adopted a 'not an inch' [of movement] stance (*Press Gazette* 21 May 2004).

Although mindful of the unit labour cost implications of bargaining, an additional dimension to this intransigence was that after reluctantly conceding recognition, employers had determined against further loss of face by being turned over again by the NUJ. This mentality was particularly strong in 2003 after the Bradford strike of 2002 (see below), where employers dug in against the first major union mobilisation in the sector.

Second, it is apparent that while the results of strikes were limited for those chapels taking strike action, the strikes had a positive, if small, demonstration effect on other employers. Consequently, many employers were rather keener than might have otherwise been the case to make some minor concessions in the face of rejection of first offers or strike ballots and strike threats. Third, the relative success of the first chapel's strike action in 2002 considerably raised the expectations of what chapels could achieve through steadfastness in the 2003 bargaining round. Fourth, outside the annual bargaining rounds, the NUJ has recorded little success in preventing a considerable number of redundancies and in ending policies of not filling vacant posts. While severance terms have been improved, the NUJ has been able to exert no significant influence on controlling the resultant increased workloads for remaining staff. Fifth, the settlements achieved by re-recognised chapels compare favourably with those made by non-derecognised chapels. However, continuing recognition should not be viewed as a sine qua non of union strength, given employer discretion and the recent decline in the union (wage) 'mark-up'. Neither should the settlements gained by these non-derecognised chapels be seen as equating to significant gains from collective bargaining.

Three cases of bargaining

To provide a more detailed and richer picture of bargaining post-recognition, three cases are illustrative. The most aggressive and militant 'surface bargaining' has taken place in the Newsquest Group at its Bradford and Bolton centres. The first to regain recognition in Newsquest was the Bradford chapel. Nonetheless, and without consultation or any reference to the newly signed recognition agreement, the company attempted to impose new contracts that represented a significant worsening of conditions. Under these contracts, the amount of paid sick leave for those in their first year of employment was reduced to three days, the retirement age was raised from sixty-two to sixty-five and new working hours stipulated that journalists were to be on call to work any time. The chapel rejected the new contracts, most members refused to sign, and each of the 'refuseniks' took out an individual grievance against the company under company procedures. Two months later, the contracts were withdrawn but redundancies were imposed without consultation. Eighteen months after winning back recognition, the NUJ was offered a 2 per cent pay increase in late 2001, in response to its claim for a 7.5 per cent pay increase, one day's extra holiday and rises in mileage and sick pay rates. The chapel balloted on strike action, producing a 'yes' vote. The company improved its offer to 2.5 per cent and an increase in minimum starting rates. The NUJ rejected this and reduced its claim to a straight 4 per cent pay increase. It then took a half-day strike action and gave notice of two further one-day strikes. The company moved slightly by increasing further the minimum starting rates and offering a pay rise of either 2.5 per cent or £500, whichever was higher, and talks on mileage rates, redundancy criteria and training. Nonetheless, the response of the company was robust, emphasising the normal continuation of production (*Press Gazette* 18 January 2002), offering a bonus to strikebreakers and warning new and trainee staff about the impact of striking on their careers. After the strike, the Mother of the Chapel (MoC) reported a mixed picture: 'Our strike won us more money, solidified the chapel, raised morale and widened the scope of the recognition' (*Socialist Appeal* April 2002), and, 'Managers still treat us with contempt. . . . We are still fighting to hold union meetings on the premises and [obtain] a decent pay structure' (*Socialist Worker* 16 March 2002).

Prior to 2003, the MoC was disciplined over her use of email for union purposes. In 2003, the chapel submitted a claim for a £2,000 across-the-board rise, with increases in mileage rates and annual leave. The company offered a 2 per cent rise and a one-off payment of £400, or an inflation rise so long as this was funded by increases in productivity rises and/or cost cutting. In response, the NUJ chapel reduced its claim to a straight £1,500 but the company made no movement. Following this, it took forty-seven days of strike action without the company changing its offer. The strikers ended their strike for fear of being sacked after the eight-week protection of the ERA ended and reballoted for strike action to renew the protection. However, they did not renew their strike action. During the dispute, the MoC and two activists were disciplined for handing out strike leaflets and the company responded again robustly, blaming the strike on a militant minority and highlighting its lack of impact on production (*Press Gazette* 25 April, 2 May, 30 May, 11 July 2003). Newsquest took this hard line as a result of being portrayed as having made significant concessions in 2002, where this acted to spur sister chapels to move towards strike action. Subsequently, the Bradford chapel then began focusing on its next annual claim, leading to a two-year deal for 2004–06. Both sides appeared keen to avoid further prolonged industrial action. However, this new-found commonality did not prevent the company making more redundancies in 2004 without adequate consultation.

At its sister centre in Bolton, Newsquest imposed a 3 per cent increase in

2001 and unsuccessfully tried to remove the journalists' nine-day fortnight working arrangement. In 2002, as pay negotiations dragged on for six months, the chapel balloted for strike action but did not implement the mandate when a 2 per cent offer was increased to 2.5 per cent. However, this sharpened the degree of antagonism felt by the chapel towards Newsquest. In 2003, the chapel asked for a 7 per cent pay increase but was offered 2 per cent. Following thirty-one days of strike action (which ended for fear of moving outside the eight-week protection period), the company offered a two-year deal of a 2 per cent rise for 2003 and an inflation rise for 2004, with a one-off payment and a 3 per cent increase in minimum starting rates. Contrary to the statement of the Newsquest chief executive that it operated a decentralised management decision-making process in industrial relations (*Journalist* June 2001), the imposition of a standard 2 per cent pay offer in 2002 and the similarity of 'surface bargaining' across the group suggests a centralised and uniform approach.

At the Trinity Mirror Birmingham centre, something more akin to 'hard-nosed' bargaining rather than consistent 'surface bargaining' has existed. Following the signing of a partnership agreement in 2001, the chapel was able to gain an increase in mileage rates, access to company information for bargaining, access in order to recruit at staff induction courses, and equal representation on a working party to restore the pay grade system after protracted negotiations. The bargaining round in 2003 was marked by toughness. The company offered a 2.5 per cent increase and improvements in other conditions (i.e. improved maternity/paternity leave, premium for night working) but no movement on the basic starting rate of £11,000. This offer was rejected in a consultative ballot by the chapel, but it was unable to compel the company to use third-party arbitration as stipulated in the recognition agreement. Later in 2003, the chapel staged a one-day strike to protest against the ending of the final-salary pension scheme and its replacement with a defined contribution scheme for new entrants, as well as reductions in company contributions into the existing scheme for existing staff. Trinity Mirror's response was robust and abrupt: 'Staff understood the reasons behind the changes. In any case, action will not achieve anything as the company has made its decision' (*Press Gazette* 7 March 2003). Before the year was out, the chapel engaged in industrial action short of a strike by carrying out a work-to-contract against redundancies and the inadequate process of consultation over these. The action resulted in the numbers of redundancies being reduced from twenty to fifteen, but the company at the same time refused to negotiate on a freelance agreement and attempted unsuccessfully to victimise the FoC for union activities. In 2004, the sixty-nine strikers in 2003 were penalised by being excluded from a profit-related pay bonus as a result of having discontinuous service. In response to the NUJ's appeal to give the bonuses to charity or its hardship fund, the company stated, 'The NUJ has no right to dictate how [the company] manages its finances' (*Press Gazette* 2 April 2004).

Therefore, the cases in Newsquest and Trinity Mirror are illustrative of a wider phenomenon where provincial newspaper employers have successfully set the parameters for bargaining after conceding recognition. These employers were not prepared to capitulate to the NUJ's demands, although all were prepared to engage in what outwardly looked like the conventional process of collective bargaining.

Union revitalisation or continuing stasis?

After years of enforced disorganisation and quiescence, the NUJ enthusiastically greeted the re-emergence of strike action amongst its provincial newspaper members with the positive characterisation of 'a wave of militancy' (e.g. *Press Release* 14 March 2002, *Socialist Appeal* April 2002) and likewise categorised the concessions in bargaining as 'stunning' and 'huge' victories (e.g. *Socialist Worker* 16 March 2002, *Press Release* 30 April 2002, *Journalist* June 2002, *Morning Star* 22 May 2002, *Tribune* 4 April 2003). In late 2002, the NUJ stated,

> We have done more to tackle low pay in the last year than at any time in the last decade. . . . There is a new realisation at all levels in the union . . . that through collective action we can improve our working lives – whether it be standing up to bullying [or] fighting low pay.
>
> (*Journalist* December 2002)

Even a more sanguine assessment by the Oxford branch was 'optimistic': 'The NUJ has scored success in a series of battles . . . but has still not won the war' (*Journalist* May 2004).

The preceding analysis of bargaining and union mobilisation outcomes suggests that this rhetorical practice of 'talking up' the strength of action and extent of the results was for the purpose of internal consumption where there existed four specific audiences. First was the activist milieu that had maintained union organisation throughout the lean years and had enabled the NUJ to be in a position to regain recognition using the influence of the ERA. Of an activist mentality, this milieu often had raised expectations of what the union could achieve in the flush of success of regaining recognition. Making assessments of its success commensurate with their expectations formed a key part of the NUJ's maintenance of their motivation for activity. Second were the members who had partaken in mobilisations. The NUJ felt the need to support and affirm the actions of these members who had been in the vanguard of the attempt to swing the pendulum back in favour of the union, primarily because they were the likely bedrock of union organisation in the coming years. Third were the new and potential union members who, the NUJ believed, required the efficacy of the union to be proved in order to affirm the value of union membership. Fourth, the union as a whole needed to reaffirm not only its industrial purpose but its industrial prowess after years in the doldrums. This tendency was heightened with the recent election of a new, young and energetic general secretary. In addition to these internal audiences, the NUJ also bore in mind its external audience of the employers. While employers in the media (inside and outside the provincial newspaper sector) are unlikely to have found the NUJ's assessments particularly convincing, they served the purpose of showing that the NUJ was not suffering from a crisis of anxiety and low self-confidence. Rather, the NUJ sought to convince employers that its fighting spirit and tenacity were undiminished and so it was a force to be reckoned with.

Nonetheless, and despite not winning a significant amount of their bargaining agenda, some chapels and the national union rightly appraised themselves as having achieved a measure of self-dignity and self-respect by being able to mobilise collectively through strikes, industrial action and mass meetings after a decade of a management offensive. To 'fight the good fight' was in some respects sufficient in itself for the years immediately after re-recognition. Chapel officers reported that industrial action had helped solidify chapel organisation and members' commitment to it. Meanwhile, the union had established productive and mutually supportive links between chapels in the various newspaper groups through organisations like the Northern Low Pay Committee and its *Northern Soul* email newsletter, and had financially supported chapels via its 'Fighting Fund', which stood at £0.8 million in 2002. Whilst there has been some internal debate and criticism of union strategy and activity, this has been muted compared to previous occasions of fratricide in the 1990s (see, for example, Gall 1992). Rather, the NUJ has been united by conflict with a common enemy, the employers, and as a result of the difficult and lengthy period from which it has recently emerged. Moreover, compared to the early 1990s, the union was in a sound financial position. In this sense, no *internal* limit was placed on the extent of resources made available by the national union for mobilisation. Allied to the dominance of an assertive and outward-looking, left-wing national leadership, the NUJ was in a better position than at any time since the mid-1980s to contest employer actions.

However, further sober analysis indicates that a number of the NUJ's long-standing difficulties have not been resolved. Two of the most important of these are the ineffectiveness of strike action and the disaggregation of (potential) union strength under decentralised collective bargaining. These had been acute both prior to derecognition in the 1980s and in the struggle against derecognition itself (Gall 2002). The year-long strikes at Aberdeen and Chelmsford between 1989 and 1990 over recognition epitomised these problems. Taking strike effectiveness first, journalists' strikes had never succeeded in halting production. Prime amongst the explanations for this outcome are that, on the one hand, the strikers have not constituted a high enough proportion of all staff, and on the other hand, journalists alone have been on strike. While majorities or significant proportions of staff have struck, the most senior staff (often on personal contracts) have not, enabling origination of copy, albeit of a slimmed and dumbed-down nature, to continue, aided by syndicated copy from the newspaper group's other sources like the Press Association. For example, in the case of Bradford, forty-eight of the ninety-nine staff struck. while in Bolton sixty of the eighty-five staff struck. The length of the actions (five days, ten days, indefinite) indicates that the proposition that longer strikes would produce more effective action is not tenable. If NUJ chapels were unable to secure their bargaining objectives by significantly disrupting or halting production on their own, what were the prospects of aligning themselves with the GPMU chapels in order to do so? In nearly all of the newspaper centres where the NUJ had regained recognition, the GPMU had also regained recognition for its members in the prepress areas, press halls and distribution. Moreover, in a number of cases, GPMU chapels had also rejected their pay offers at the same time as the NUJ chapels had (as at Bradford in 2003). But the prospects of the NUJ using the possibility or actuality of GPMU unrest to support its struggle were slight, because of the much slower rate of recovery in the industrial confidence of GPMU members. Whilst GPMU chapels have regained the organisational rights associated with recognition, they were in less of a position to pursue and operationalise these, compared to the NUJ. This situation arose because of the deep malaise affecting their occupational group and that of their union due to the social dislocation resultant from the employers' aggressive implementation of new technology to displace them (Gall 2000a).

The NUJ recognised the seriousness of employer intransigence and ineffective industrial action, such that it produced a booklet called 'An NUJ guide to organising effective industrial action' in 2003 that stated,

> When negotiations fail and dispute procedures have been exhausted members may decide they wish to ballot for industrial action. In some cases the mere threat of a ballot can be used as an effective negotiating tool and help restart stalled talks or succeed in getting an improved offer. Once the chapel has concluded that there is no other way of resolving a dispute with their employer short of industrial action, then it is important that NUJ members seek to make the industrial action as effective as possible.

Understandably, the NUJ was unable to proffer any solution to the inadequacy of strike action as practised to date. Hence, it attempted to sidestep the issue by trying to create alliances with political forces such as MPs (through early day motions in Parliament) and other members of the political elite to put extra-workplace pressure on the companies. But, as before and with other unions, this had a very limited efficacy.

Turning to the second issue, the provincial newspaper sector is dominated by a small number of very large employers (Johnson, Newsquest, Northcliffe, Trinity Mirror), each of which conducts its industrial relations at a local level, even though it is clear that a centralised steer is given to each local organisation. Under this decentralised system of bargaining, which is in turn supported by a legal framework which tightly stipulates what types of industrial action have immunity in tort, the NUJ has suffered deleteriously from its inability to aggregate its forces, while the employers are not prevented from doing so. Thus, it becomes very difficult for the NUJ to organise simultaneous or solidarity action across and between chapels, meaning that disputes arise and develop in isolation from each other. Stronger chapels cannot support weaker chapels, nor can a number of fronts or a generalised attack on companies be opened up. Consequently, bargaining in each centre within each group has developed slightly differently in terms of time, pace and content. This disorganisation has been recognised by the NUJ such that it submitted group-wide pay claims to Newsquest and Trinity Mirror in 2004, and has called for the reintroduction of national collective bargaining by group. However, none of the requisite conditions (union strength, labour market, public policy) exist by which the newspaper groups could be compelled to do so.

Cumulatively, the NUJ is as yet unable to produce solutions to these long-standing challenges and this will constrain the extent to which it can advance and protect its members' interests. In the absence of an appropriate national strategy, the most credible option is for chapels to engage individually, or collectively in tandem with each other, in a series of unofficial actions (strikes, industrial actions short of a strike). The merit of unofficial action is that it has the element of surprise which counters employer preparations to withstand lawful and official, and therefore notified, strikes, and that it can be organised by the union as a legitimate and supported action if preparations are carried out surreptitiously. However, there are of course obvious problems: the union could be subject to legal injunctions (and thus fines and sequestration) for organising unlawful action, unofficial actions could be disowned and isolated by the union if carried out without its permission and there is almost no tradition amongst journalists of unofficial action in the last twenty years. Compared to generating simultaneous but 'localised' collective industrial action at each centre across a single newspaper group, the unofficial approach is more likely to succeed because the former depends on synchronising disputes where the local employers heavily influence their timing. But the most credible option is still not necessarily an easy or easier option to take.

Journalists' strike action has been of some importance directly and indirectly in recent years, and subject to the assessment of awards above, the majority of chapels have 'gained' pay settlements through 'straightforward' bargaining involving no industrial action. In this process and that of representing members' workplace interests generally, chapels have had certain advantages and disadvantages in doing so vis-à-vis resources and expertise. The milieu of lay activists, the chapel officers, are experienced and battle-hardened and had the support of a proportionately increased number of national FTOs, of whom most were ex-journalists. Moreover, activists and

FTOs operated in a situation where recognition had been regained rather than being gained for the first time. These represented, in addition to the earlier discussion, fairly favourable grounds on which to pursue members' interests. But as intimated earlier, these were outweighed by a series of 'imbalances' between employers and journalists in the three key arenas of union influence, these being labour scarcity, disruptive capacity and political influence (Batstone 1988). In cognisance of the slight movement in the balance of power towards the journalists within the continuing imbalance in favour of the employers, this suggests that the predominant employer strategy of derecognition has now been superseded by the predominant strategy of marginalisation, whether of outright surface bargaining or hard-nosed bargaining.

Conclusion

The case of the provincial newspaper journalists provides a salutary lesson in demonstrating that *de jure* recognition should not be made synonymous with de facto recognition. For employers with a deep-seated and historically situated antipathy towards trade unionism (Gall 2000a, 2002), merely conceding recognition has been the demonstration of tactical deftness in engaging in a longer and more drawn-out war. Indeed, some in the NUJ were far-sighted to recognise this early on. The NUJ's northern organiser told the 1998 NUJ annual conference, 'Recognition is not the panacea. When we get it we will still have to fight for higher wages and better conditions. On its own it will achieve nothing' (*Journalist* April 1998). For the NUJ to become a match to the financially, ideologically and organisationally well-resourced employers would entail the NUJ developing its industrial prowess far more. While professionalism may have some role to play in cohering journalists into a significant industrial force (Gall and Murphy 1996), this is an extremely contingent process. Far more germane would be the process of deepening the degree of 'unionateness' (Blackburn 1967) or 'union militancy' (Allen 1966). In this regard, the theme of mobilisation per se being necessary but not sufficient was explored in the case of the oil workers seeking union recognition against recalcitrant employers in the late 1980s/early 1990s (Gall 2003e). It is equally relevant to the case of the journalists, for it focuses attention on two points: first, the generalised need to achieve higher levels of aggregation of the forces of organised labour in acts of mobilisation to overcome employer will and resource; and second, consideration of which particular tactics offer the application of the highest forms of pressure. Unlike the oil workers, provincial newspaper journalists have operated in the more conducive environment of being a small, homogeneous and tightly knit union with a common sense of identity and grievance. Moreover, the potential ability of strike action to halt production of an extremely perishable product offers significant leverage. But the forces ranged against the journalists, and their relative union disorganisation, have so far outstripped the potency of these components.

8 Union recognition in Asian workplaces

Springboard to further organising and recognition campaigns?

Jane Holgate

With few exceptions (e.g. Wrench and Virdee 1996; Virdee 2000), research on the union organisation of black and minority ethnic (BME) workers and migrant workers in Britain has been absent. Despite much research into union renewal and union organising methods, this absence is also marked in the US (see Milkman 1998; Mitchell 1996; Savage 1998). While this limited number of studies are welcome additions to the literature on the process of unionisation of BME and migrant workers, there is little understanding of what happens to worker organisation post-recognition, or after first contracts are signed. This chapter attempts to help bridge this gap by exploring post-recognition outcomes in five factories in west London, comprising workers from the large well-established Asian communities[1] in this part of the capital. It explores the process by which collective identity developed among this group of workers, drawing on a key aspect of mobilisation theory, that of social identification (Kelly 1998). In outlining the process by which individuals move from a sense of injustice to developing a collective interest, Kelly (1998) notes that workers first need someone to blame (attribution), a sense of 'we' defined in opposition to 'them' (social identification) and, in order to combine these into collective interest, leadership. Central to each recognition campaign was the construction of identity based around an 'Asian community'. One social theorist who has considered the use of cultural networks and resources in political formation notes that collective mobilisation through a 'politics of identification' is possible through commonalities of experiences, be these 'race', gender, class, caste or religion (Brah 1996). Although workers in this study broadly identified themselves as part of the diverse Asian community in London, their 'politics of identification' was clearly expressed in class terms when organising for union recognition. The fracturing of community along class lines was evident as workers made clear distinctions about their relative economic position and that of Asian managers and bosses who sought to undermine their attempts at unionisation.

The chapter then analyses how the GMB union, largely through the use of Asian leaders, used this notion of an 'Asian community' as means of mobilising workers in west London around a 'shared identity' in a number of recognition campaigns. It begins by examining how unionisation at a large Asian food factory led to recognition at a number of other Asian factories in the locality. With high union density and relative autonomy from the national union, it could be viewed as a model example of organising unionism (see Bronfenbrenner 1998; Heery *et al.* 2000c). Other campaigns, although successful at achieving recognition, have been less successful at the collective bargaining stage and were still reliant on FTOs to provide support. The reasons behind these different outcomes are explored, looking at the development of social identification, the role of leadership, and the relationship between members and their union.

Inherent in all these workplaces, which ranged from small to large manufacturing and service enterprises, were poor terms and conditions of employment. Union activists and workers were acutely aware that the racialised[2] nature of the labour market was responsible primarily for the immediate conditions under which they were employed (Holgate 2004a). Despite the fact that many workers were highly qualified, most were unable to find employment appropriate to their skills. In addition, more-recent migrant workers had limited English language ability, which further restricted the type of employment they were able to obtain (Haque 2002). In each of the campaigns, employer behaviour was hostile towards the union and the common message conveyed to workers was that they were easily replaceable as a result of the large pool of unskilled labour on which employers were able to draw. Many workers were therefore vulnerable and fearful of losing their jobs. In addition, most had little or no prior experience of collective workplace organisation.

Methods and context

Data for this chapter was gathered from participant observation of union activity within the London region of the GMB union over a three-year period, involving attendance at union meetings, factory gate recruitment and leafleting, and discussions about tactics with union activists. In addition, sixteen formal interviews were undertaken with shop stewards, union members, lay activists and union officials involved at the Video Duplication Company (VDC). All union members interviewed at VDC were male and were largely representative of the many different ethnic groups in the workplace: Indian/Kenyan, Sri Lankan, Punjabi and Somalian. Of the FTOs interviewed, two were female, one of whom was white British and the other black British Caribbean. Three of the male officials were white British and two were Asian, both Pakistani. Other material was gathered from union organising meetings and conferences, and from analysis of literature produced by the GMB. All quotes used in the chapter are derived from interviews and meetings.

At the heart of GMB London region's strategic organising plan, developed in 2001, was an understanding that its membership did not reflect the ethnicity of the local labour market and that this needed rectifying. Previous organising approaches had been concerned with in-filling unionised workplaces and had tended to avoid those 'difficult to organise' workplaces where many BME workers are located in jobs such as food manufacturing, security and cleaning services. The initial success at Noon Products provided the union with a substantial increase in membership and a greater profile among the west London Asian communities as well as a number of experienced activists. This convinced the GMB London region that it could and should develop a specific organising strategy for workers in these previously neglected parts of the labour market. It was as a consequence of the GMB's explicit acknowledgement of racism in the labour market and in the workplace that union organisers successfully conveyed the message that the struggle for unionisation was a collective community issue for Asian workers in this part of London.

Noon Products: a catalyst for future organising campaigns

In early 1999, the GMB London region finally signed a voluntary recognition agreement with Noons, following a long and difficult battle. The predominantly female Asian workforce at Noons campaigned for over a year for their union to be recognised and, more importantly, to be treated with dignity and respect at work. Idiosyncratic employment practice and discretionary pay to favoured employees caused huge resentment among staff, leading to calls for union representation. The campaign generated considerable local and national media notoriety and received widespread support from the local Asian community, where thousands signed petitions and demonstrated in their support. The campaign began when a group of workers felt that they could no longer sit back and watch as their fellow workers were treated badly. Although a culture of bullying and fear prevailed, it was lack of respect from managers that created a sense of injustice and brought workers together. Assuming a leadership role, a couple of activists regularly met with small groups of workers to listen to their grievances, persuading them that only by unionisation and collective action would they be able to change the situation in the factory.

As many workers lacked the confidence to attend open meetings, home visits allowed union activists to speak to workers. Lack of respect from management was used to build a collective sense of injustice, where union organisers were careful to counterpoise the union's behaviour with that of the employer by demonstrating sensitivity. Realising that the wider community could be a source of support, the campaign at Noons extended into its locality, Southall. Through community events, union organisers encouraged workers' families and friends to become involved and, at the same time, built the GMB's profile as the 'union for the Asian community'. To overcome the fear that many had about joining the union, organisers arranged meetings in community centres and mosques, and recruited door-to-door, where they were away from Noons' watchful eye. It was this appeal for community support and the work of key activists in building the membership that eventually persuaded the employer to recognise the union.

Throughout, the pressure on the company was fairly constant and intensive, but the mobilisation was also a great challenge for the union, which had not previously run a 'community' campaign. The lessons learnt here helped to crystallise further the GMB London region's development of an organising culture among its members, activists and FTOs. The shift towards community organising or social movement unionism began to open up a new geographical space in which the GMB could operate and, at the same time, provided a way to reach those unorganised workplaces which had until now been inaccessible to many of the union's white officials. And consequently, the two leading activists at Noons began working full-time for the GMB because of the recognition that they were rooted in the geographical and cultural space of the local community. A senior GMB organiser commented,

> The two Asian organisers both live in Southall. Zaheer will sometimes disappear for a couple of months and come back with 200 membership forms from some firm that we have never heard of. When you ask him how did it go – he said it was all done in front rooms. . . . We would never really dream of knocking on people's doors. . . . [H]e understands the culture and the gender politics. He knows the way in. We can never intervene on this level.

While the workplace has remained the focus for securing improvements in terms and conditions, some recent organising campaigns within the west London Asian community have been conducted at a wider scale. The normal geographical boundary of unionisation campaigns has now been extended to include public and private spaces outside of the workplace, encompassing community space as well. Links between campaigns have helped to engender a degree of trust in trade unionism among Asian workers, which had hitherto not existed.

Community links and further unionisation

Over twenty workplaces have been organised since the Noons campaign, using social networks in the west London Asian community, including food processing factories, security services, manufacturing factories, cleaning companies, hospitals and hotels. In one campaign, at Renolit, a worker who was not a union member contacted the GMB for advice after being treated badly by a manager. After several attempts to get help, he was passed to an Asian organiser:

> I said if the GMB didn't reply today then I will leave [work]. . . . Zaheer . . . came to my home and he explained about rules and regulations and about recognition. He gave me some forms and said he would come back in two weeks' time to collect the forms.
>
> (Vishram, subsequently GMB lay organiser)

With the support of Zaheer, this new union member recruited 80 per cent of the workforce within two weeks, securing a voluntary recognition agreement shortly afterwards. After successfully organising his own workplace, Vishram decided to repay the GMB's support. He was concerned that the disadvantage Asian workers experienced in the labour market made them particularly vulnerable to exploitation and discrimination and set himself the task of ensuring that other Asian workplaces were aware of the benefits of joining a union:

> My aim is [to recruit in] my community and I know where the problems are and where the workplaces are. . . . It is like a chain cycle . . . some of the men's wives work at [company A] and at [company B] . . . so this is the cycle . . . the connection. I use this connection and explain about the union and what the benefits are. Anybody, who sits down with me for an hour, I convince them about the union. For example, in one place I recruited 160 people in one day.
>
> (Vishram, GMB lay organiser)

This identification and mobilisation of stewards who can play a leadership role in the community has been one of the major successes achieved by the GMB. At Katie's Kitchen, another food processing factory, it was again through community contacts that workers approached the GMB, seeking assistance. Many workers there had family or friends who worked at Noons. Similar community connections led to a successful union recognition campaign at a small factory, Richmond Mirrors, and at VDC, a large video production company with over 300 workers. The use of union activists in other campaigns, either as means of support, or as examples of how collective organisation could be achieved, soon became a common occurrence:

> As we have seen, the ability to use a trained rep from another company to speak to other workers works really well. They are usually happy to do it because it is their community. If you look at the mirror factory, they only came on board because Vishram [from Renolit] had won recognition at his workplace and he had achieved many gains. Word went out around the community. . . . They then thought 'well if that happened there, then perhaps we can do it here'.
>
> (Paula, GMB FTO)

Thus, the dynamic of the Noon campaign began a series of events which, through social networks in the community, led to a number of subsequent workforces becoming unionised, substantially increasing the GMB's Asian membership and its activist base. One of these campaigns provides a contrast to the organising success of Noons. While successful at achieving recognition, workers at VDC were faced with a virulently anti-union employer who constrained union members from mobilising collectively. Consequently, it was difficult to find individual workers prepared to adopt leadership roles, reducing the union's ability to call upon support from the wider community.

Organising for union recognition but not collective bargaining?

VDC, located on a large industrial estate in west London, produces CDs, videos and DVDs for retail stores. It employs an Asian workforce of approximately 170–200 production workers, and between 100 and 200 mainly Asian casual workers through 'agencies', on a casual, but regular, basis. The recognition campaign began as a consequence of local networks in the Asian community but took two years to come to fruition with the GMB, eventually winning an award through the statutory procedure. Throughout that time, shop stewards operated in secret because the company was actively hostile to the union. This section examines how the GMB won recognition but was nevertheless unsuccessful in gaining de facto collective bargaining.

Within a few days of the first meeting with union officials, one VDC worker convinced eighty of his fellow staff to join the GMB. Despite this positive beginning, the campaign developed slowly and floundered on a number of occasions. In early 2002, membership dropped to fifty and union officials began to doubt whether there was sufficient support to proceed. This view was reinforced when the company began making threats against individuals, warning them not to join the union. Activists were disillusioned and were unconfident about continuing, until an activist from Noons spoke to them about his experience of collective organisation when he was sacked for his union activities:

> When the other reps heard the news [of my dismissal], the whole factory was closed in a couple of minutes. There was a sit-in . . . Noons had to call the GMB official to ask him to come down and stop the members' sit-in. The members said: 'No, we are not going to walk away until Aasim comes back in the canteen to tell us that he is going to stay.' Noons then called me on the phone and said, 'Can you come back?' This was just in half an hour! What I am trying to say is that if there is the right union, then the people will realise what strength they have. First of all you have to understand about unionism yourself, then you can motivate other people.
>
> (Aasim, subsequently GMB FTO)

Had it not been for Aasim's intervention, it was likely that the campaign would have disintegrated at this point. This intervention precipitated a change in attitude as messages of respect, trust and community support resonated. From this meeting one activist proceeded to collect ninety-four signatures from fellow workers requesting union recognition and this was used by the GMB within its statutory recognition application. But despite Aasim's activity, the support and leadership in the campaign was largely provided by GMB FTOs and a number of Asian lay activists from outside VDC. Workers were particularly fearful of their employer and because it employed a large number of agency staff, which made workers feel vulnerable for their jobs, there was also a reluctance to make a wider appeal to the community as had been the case at Noons. Nevertheless, a common refrain to convince workers to join was: 'We are all Asian. You must do this for our community.' An aspect of this appeal to community solidarity was the construction of an Asian identity as an organising tool. It was developed around an understanding of a common experience by Asian workers in the London labour market which involved an acute awareness of the impact of racism on their opportunities for employment and their level of exploitation.

However, there were limitations to this common experience and the mobilisation around a collective 'Asian' identity. There were divisions between the established migrants who were the permanent staff and the more recent migrant workers who were employed through agencies. The status of these agencies was questioned by the GMB, who provided a dossier to the Department for Trade and Industry (DTI), alleging that the recruitment companies were not legitimate employment agencies but were, in fact, operating as gangmasters, much in the way that casual staff were employed on the docks before decasualisation (see Blyton and Turnbull 1998). Throughout the campaign, the presence of 'agency' workers caused problems, as workers claimed that the number of permanent staff was reduced and the number of 'agency' staff increased, in order to make it difficult for the GMB to build the critical mass necessary to achieve recognition. The problem of how the union should address the issue of the casual workers was one that arose constantly during the campaign. It was evident that the social identification referred to by Kelly (1998), whereby workers develop a sense of 'we' (workers) defined in opposition to 'them' (employer), did not include the agency workers as part of the workers' collective. The overwhelming view of workers was that employing agency workers made it more difficult to secure unionisation, recognition and the benefits of collective bargaining. The debate over whether to report the 'illegal' workers to the various authorities caused difficult moral decisions for union officials:

> Do we blow the whistle on people who are trying to earn a living? . . . [A]t the end of the day, the chances are that we would. . . . As long as [VDC] is able to prop up the system, which invariably exploits people, then it's a problem. . . . So when you start to weigh up the pros and

> cons, my conscience tells me that we have to.... [Y]ou come to a point when you realise that doing nothing is effectively condoning that situation.
>
> (GMB Regional Secretary)

Despite many workers' fear about being identified with the union, the CAC ballot showed overwhelming support for the GMB: 75 per cent of the 170 workers voted and, of these, 86 per cent voted for the union. Thus, in spring 2003, the CAC awarded the GMB recognition at VDC for collective bargaining. Workers were understandably jubilant but their anticipation of improvements in terms and conditions was short-lived when it became apparent that the GMB was encountering difficulty in persuading VDC to enter into meaningful collective bargaining. The nature of the statutory process and the high numerical membership thresholds required to gain recognition often result in recruitment becoming the sole focus on campaigns, particularly in the later stages. Hence, there is a tendency to neglect the process of educating workers about the skills and activity needed to undertake collective bargaining. In this case, the passivity of members and their fear of being identified with the union meant that they were reliant on the GMB to undertake this representation and negotiating work. Thus, the nature of their sense of collectivity formed in the process of organising for recognition cannot necessarily be taken as being sufficient or appropriate for process of internal agenda setting and mobilisation needed for representation and collective bargaining.

What strategy when an employer refuses to bargain?

It took six months following the CAC ruling before a recognition agreement was signed, and it was achieved only after the GMB made a request to the CAC to intervene. However, if the union hoped that this would result in subsequent 'good faith' collective bargaining negotiations, it was soon to be disappointed. VDC would not disclose financial information to the GMB and flatly refused to negotiate over the first pay claim submitted. Indeed, while 'negotiations' were continuing, VDC wrote to staff inviting them to 'opt out' of the bargaining unit if they wanted to receive their pay increase. At this stage, union organisation inside the factory was still weak, and hostility from management had increased. The problem the GMB faced in this breakdown of negotiations was how to respond. After calling a meeting of union members, it was clear that workers did not have the confidence to take industrial action to try to break the impasse. The presence of 'agency' workers led members to conclude that the company could probably hold out for a long period in the face of any strike action. In the absence of internal workplace unionism and leadership, members had become reliant on FTOs to try to secure improvements to terms and conditions, with the consequence that after three years of battling to secure recognition and without any discernible material gains, their sense of collectivity and confidence had become diminished. Moreover, the workplace union was unable to represent or defend members in disciplinaries or undertake grievances at an individual level. Membership dropped to around fifty as some workers stopped paying their union dues, which, together with the increase in agency workers, represented a drop in density to 13 per cent. It was becoming harder for the only shop steward who remained active to promote a sense of 'group cohesion' or to deal with the employer's counter-mobilisation.

This situation contrasts starkly with that at Noons, where members learned early on that collective action could achieve results, even prior to recognition. This experience of successfully wringing concessions from management gave members an understanding of how collectively to achieve their demands. VDC workers, on the other hand, had no experience of pre-recognition gains and had placed all their expectations in the legislation and the skills of union negotiators to provide improvements to their terms and conditions. Union membership was very weak and the members inexperienced, and fear of the employer had a disabling effect. As a result of its inability to mobilise its members collectively at VDC in any form, the GMB decided to adopt a new strategy. Recognising that there were few other options, the GMB undertook what it considered to be a 'last resort' strategy. In mid-2004, it compiled a dossier of alleged breaches of employment law, including the national minimum wage, working-time regulations, Inland Revenue rules and National Insurance regulations. Containing signed statements from VDC workers describing the process by which 'illegal' workers were employed and examples of how workers were employed at the factory gates without the necessary documentation, the dossier was sent to the press and relevant government departments responsible for upholding this legislation. VDC responded by threatening the GMB with legal action. In turn, the GMB pushed the DTI to act on the information provided. As a result, the DTI instructed the Employment Agency Standards Inspectorate to undertake an investigation, stating that the DTI considered the matter 'very serious' and promised to 'take all possible steps to stamp out the exploitation of these workers' (letter from Secretary of State for Trade and Industry, 3 June 2004).

By this strategy, the GMB sought to force VDC to abide by employment legislation and to end the exploitation of a vulnerable group of workers. However, this was a high-risk strategy, and even though the GMB called for an amnesty for any 'illegal' workers who might be employed at the factory, there was the chance that some workers might get caught up in any investigation undertaken by the authorities. Further, there was doubt among some workers that the company would survive if its supply of cheap labour was cut off. At a union meeting prior to the dossier's completion, there was unanimous agreement that after three and a half years of campaigning and using the statutory recognition procedure, this was perhaps the only way the company would be forced to listen to the union's demands. The decision to submit a dossier to government departments was considered a 'do or die' strategy. Members calculated that they had only a 'fifty–fifty' chance of success but, overall, felt that they had little to lose. Most did not wish to continue working long hours for little pay and were aware that they could in the current economic climate find work in one of the many companies in the area employing Asian workers through their social and family networks. As any investigation is yet to be completed, it remains to be seen if the GMB's strategy is one that is successful or self-destructive. Nonetheless, the GMB felt compelled to act, for the alternative would have been to walk away, essentially blaming union members for their lack of confidence in undertaking industrial action.

The organising campaigns at Noons and VDC were very different. The former was high-profile, had strong workplace leadership and high union density, and used the wider community for support. The latter was conducted in secrecy, reliant on FTO support, and hampered by low union density, and workers were fearful of identifying themselves as members. The next section reviews these issues in the context of other campaigns, questioning whether the process by which recognition was achieved affects the outcomes post-recognition.

Securing recognition: process and outcomes

Since the GMB London region began implementing its strategy of organising in the Asian community, it has experienced an increase of 10,000 Asian members between 1998 and 2003, and 95 per cent of its current Asian membership joined following the campaign at Noons. In some cases, campaigns resulted in increased membership at already recognised workplaces, but in others there were protracted battles to secure recognition at greenfield sites. In the five greenfield sites where recognition was won during this period, the union used the statutory procedure three times, while gaining recognition voluntarily in the other two (see Table 8.1). This section compares and contrasts these campaigns, assessing the impact of the different organising campaigns upon organisational and bargaining outcomes in the post-recognition period. Table 8.1 summarises the salient features for each and, following these chronologically, provides a method of assessing process and outcomes using the framework of mobilisation theory.

Common to all workplaces was the predominance of Asian workers who had little or no experience of trade unionism. Many were recent migrant workers whose English-language skills were limited, which restricted opportunities for obtaining other, more gainful employment. In each of these campaigns, workers feared joining the union, anticipating that they might be dismissed, with some members being intimidated by managers into spying and reporting on union activity. Nevertheless, workers did join in considerable numbers, and average union density in the five workplaces was 40 per cent, much higher than the national figure of 14 per cent for

Table 8.1 Union recognition: outcomes from five campaigns

	Noon Products	*Renolit*	*Katie's Kitchen*	*Richmond Mirrors*	*VDC*
Enterprise	Food manufacturer	PVC manufacturer	Food manufacturer	Mirror manufacturer	CD/DVD manufacturer
Recognition gained	March 1999	January 2000	November 2001	March 2003	April 2003
Recognition status	Voluntary	Voluntary	Statutory	Statutory	Statutory
Number of workers	350 (now 1,000)	100	850	48	170 (plus 100–200 agency)
Union membership (density) at recognition	295 (84%)	80 (80%)	160 (18%)	13 (27%)	60 (35%)
Union members June 2004	600 (60%)	Closed January 2004	600 (70%)	16 (33%)	55 (32%)
Workers' support for recognition	n/a	n/a	64% (petition)	57% (ballot)	87% (ballot)
Date of first pay increase	January 2000	January 2000	April 2002	January 2004	1 April 2004
First pay increase after recognition	2.9% (binding arbitration)	6–8% (negotiated)	4.5% (negotiated)	2.8% (negotiated)	3% (imposed)

Other terms and conditions benefits	Job re-evaluation. Many staff received increases of 8%–50%. Loyalty bonus of between £500–£1,500. Removal of security cameras in canteen. Recent Equal Pay Audit resulted in £150,000 back pay and 60 new members.	Improvements in health and safety. Introduction of new machinery in exchange for increase in productivity. Introduction of pension and sick pay schemes.	Introduction of fair and transparent disciplinary and grievance procedure. Secured time off for union reps. Assistance with English language training. Improvement to sick pay scheme, maternity/paternity pay. Improvements in pension scheme.	Improvements in health and safety. Regulated pension scheme (previously employer withheld payments into the pension fund). Regularised pay (previously the employer sometimes withheld employees' weekly pay).	None.
Number of shop stewards	7	1	9	1	1
Workplace organisation organisation	High. Day-to-day union activity undertaken by local shop stewards. Union office, telephone and computers.	High until closure. Day-to-day union activity undertaken by local shop stewards.	High. Day-to-day union activity undertaken by local shop stewards. Union office, telephone and computers.	None. FTO support, but no active involvement from the workers.	Low. Mainly FTO support around collective bargaining. Three previous stewards now have little/no involvement.

union density in the private sector. Moreover, in the larger workplaces – Noons and Katie's Kitchen – it was 60 per cent and 70 per cent respectively. Although common, worker fear did not have the same restraining effect on each campaign. In general, it was in the larger companies that the GMB had greater success in persuading workers to become active. From these cases, it seems that the higher the membership and density, the greater the success of achieving improvements in terms and conditions. In Richmond Mirrors, where there were only sixteen members, they felt exposed and vulnerable. At each workplace, there was a sense of injustice which in addition to low pay and poor working conditions, was manifested in an experience of a general lack of respect towards Asian workers. Workers and union activists continually expressed this by reference to the way that they were treated less favourably because they were Asian workers. Mobilisation theory highlights that a prerequisite for collective action is not only a sense of injustice, but that workers must develop a sense of their grievances being collective. These recognition campaigns used the discourse of community to achieve this, drawing on the lived experience of Asians as low-paid, racialised workers to solidify a social identification.

But despite these commonalities, there were different positive and negative aspects to the campaigns that determined later outcomes. The Noons campaign benefited from high profile and committed workplace activists who were trusted and respected and in charge of the campaign from the beginning. Since the company was the largest Asian employer in the locality, with an Asian workforce, community pressure, in conjunction with negative publicity generated by the GMB, inclined management to reach a voluntary recognition agreement rather than being forced through the legal procedure. Consequently, recognition was agreed in 1999 and workers saw their first benefits from unionisation when they received a pay increase in 2000, some three years after the start of the campaign. But members soon became disillusioned. The two main activists left to work for the GMB and FTOs negotiated the first pay increase which was regarded as disappointingly low at 2.9 per cent, and was settled only with resort to binding arbitration, and few improvements to other terms and conditions were secured. Membership dropped rapidly to around ninety as members began to lose faith in the union's ability to achieve results. Although it took some time for the union to recover its strength, it did manage to rebuild itself by developing new activists who refocused on developing a new organising strategy. They managed to secure a job re-evaluation exercise and conducted an equal-pay audit that saw significant improvements in pay for many workers. Since then, workplace organisation has become largely self-sufficient, with seven trained shop stewards who, through hard work, have brought 600 workers into membership.

At Renolit, voluntary recognition was achieved after a short campaign. Almost immediately thereafter, the steward negotiated pay increases between 6 and 8 per cent, along with the introduction of a sick pay and pension scheme. When the steward went to work full-time for the GMB, the factory remained well organised, with another steward taking his place. But, following a spate of redundancies, the factory closed in January 2004. However, by using steward networks within the Asian community, the remaining workers were all found jobs at other Asian workplaces in the locality. This significantly enhanced the union's credibility in the eyes of those workers, who have since gone on to assist in unionisation campaigns in their new workplaces. Again, the key determinant in the post-recognition outcome was the leadership provided by the steward.

Katie's Kitchen followed a similar pattern to Noons in terms of employer hostility, but the campaign got off to a much slower start, achieving a membership of only 160 out of a workforce of 850 by the time of recognition. Workers were divided, with some managers and supervisors using social and family networks within the Asian community to argue against recognition. Although the campaign had strong support from the Asian FTOs, there was no visible internal leadership to challenge the counter-mobilisation. To address this, the GMB took the campaign outside the workplace and into the wider Asian community, as they had done at Noons. Although the campaign was not as high-profile in the media, regular meetings and social activity were nevertheless used to develop membership confidence and cohesion. The two Asian FTOs who had run the Noon campaign had considerable standing in the community. Consequently, when an application requesting recognition was submitted to the CAC, 492 workers out of 769 signed a petition supporting the right to GMB representation. Since recognition, skilful bargaining by an experienced FTO, and the employer's desire to eliminate the practice of favouritism, which created so much discontent, saw membership rise to 600. This led to a relatively self-organised workplace, where terms and conditions have improved and most union activity is conducted through nine fully trained shop stewards.

The campaigns at Richmond Mirrors and VDC have, so far, been less successful, both in terms of member mobilisation and workplace self-organisation. Richmond Mirrors, a small workplace, was largely organised by the women employees. Male workers appeared reluctant to get involved in the union for, according to women union members, they had better-paid jobs and were treated more favourably. Nevertheless, women workers were not put off and stood together, eventually winning recognition through a CAC ballot. However, Richmond Mirrors resorted to legal manoeuvres to overturn the award, claiming that, since the ballot, the bargaining unit had been substantially changed as a result of the requirements of the business, necessitating another ballot. The employer also submitted another challenge, in which it claimed that the company was now a different business and therefore this made the ruling invalid. However, these were withdrawn when it was pointed out that these two positions were contradictory and, since then, the company has reluctantly entered into limited bargaining. Although there have been some improvements to terms and conditions, the steward was inexperienced and consequently felt intimidated by employer hostility, particularly with only a third of workers in membership. In this case, there was not sufficient 'critical mass' to instil a sense of confidence leading to any form of collective mobilisation. Both Richmond Mirrors and VDC displayed hostility towards the union and, in both, union density and workplace self-organisation were more fragile, with reliance on FTOs to undertake negotiation and representation. With a climate of fear pervasive, few individuals were prepared to come forward and be identified as workplace activists, which restricted the level of mobilisation among workers. Finally, it appears that while ERA provides a means for achieving statutory recognition and can be a useful mobilising tool, it provides little redress when an employer refuses to enter into meaningful collective bargaining (see also McKay, Moore and Wood, this volume). In such cases, unions are either reliant on traditional forms of industrial action or, in the case of VDC, attempt to deal with membership weakness by deploying pressure through alternative, outside means.

Conclusion

Since adopting an organising philosophy akin to social movement unionism, the GMB London region has organised Asian workers in a considerable number of new workplaces, five of which were analysed in this chapter. The first, at Noons, became a catalyst, sparking a chain reaction and highlighting the importance of social networks to initiate, sustain and mobilise other workers in unionisation campaigns. Although it had been the intention to organise more BME workers for some time, it was the unpredicted contact from those workers at Noons that made this happen. The use of social networks in the community was an important development for the GMB in unionising what were considered 'difficult to organise' workplaces, highlighting how culture and identity can be important tools in union mobilisation. Mobilisation theory suggests that groups develop a social identity around which to coalesce as they move from a sense of injustice to collective activity. Trade unionism has often presumed that 'class' is the most salient feature in developing workers' consciousness as workers. Yet this prioritisation has often neglected how gender, 'race' or other identities intersect with class to create a different focus in collective organisation (Holgate 2004a). Although the issues faced by workers in these case studies could be described as 'class-based' – low pay and poor conditions – these were often experienced within the context of the racialised nature of employment, which saw many Asian workers restricted to, or trapped in, certain types of work. As a consequence, 'the community' can at times, and did in these particular circumstances, provide a source of strength and support, and a degree of collectivism in the absence of other support networks. In the campaigns in this chapter, a sense of injustice based around lack of respect, racism and job segregation from white workers was highlighted and used as a means of collectivising workers.

US observers of union renewal have noted how social movement unionism, which is described as a type of unionism based on member involvement and activists, can open up possibilities for involvement and mobilisation in wider communities beyond the specificity of the workplace (Turner *et al.* 2001). Other writers have also called for unions to pursue renewal strategies that give a greater focus on the benefits of linking up with communities in their broadest sense, if unions are to reach low-waged workers who have been left without union representation. Wills (2002: 54) calls for 'a new strategy that unites trade unionists, non-members and their supporters around the battle for justice in the labour market' as a 'more promising way to reach and mobilise such workers today'. The 'geographic and strategic gaps' that Wills refers to in contemporary union organisation could be filled, in part, by building a form of networked trade unionism that reaches into the diverse communities within wider society. This raises the possibility of a renaissance of local geographically based trade unionism. The cases in this chapter give just one example of how a union has expanded its social movement unionism into one particular community. However, it is important not to assume that 'community' is necessarily always a progressive force for worker mobilisation. At Katie's Kitchen, groups within 'the community' used social networks to mobilise against unionisation. As mobilisation theory suggests, the process is contingent on whether strong union leadership is able to defend collective action and social identity in the face of counter-mobilisation.

The role of leadership was crucial to the success of all five campaigns, but there was a significant difference between those campaigns that had strong workplace leadership and those that relied on outside FTOs. Noons, Renolit and Katie's Kitchen had committed and competent workplace activists who were able to sustain union organising in the post-recognition period. The two stewards at Noons displayed an understanding of the ideology of class and the need to collectivise members. This was evident in their approach to union-building, whereby they organised workers in small groups before bringing them together at larger meetings in an attempt to build collective confidence. Throughout the campaign, these stewards openly stood up to management, telling workers they need not be afraid. However, both Richmond Mirrors and VDC were without stewards who were capable of challenging management hostility, and consequently, union membership was much lower. In these cases the activists were good at appealing to workers on an individual level and had success in getting them into membership, but were less successful at transforming that 'individualist' orientation into a collective force. Collective action by workers was generated through social networks constructed around a shared 'Asian' identity. Community, defined in terms of 'race' and 'class', was used as the primary social identity around which to organise, although demands for improvements in terms and conditions were class-based as workers challenged their economic marginality as workers. Such communities necessarily possess a geographic dimension.

But the way in which the GMB approached its campaigns is not necessarily readily transferable to other places or communities. Nevertheless, the chapter has highlighted issues that have been under-theorised with regards to worker mobilisation – those of place-specific and identity-specific union organising. Too often, the social and spatial geographies of workers have been ignored and we are reminded that 'the failure to theorise the spatial nature of socio-political life hampers us from providing a satisfactory explanation for political mobilisation' (Marston 2001: 925). The case studies suggest that a more geographical and identity-sensitive approach to union organising can, in some circumstances, produce significant gains in union membership, union organisation and representational outcomes.

Acknowledgements

I am grateful to the ESRC's financial support (award S42200134047) and to my co-sponsors, the TUC and SERTUC. Thanks are also due to officials and union members from the GMB, and to Gregor Gall for comments on an earlier version.

Notes

1 In using the term 'Asian community', it is not intended to suggest a homogeneous ethnic group, nor to essentialise 'community'. Rather, Asian union activists used the term to describe the Asian community of west London. In British discourse, Asian generally refers to people who originate from the Indian subcontinent.

2 The term 'racialised' is used to denote BME workers are represented in some jobs or employment sectors – disproportional to white workers – primarily because of their ethnicity or skin colour, rather than their qualifications or skills.

9 Two strategies, two divides

Employer and union strategies towards non-union employee representation at Eurotunnel and News International

Paul Gollan

It is evident from existing research in Britain that relatively little is known about management strategies towards non-union employee representation (NER), sometimes also referred to as 'union-independent' or 'alternative' forms of employee representation, either in terms of its independence from managerial influence or its effectiveness in representing employees' interests (Gollan 2000, 2001; Terry 1999). Building on earlier work (Gollan 2001), this chapter addresses the deficit by examining the experience of non-union and union representation arrangements at Eurotunnel (UK) and News International Newspapers. These organisations were chosen to generate data on management strategies in establishing NER structures and union responses to such arrangements, and to shed some light on the outcomes and implications of these arrangements for management, unions and employees. The importance of NER arrangements in Britain has been highlighted by the European Union's Information and Consultation Directive. The Directive applies to undertakings or businesses with at least fifty employees (or establishments with twenty employees or more), and will require them to inform and consult their employees in good time about issues directly affecting work organisation, job security and employment contracts regarding terms and conditions. More specifically, the new directive will require employers under a legal obligation to inform their staff on an ongoing basis about matters such as firm performance and strategic planning. In Britain, the Directive is being introduced as a regulation and in phases: firms with more than 150 employees had until March 2005 to set up information and consultation procedures; those with more than 100 employees have until March 2007; and those with more than fifty employees have until March 2008.

While the Directive offers substantial flexibility in relation to the shape of information and consultation arrangements, some commentators have suggested that this proposal implies the establishment of national-level works councils in Britain or at least, in non-union establishments, some form of non-union employee representation (Gospel and Willman 2002, 2003). For some Member States, notably Britain, it will require organisations to have much more extensive employee consultation processes than are currently in place. The Directive requires workplace bodies comprising elected representatives and consultation to be undertaken in such a way that these representatives and their constituencies can influence management decisions. Notwithstanding the motivations of employers in setting up NER arrangements, the Information and Consultation Regulations requires effective voice for all employees in an establishment covered. Thus, it is important that an assessment is made of the appropriateness of existing NER and union arrangements in satisfying these requirements. Under these arrangements, the implications of not satisfying these requirements may be greater legislative intervention in management decision-making processes and greater challenges for unions. Furthermore, not meeting these requirements could increase dissatisfaction towards management and result in lower productivity and performance and increased instability in industrial relations environments.

While it can be argued that firms set up NER to provide a more structured method for employee involvement and for purposes of union avoidance, this chapter will focus on the effectiveness of NER arrangements in providing voice through bargaining, consultation and representation of the needs of employees. 'Voice' is defined here as a communication that has the power to persuade and is a legitimate expression of the collective aims of those workers (Greenfield and Pleasure 1993: 193–4). As a means to explore these issues, a review of the union strategies and tactics of 'colonisation' and 'marginalisation' of NER arrangements is carried out. In addition, management strategies of either union representation (e.g. Eurotunnel) or establishing an alternative non-union bargaining structure (e.g. News International) are assessed. Issues of industrial relations instability and management and union intentions are also explored. These tasks are undertaken by reviewing representation arrangements before and after union recognition and alongside a company council at Eurotunnel, and with regard to increased union influence on the News International Staff Association (NISA).

Thus, the chapter addresses a number of research questions. First, how effective are NER and union arrangements at representing the interests of, and providing voice for, employees? Second, in the absence of union representation, how independent are NERs from management influence? Third, are NER arrangements a complement to union representation or do they act as a substitute for union-based voice arrangements? Fourth, what are the potential implications for employers, unions and NER-based voice arrangements in the future?

Management approaches to NER and relationships to trade unionism

Two main approaches to NER can be identified. One suggests that structures representing the interests of employees through collective bargaining, legally enforced or not, may give more legitimacy and efficacy to the decision-making process (Hyman 1997), ensuring greater organisational commitment and acting as a complement to existing union structures. Hyman (1997) also suggests that NER forms have the capacity to assist unionism in workplaces where they are given many responsibilities and especially when enforced through statutory rights. Others have suggested that the issue is not whether works councils will weaken unions, but whether unions will be prevented from developing a stronger presence where there is a works council (Terry 2003). In essence, this contention is premised on 'confident, assertive unionism . . . still [being able to] make effective use of collective action to obtain management concessions' (Terry 2003: 491). This view is often linked to the notion of 'partnership' that stresses the need to transform traditional adversarial behaviour to a consensus-based approach (Terry 2003).

In contrast, some commentators have argued that works councils have 'consolidated a more recent shift to non-unionism' (Kelly 1996: 56). This rationale is premised on the belief that employer-initiated structures are based on employers' terms and cannot be effective in providing an effective voice for employees' concerns because they institutionalise worker cooperation, thus limiting scope for union action (Kelly 1996; Lloyd 1999). Others argue that NER structures such as works councils are used by management as 'cosmetic' devices (Terry 1999) or are little more than 'symbolic' forms of representation (Wills 2000) as a means to avoid unions. Another important debate around collective representation is the notion of 'fairness' and the sense of injustice. Kelly (1998) has advocated the approach that emphasises workers' perceived injustice as the basis for mobilisations for the representation of workers' interests. He argues that in order to mobilise collective action, workers need to acquire a sense of injustice or grievance in their work environment. This process, he argues, requires leadership and a collective organisation and structure.

This debate has focused on the intention behind, and results of, management approaches. Various writers (see, for example, Gall and McKay 2001; Gollan 2000; Marchington *et al.* 1992, 2001; Oxenbridge *et al.* 2003; Terry 1999) have examined whether NER acts as a 'substitute' for unions and/or as a 'complement' to management decision-making (see Table 9.1). One notion of a 'substitute' is that it serves in place of a union. It assumes that employers create an alternative form of employee representation which employees will prefer to a union. However, this view has been challenged because for many employers it is not important whether NER structures approximate to unions as part of a collective bargaining process, since this may not be the objective or desired outcome. These issues are linked to Ramsay's (1977, 1983) notion of 'cycles of control' where consultation (and participation) are introduced by employers when they feel under threat from organised workers, and discarded when such a threat is reduced or dissipated (see also Marchington *et al.* 1992, 2001). Nonetheless, as Watling and Snook (2003: 268) noted, management pragmatism towards union recognition often

Table 9.1 Characteristics and objectives of non-union employee representation forms

	Characteristics	*Complement*	*Substitute*
Representative interest	Mutual	Conflictual	Mutual
Process	Co-determination/ joint consultation	Representation of employee interests	Cooperation
Power base	Legally imposed or management initiative	Legally imposed or management initiative	Management initiative
Channel of representation	Dual	Single	Dual
Rights	Information, consultation, co-decision making, limited veto powers	Information, consultation, limited workplace decision-making	Production line information, suggestions schemes, problem identification
Outcomes	Procedural justice	Internalisation of employment relations	Productivity improvement

Source: Adapted from Gollan (2000: 415).

concealed a covert employee-relations strategy to bolster non-union structures as a process of union avoidance or substitution.

A different notion is that alternative forms of employee representation make traditional union structures unnecessary, in that they transform the employment relationship, with other high-commitment practices, into a mutually productive relationship. This notion is premised on employees not desiring or needing a protective agency through traditional bargaining per se (since this emphasises the adversarial, distributive element of the employment relationship), because their basic interests are satisfied. In this approach, the purpose of NERs is to encourage and foster an alignment of interests between employer and employees. An alternative strategy is evident when traditional union structures and alternative forms of employee representation 'complement' each other, dovetailing in terms of form and function, as in the case of German works councils through the co-determination process and industry-wide trade union bargaining (see Jacobi 2003).

However, such debates can oversimplify union avoidance strategies that are in practice very diverse and complex (Dundon 2002). Dundon (2002: 236) highlighted that the 'absence of industrial discontent or union membership "may" point towards some level of commitment or trust between an employer and employee'. Alternatively, it could reveal fear of management and abuse of management prerogative, or union membership may be less attractive to workers because employees in non-union workplaces can potentially earn market premiums underpinned by more individualised and productivity-driven remuneration arrangements.

The chapter now addresses such issues by examining the background of the consultation and representative arrangements at Eurotunnel and News International and by outlining the results of employee surveys carried out in each organisation, which were supplemented by interviews with managers and employees, and company documentation. Following this, the chapter discusses the themes of effectiveness, independence, management strategies towards representation, and union responses of NER arrangement in each organisation.

Eurotunnel UK

Eurotunnel, with a ninety-nine-year lease to operate the Channel Tunnel between Britain and France, has a complex structure, consisting of two legal entities, to meet company law requirements in both countries. It is owned by private shareholdings in Britain and France and employs a total of 2,300 staff, with approximately 1,300 based in Britain. The British head office is in Folkestone, with a separate office nearby for some administration activities and the call centre. Eurotunnel (UK)'s company council was established in 1992 as the sole channel of employee representation. As the company's communications forum, it has three main aims: to give information and consult on matters of common concern to employees; to manage the social and welfare budget equal to one per cent of payroll (approximately £250,000–£350,000 p.a.) where the company councillors are the trustees; and to represent all employees at Eurotunnel, where before June 2000 this included bargaining and negotiation over pay and conditions.

As part of an early policy choice to integrate its two workforces, the company council for UK-contracted employees was broadly similar to the enterprise committee under French legislation. Until 2000, Eurotunnel (UK) recognised only the council for negotiation purposes, with one representative and one deputy elected from each of eight geographically or functionally based constituencies by secret ballot for a two-year period. In addition, a European Company Council (ECC) was created in November 1998, comprising sixteen members (eight British and eight French) drawn from the national committees, which meets at least twice a year and is informed or consulted on all matters of general bi-national interest within the company, without encroaching in any way on the autonomy of the national committees, which this preserves all their prerogatives.

Thereafter, a recognition and partnership agreement was signed with the Transport and General Workers Union (TGWU) to cover all non-managerial staff. The agreement included negotiation rights, confirmed the acceptance of the existing consultation framework and established a joint management–union forum. Consequently, there are now two representation structures. A modified company council with eight representatives, meeting six times annually, represents all employees at Eurotunnel. The TGWU's attitude to the council was:

> We are a pragmatic union and we would complement it. We would not want to bypass it or undermine it. We, as a union, could enhance the role of the company council. The recognition agreement is a new significant development for Eurotunnel and the T&G. We see this agreement as a model agreement, looking at it as a basis of a very good example of best practice.
>
> (TGWU FTO).

The joint management–union forum represents TGWU members at Eurotunnel covering all issues of concern, and negotiates company-wide pay levels for all employees (union and non-union). The then HR director indicated that the impetus for recognising the TGWU was the industrial action taken by the train drivers' union ASLEF in 1999, which created operational upheaval and a situation of crisis management. Other important influences identified included the ERA's recognition provisions and the forthcoming regulations over information and consultation.

Employee views

The findings are derived from two employee surveys, one undertaken between December 1999 and January 2000, and the second undertaken in late 2002. The first, a self-completion questionnaire, was distributed to 400 of the British-based workforce by company council representatives and deputies, with a 31 per cent usable response rate. The second replicated the first, but included additional questions relating to union recognition and union presence. It was distributed to all British-based employees through attachment to employees' pay slips by the company council, and returned a 40 per cent usable response rate.

On the issue of the effectiveness of communication at Eurotunnel, over 60 per cent in the second survey indicated that they were either not well informed or not informed at all about workplace issues at Eurotunnel. These results were similar to those findings in the first survey (58 per cent). Nearly 60 per cent of respondents in the second survey indicated that company council representatives were not helpful (50 per cent in the first survey) and 70 per cent of respondents suggested that union respondents were not helpful. This would suggest that neither company council representatives nor union representatives have effectively dealt with employees' concerns. Overall, the majority of respondents were dissatisfied with the amount, type and timing of information from management, although the second survey showed a slight improvement. When asked, 'Typically when management communicates with you, to what extent do you believe the information you are given?', there was little change in employee attitudes, with around 40 per cent of respondents from both surveys stating that they did not believe information from management. In regard to the level of influence, nearly 80 per cent of respondents in both surveys stated that they had no or little chance to influence management at Eurotunnel.

On the issue of which organisation would best represent staff on major workplace issues, in both surveys the strongest support for a union was on pay increases. However, this fell from over 70 per cent in the first survey to under 50 per cent in the second. This fall was also apparent on other workplace issues: making a complaint about work – 55 per cent to 35 per cent; dealing with disciplinary action – 61 per cent to 43 per cent; and objecting to changes to workplace environment – 46 per cent to 32 per cent. Support for the company council stayed relatively constant between the two surveys. The proportion of respondents who stated that they were best placed to deal with these issues on an individual basis increased: making a complaint about work – 15 per cent to 38 per cen; dealing with disciplinary action – 10 per cent to 26 per cent; and objecting to changes to workplace environment – 26 per cent to 46 per cent.

In the second survey, 35 per cent of employees indicated that they were union members, compared to 12 per cent in the first. Union presence had also increased greatly, with 55 per cent of respondents suggesting that they had an active union presence in their workplace, compared to 6 per cent in the first survey. In regard to union effectiveness in representing general employee interests, only 29 per cent suggested that the union was 'effective' or 'very effective', with 27 per cent suggesting it was 'not effective at all'. Union effectiveness was recorded to be low on specific representational issues: improved pay and benefits (11 per cent), work conditions (13 per cent), health and safety (14 per cent), training (6 per cent), individual grievances (19 per cent) and job security (11 per cent). These findings contrast with those from the first survey (prior to union recognition), where many employees believed that union representation would improve their position over these issues: pay and benefits (72 per cent) and work conditions (73 per cent).

In common with the first survey, two-thirds of respondents in the second stated that the council was not effective in representing general employee interests or those of employees in individual sections. Finally, 50 per cent of respondents suggested that the council should retain a consultation role. This view was strongest in relation to pay and benefits and employee grievances. Few respondents believed that the council should have no role. One respondent expressed this as: 'The idea of the council is a good one [but it] doesn't have the power to achieve a great deal. [It] needs to evolve with the company and be given more power on certain issues.'

Comment

The views of survey respondents and interviewed employees suggest that the company council prior to recognition had been ineffective as a substitute for union representation, as a result of its limited role in negotiation and decision-making processes. The council's prime focus was to provide information on performance or 'business' issues (improving quality, productivity, customer service and/or sales), to communicate the benefits of change and to persuade employees of the need for such change, rather than addressing employees' interests and meeting their expectations. It was, thus, ineffective as a vehicle for two-way voice for employee concerns, leading to frustration and creating an environment for wider union activity. Subsequently, there was strong support for trade unionism across Eurotunnel, with most respondents believing that union representation would improve their overall position. One employee commented, 'the power and inclination [of company council representatives] is limited. It was hoped the union coming in would change all that . . . The TGWU seems to be more compliant than the company council.' But a perceived lack of progress by the TGWU manifests itself in respondents' belief that their expectations had not been met and that the TGWU had failed to address employees' concerns. This highlights the pitfalls of what a union might regard as 'unrealistic' employee expectations, whatever the source of the scale of those expectations. Consequently, many respondents favoured continued (TGWU) recognition and a continued, but expanded, role for the company council because there remains doubt that the TGWU alone will achieve greater benefits for employees.

News International Newspapers

News International Newspapers (UK) is part of the Australian-based News Corporation, one of the world's largest media companies, with operations across the globe covering, *inter alia*, production and distribution of motion pictures and television programming, television, satellite and cable broadcasting, publication of newspapers, magazines and books, and production and distribution of promotional and advertising products and services. In 2000, News International Newspapers employed 3,600 staff in London, Manchester and Glasgow. There have been no recognised unions at News International following the Wapping dispute of 1985–86 (Gall 1998b). In that dispute, Rupert Murdoch sacked 5,800 print workers and derecognised the unions when production moved out of Fleet Street. Management has estimated that at Wapping there are approximately 500 union members out of 750 production workers, while of the 1,000 journalists, a significant majority are NUJ members, although management doubts that many are active members.

In 1999, the company held a ballot to win support for the establishment of NISA as a means to expand the role of its Employee Consultative Council (ECC), which was established in 1994 to provide sole representation for employees. The HR director was open about his rationale for the ballot: 'We don't want external unions. That's the driver. And with all the employment relations legislation coming through, we needed to do something.' Overall, 60 per cent of employees on a 73 per cent turnout voted for NISA's establishment. Some employee representatives believed that staff saw NISA as the best form of representation they were likely to get from a virulently anti-union company (Gall and McKay 2001). Following this, in 2000, News International set up the company-sponsored 'independent union'. To satisfy the 'independence' requirements of the certification officer, News International gave NISA £250,000 in lieu of membership subscriptions for employing a full-time general secretary and provided it with facilities, including an office. (According to company figures, NISA would cost up to £100,000 p.a. to run.) In addition, News International also provided money for legal support. If independence were granted by the certification officer, the HR director indicated that News International would provide a charitable donation of £1m–2m as further support, although conditions would be attached: 'Of course, we would write conditions into the funding. In the event of an external union gaining favour here, the money would be stopped and then we would ask for the money back. The point is we have to fund it, and for independent status, employees have to pay subscriptions, even if it's only a penny a year.' Following establishment, the NUJ Father of the Chapel was elected unopposed as the NISA chair. In addition to the previous 'consultation' powers of the ECC, the NISA charter (formally) encompasses collective bargaining over matters covered by the ECC and hours of work, rates of pay, benefits and other terms and conditions of employment.

Employee views

The ECC employee attitude survey was carried out by PricewaterhouseCoopers in 1998 for the ECC. Questions covered issues of work satisfaction, communication, management style representation and the ECC. Of the 3,553 questionnaires sent out, 1,656 were returned, representing a 47 per cent response rate. However, Wapping (39 per cent) and Manchester (33 per cent) had lower response rates and nearly half of respondents were from production areas.

The survey found that 66 per cent of respondents were very or fairly satisfied with their present job. However, regarding communication, only 33 per cent felt that they were fully or fairly informed at company level, and on nearly all important performance and strategy issues more respondents reported that they found there was 'too little' information, compared to those who found they had the 'right amount'. The survey also revealed that the majority of respondents preferred to receive information from their boss, team briefings, directly from management, email or the company newsletter.

Only 34 per cent indicated that they would prefer to receive information to a 'great or fair extent' from their ECC representative. With regard to senior management, 67 per cent of respondents reported that there was not enough opportunity for employees to express their views about issues that affect them and their work. Over 69 per cent indicated that speaking up on issues where they disagreed with management could damage their career prospects. Nearly 50 per cent also disagreed with the statement that 'senior management explained the reasons behind major decisions', 66 per cent wanted to see more evidence of senior management taking an interest in employees' role in the company, and 37 per cent disagreed with the statement 'senior management lead our organisation by example', compared to 25 per cent who agreed. Some 37 per cent of respondents stated that they wanted representation by a third party (such as a union), while 35 per cent did not. Just over 40 per cent agreed that such representation would improve management and staff working relationships, while only 28 per cent stated that it would improve business success. There was a high level of employee awareness of the ECC, with 76 per cent of respondents knowing whom to contact if they wanted to raise an issue of concern, and of these respondents 83 per cent felt able to raise the issue through the ECC representative.

In relation to improving the ECC, 67 per cent favoured giving the ECC pay negotiating powers, 80 per cent negotiating powers over working conditions, and 67 per cent the power to negotiate directly with senior management. Over two-thirds also suggested that fair representation could be achieved if the ECC could represent staff on grievance and disciplinary issues. In addition, 60 per cent stated that fair representation could be achieved if the ECC became a staff body independent of senior management, with 70 per cent also suggesting that overall representation could be improved if the ECC properly consulted prior to meetings. Only 24 per cent stated that the ECC in its current form was successful in its consultation with management, with 32 per cent reporting that it did a 'good job' of representing employees' interests, and only 22 per cent stated that the ECC 'does not need to change significantly to achieve fair representation'. Around three-quarters of respondents stated that they would like to hear more about how the ECC helped to improve work conditions. While 65 per cent understood what the ECC does, only 38 per cent indicated that the ECC representative did a good job in their area.

Comment

In an internal staff email, the HR director stated, 'If a union made a claim for recognition, they would argue that the ECC is not totally independent. In all honesty, they would probably be right. If you do nothing you would almost certainly end up with a union. It is not an option if you want your interests to be represented without the involvement of an external third party' (*Journalist* May 1999). Behind this lay his normative belief that 'A staff association is in-house, it's an internal body, not an external body which may have prejudices. The problem is history: it's that strong. Unions have changed, but so what? No partnership deals even with a no-strike clause can be overturned under legislation with a ballot', and 'we would rather give our own staff a body that can represent their interests and interface with management without having to go to an association or union and be overturned' (interview). This strategy has been successful in invalidating a CAC application for recognition by the NUJ at the Times Supplement's series of professional weekly papers within News International, where NUJ membership was high: the application was rejected because of the existence of NISA.

Discussion

Effectiveness

Overall, the findings of both studies suggest that there is widespread dissatisfaction with management, especially the unwillingness to involve employees in decision-making and lack of consideration regarding employee concerns, highlighting the perceived lack of effective voice in the decision-making processes.

Eurotunnel provided an opportunity to explore the impact of consultative structures as well as to assess employees' attitudes towards the company council and trade unionism, both before and after union recognition. In regard to the effectiveness of NER, the company council (before recognition) had been ineffective as a substitute for union representation and as a vehicle for two-way voice for employee concerns, which subsequently led to increased frustration and created an environment for greater union activity. But, when examining objective and tangible measures of effectiveness, such as the ability to secure negotiated pay increases, it would appear that the union was less successful than the company council. The 1999 salary review gave a 3.5 per cent across-the-board general increase, and in 2000 (the first year of union recognition) there was 2.5 per cent increase. In 2001, a 3 per cent general increase was given and in 2002 a 1.8 per cent general increase was negotiated with the TGWU. In addition to these payments, in 2002, an additional 1 per cent of total salary was given for career development. This raises the issue of whether conditions of trading and profits, or the strategy of management, primarily account for the difference.

News International provided a means to explore how effective the ECC was perceived to be before the establishment of NISA, and to establish the initial outcomes of NISA arrangements. Overall, the findings from the employee survey suggest that there was widespread dissatisfaction with management, especially with their lack of understanding, unwillingness to involve employees in decision-making and lack of consideration regarding employee concerns. The findings also highlighted the perceived lack of effective voice of the ECC, with representatives lacking sufficient training and experience in negotiating with management. Concerning NISA's potential effectiveness, the HR director stated at the time, 'If it's not influential it will fail. If it does not get results on behalf of its staff it will fail. . . . [NISA] ha[s] to get some prizes out of this and some early gains so they can go back to staff to say what they have secured.' As a result, in mid-2000, News International reached an agreement with NISA over a package of changes to terms and conditions of employment, including a three-year pay deal. This consisted of a 5 per cent increase in the first year and a 3.75 per cent rise the year after (or if inflation was higher, an inflation plus 1 per cent increase, up to 5 per cent) (IDS 2000: 4). The timing of the three-year deal coincided with the establishment of NISA and the introduction of union recognition legislation through the ERA. Again, this raises issues over the role of management intention when accounting for the favourable outcome.

Independence

The NER arrangements at both organisations highlight the important but contentious notion of 'independence' in workplace representation. Perception of a lack of effective independence from management, and the lack of effective sanctions, such as the ability to use collective and industrial action against management, have further undermined the legitimacy of such bodies in the employees' eyes. This seems to reconfirm Greenfield and Pleasure's (1993: 193) view that 'without power and legitimacy the concept of voice is rendered virtually meaningless'. For some commentators, independence is critical, given that unions' collective voice has its origins as a vehicle of protest against injustice, or as some have argued, its reliance on various forms of mobilisation theory (Kelly 1998). Accordingly, an ability to exert influence over terms and conditions of work depends on a sense of collective capacity and identity (Hyman 2001b).

Kelly (1996) argues that cooperation at workplace level may lead representatives (including union members) to identify their interests ever more closely with those of their employers, underlining the fear that such non-union structures may provide employees with 'voice', but on the employer's terms. Such concerns over independence were highlighted by the Certification Office's refusal to recognise NISA as an independent union, especially regarding its genesis, lack of voluntary membership, structure and dependence on management for financial resources. Indeed, the NUJ pointed out, '[News International is] insensitive to the obvious paradox. . . . [It is] making NISA "independent" while constantly warning of the dangers of independent unions to News International prosperity. That is the proof that it is not, because if it really was they couldn't allow it' (*Journalist* November 2000). At Eurotunnel, employees' perception of a lack of independent voice undermined the legitimacy, authority and trust in both management and the company council. One worker stated, 'The Company Council has failed to deliver independent and worker orientated programmes and policies. . . . [It] has lost its credibility, influence and focus and must be replaced by new structures.'

Management strategies

One of the reasons that management establishes NER arrangements is a desire to have a more direct relationship with employees, without the mediating forces of a 'third party' through union representation. Eurotunnel's substitution approach failed to stop the forces for unionisation, the catalyst being ASLEF's presence in the train crew section. At Eurotunnel, an important underlying force in the unionisation process was management's ambivalent behaviour towards employees' views and concerns, rather than any employee perceptions of potential financial advantage to be gained by unionisation. Dissatisfaction with certain issues considered by employees as important and the lack of trust between management and employees appeared to have been an even more critical impetus to the unionisation process. Management's response was a 'partnership' recognition agreement with the TGWU. However, this did not alleviate the considerable frustration among employees, for there were two underlying sources of discontent. First, management preoccupation with cost-cutting due to share market demands, high continuing debt, pressure on market share and the highly centralised nature of the decision-making process were all incompatible with the norms and expectations developed through Eurotunnel's growth phase. This resulted in a loss of faith in the company council and the TGWU, and a loss of trust in management. Second, the clash of an autocratic management culture and style with the perceived lack of effective voice. This further undermined employees' trust in management. Unilateral management announcements regarding the partnership recognition deal were not considered to be a positive employee gain by many. Indeed, many employees and representatives felt it showed further erosion of employee voice and influence, being often greeted with cynicism.

As part of News International's union avoidance strategy, it sought to expand its ECC into an 'in-house union', giving rise to NISA and bestowing upon it formal bargaining power and rights similar to those of an independent union. Management indicated that this was an initiative that had come from its employees on the council and had staff support, following a staff survey carried out for it by PricewaterhouseCoopers (Gall and McKay 2001; *People Management* 25 February 1999). However, it was an idea that the company helped formulate, and then support was canvassed for it through the survey, in order to provide the basis for the claim that it resulted from the demand of the staff. In spite of the attempt to maintain a 'union-free' environment, News International has been continually, if unsuccessfully, targeted by the print unions and NUJ. The size and profile of News International and its high-profile attempts to avoid unionisation have compelled these unions to maintain it as a target.

Union strategies

Two different strategies were applied by the unions at Eurotunnel and News International. At News International, they used a strategy of colonisation of NISA rather than the marginalisation of the company council adopted by the TGWU at Eurotunnel. At Eurotunnel, the first survey provided strong support for trade unionism in that the majority of respondents believed that a union would improve their pay and benefits, work conditions, and so on. However, the second survey revealed the lack of progress the union had made on these issues, with many employees indicating that the union had not met their expectations. Although their expectations were high, employees were not totally convinced that union representation alone would solve these issues. Only when management was perceived as unresponsive did the union become more of a catalyst for collective action. Before recognition, the TGWU was seen primarily as a means to protect existing wages and conditions. However, the results of the partnership recognition agreement protected the status quo and employees from the vagaries of management, but did not extract new gains for employees, such as increased wages, resulting in dissatisfaction, disenchantment and frustration. This wider context was of (a) the TGWU's strategy of marginalising the company council from negotiations and bargaining with management against the wishes of many employees, and (b) a substantial number of employees being unconvinced of the merits of union representation alone and many not becoming TGWU members. The conundrum for the TGWU is that increased union membership and presence have not been accompanied by more positive attitudes towards it by a majority of employees. More worryingly for the TGWU, the lack of belief in its ability to achieve traditional objectives of increased pay, fairness and protection in disciplinary action and so on was buttressed by many employees' belief that as individuals they were best able to deal with such issues. The danger for the TGWU is that such attitudes undermine the influence that it has been able to gain, further eroding is credibility and legitimacy, which would also create a problem for management.

With no recognised union at News International since 1988, the AEEU, GPMU and NUJ have adopted the strategy of colonisation of NISA. The NUJ Father of the Chapel argued, 'Why am I joining a body which actually uses the words "staff association"? Because I have been asked to by colleagues who agree with me it is important for the chapel to maintain some way of being allowed to talk to management and take up staff issues' (*Journalist* June–July 1999). NISA raises a number of questions for representatives who are union members, around three themes: role conflict, reconciliation of differing interests, and playing to different audiences. For the proponents of trade unionism, such employer-sponsored structures are fatally flawed as an instrument of workplace democracy because they are usually created and controlled by management and they have little or no independent power to protect workers' rights (Kaufman and Kleiner 1993). Union representatives on such structures arguably confer legitimacy on management action through their involvement in visible processes of consultation as accredited representatives (Terry 1999). In addition, even if such representatives can influence the agenda, but not the outcomes, there is a risk that representation on such structures could be seen as pseudo-participation, thus surrendering the legitimacy and power that unions have as an instrument of employee voice (Kaufman and Kleiner 1993; Hyman 2001b). As Kelly (1996) suggests, workers require effective voice based on the right of workers to exercise collective power through independent organisations that they regard as legitimate.

Implications

Overall, the studies show that employees were satisfied with neither the NER nor union voice arrangements at Eurotunnel, nor the previous ECC arrangements at News International. Furthermore, neither arrangement appeared to address employees' expectations in providing effective employee voice. There may be a number of reasons for this. Environmental conditions (financial situation, cost-cutting, competition and so on) may have restricted management's ability to address employees' concerns, regardless of their capability and willingness to develop good employee relations. Nonetheless, it can be doubted whether management possessed the capability and experience to address and deal with the complexity of employees' concerns through either the NER or union arrangements. The perception of a lack of independent voice and failure to act on employees' concerns resulted from the subordinate nature of, and further undermined the legitimacy, authority and trust in, the NER and union representation arrangements.

Conclusions

The two cases suggest that union substitution and avoidance strategies can have serious limitations, for they highlighted the fact that many employees felt their respective representation structures lacked the effectiveness and power required for effectively representing their interests. The implications for employers not recognising this are, *inter alia*, greater union influence, industrial relations instability, poor employee attachment and greater employee dissatisfaction. Overall, the two cases question the legitimacy of NER to claim to be a 'true' alternative to unions in effectively representing the interests of employees. However, the cases also indicate that while a significant proportion of employees may favour union recognition, not all are convinced that union representation alone would achieve greater benefits for employees. This would suggest that unions have not won the argument that sole union representation is desirable or productive, and highlights the quandary that unions in weak positions face.

These findings have implications for employers, unions and government policy regarding the structures and processes needed for providing effective consultation and representation. Given devolved organisational decision-making and the focus on employee commitment and effective organisational change, these findings suggest the following. First, if employers wish to encourage an alignment of employee behaviour to organisational goals, greater emphasis is required on giving employees a greater say in the decision-making process and influence over workplace issues. At times, an acknowledgement of differing interests may be an essential condition for a more effective decision-making process. Second, union strategies of marginalisation of NER may be problematic, giving employees heightened expectations which are difficult to satisfy where unions are weak. This suggests a need for unions to manage and condition employee expectations to be sensitive to available resources. Third, the existence of mechanisms, union or non-union, for communication between management and employees at the workplace may not be a sufficient condition for representation of employee interests. This may open up a route for employees to use the Information and Consultation Regulations to challenge both management and unions. Fourth, unions may become contaminated in employees' minds as a result of their involvement in subordinate, employer-created institutions. The prospect of such contamination and incorporation are apparent in colonisation strategies, even if union weakness compels involvement in these institutions. Fifth, while unions may provide greater voice than non-union arrangements, their strength of voice is dependent on their legitimacy and effectiveness in representing employees' interests at the workplace, which in turn depends on the unions being perceived by the workforce as both representative and able to act independently. If unions cannot, they will not meet the needs of either employees or management – and could run the risk of being supplanted under the provisions of the new regulations on information and consultation.

Acknowledgement

My thanks are to Gregor Gall for his help in substantially revising this chapter.

10 The transition from organising to representation

A case study

Melanie Simms

Increasing academic attention has recently been paid to union organising in the USA and Britain (for overviews see Bronfenbrenner *et al.* 1998; Gall 2003a), largely prompted by trade unionists discussing how to address the challenges they face as a result of membership decline and changing labour markets. The shift away from manufacturing to the service sector has meant that employment growth has been strongest in areas where unions have been weakest. Moreover, the growth of female participation in the labour market, combined with the associated development of 'atypical' forms of employment, has meant that, if unions are to (re)establish their relevance in contemporary workplaces, they increasingly have to recruit groups of workers who have traditionally been underrepresented in the union movement. Reflecting these developments, academics have been interested in the conditions necessary for union renewal (see, *inter alia*, Fairbrother 2000; Heery *et al.* 2000a; Hyman 1997; Kelly 1998), agreeing that increasing membership and activism amongst these currently underrepresented groups are significant challenges. Women and part-time employees are two related groups that have been growing in the British labour market in recent decades, but which unions have struggled to recruit and represent effectively. Consequently, unions have invested resources in specialist training programmes (Heery *et al.* 2000b), often with an emphasis on ensuring that groups of workers that are underrepresented are effectively targeted (see Freeman and Diamond 2003; Holgate 2004b; Simms *et al.* 2000).

A body of literature has explored the development of organising campaigns in British workplaces (Findlay and McKinlay 2003a; Simms 2003; Taylor and Bain 2003; Wills 2003). These case studies and others from abroad (Bronfenbrenner *et al.* 1998; Oxenbridge 1997) highlight the importance of building workplace collectivism during an organising campaign, particularly where there is employer hostility. Although most union campaigns seek to develop some form of workplace collectivism, the distinction is one of emphasis rather than of absolutes. Specifically, where unions can develop collective responses to relevant workplace issues, research suggests that they are more effective at countering employers' claims that the union is an 'external' influence in the workplace. These studies suggest that

Kelly's mobilisation theory (1998) has considerable merit in explaining the process of developing workplace collectivism, placing emphasis on building collective support for key workplace issues, with the role of leaders in identifying, framing and articulating issues being particularly important, if rather underexplored at present. In contrast to debates about broadening union membership and activism, this literature gives comparatively little systematic attention to attempts by unions to increase participation, membership and activism amongst underrepresented groups. Indeed, in giving an overview of much of the research to date, Gall (2003d) assumes that Kelly's theory is equally applicable to all groups of workers, an assumption that Kelly (1998) himself implies. It is necessary, therefore, to attempt to draw links between these literatures in order to examine the ways in which organising campaigns can be successful in increasing membership and activism amongst underrepresented groups.

But what has received significantly less attention in recent research has been the transition of a union campaign from the pre-recognition 'organising phase' to the post-recognition 'representation phase'. This can largely be accounted for by the wide meaning of the term 'organising' amongst both practitioners and academics in Britain. Organising campaigns can take place within recognised workplaces where the union is seeking to increase membership density and within unrecognised workplaces where the union is seeking to establish collective bargaining for the first time. This contrasts with the USA, where the term refers almost exclusively to the pre-recognition phase of a campaign. Despite this wide usage, this chapter takes 'organising' to refer to the pre-recognition phase of a union campaign. It can, therefore, be contrasted with the work of the union after it has formally been granted recognition for collective bargaining. This is an important distinction, as the status of the union differs significantly between these two phases (see Gall Chapter 1, this volume), and it is the dynamics of this transition that is the focus of this chapter.

One study from the USA is particularly useful in providing a starting point for understanding the issues involved. Markowitz (2000), using two case studies of organising in 'right-to-work states' where there is no compulsion on workers to become members of the union after the union has been certified, considers the transition between organising and representation. Her study is helpful, for it provides a comparison that is more similar to the British legal status of unions than would be the case in states where closed shops exist. She shows how the unions' approach to the organising phase of a recognition campaign can build norms and expectations amongst members that are often abruptly challenged by the actions of union officials during the early negotiations with managers. Markowitz found that workers expressed dismay at the changing roles and expectations placed upon them during this transition. In particular, campaigns based on ideas about increasing 'participatory democracy' (Pateman 1970) may struggle to maintain this emphasis during the transition, as the specialist skills required to negotiate with management are unlikely to be developed by workplace activists during the pre-recognition phase. Reflecting Kelly's (1998) stress on the importance of leaders in developing collective workplace mobilisation, this suggests that the role of both FTOs and workplace activists needs further examination in order better to understand the complex interactions between these groups.

This chapter, therefore, explores a campaign where the union has been successful in achieving recognition for collective bargaining. The bargaining unit is majority female (over 80 per cent) and has a high proportion (over 40 per cent) of part-timers, and is thus suitable for exploring some of the issues relating to organising and representing these groups. The factors underlying the campaign's successful outcome are explored, as they provide important contextual detail to the transition from the 'organising' to 'representation'. The transition between these was complex and contested. The chapter concludes by considering the implications of the case study for broadening union membership and activism. Dealing with this transition effectively is important because previous work has examined the ways in which unions' structures, cultures and negotiating priorities have usually been geared towards full-time, male workers (see, *inter alia*, Cockburn 1995; Colgan and Ledwith 1996; Colling and Dickens 2001; Kirton 1999). Particular challenges facing unions include not only encouraging membership amongst women and part-timers, but also ensuring that they answer the charge of being fundamentally undemocratic because of their failure to represent effectively the interests of a large and growing proportion of their members (Terry 1996). This places an emphasis not only on the ways in which unions engage these workers during the organising phase of a campaign, but also on whether they are able to sustain this engagement into the post-recognition representation phase.

Research methods

The research took place between 1998 and 2003, using a wide range of techniques. Participant observation of 120 hours between 1998 and 1999 was centred around the lead FTOs whose primary responsibility was this campaign, and included attending recruitment events, campaign planning meetings, public union meetings, branch meetings and training events. Nineteen semi-structured interviews with key actors, including FTOs, branch officials and workplace activists, were supplemented with written material, such as literature distributed by both union and employer. All quotes used in the chapter are derived from interviews and observation. This approach provided insight into the decision-making processes involved in the work of union organisers that then allowed a detailed understanding of the social processes involved in the campaign. Several methodological points need noting. While the campaign took place in a call centre run by a large charity, staff were employees and not volunteers. Therefore, the workers targeted by the union had a normal contractual relationship with their employer. In many respects, particularly in their labour process, they shared more in common with other call centre employees (cf. Taylor and Bain 2003) than with other voluntary sector workers. Since the unit of analysis for the case study was the union campaign, access to managers was extremely limited. This was countered by the fact that the rich detail concerning the union's behaviour and the research's longitudinal nature allowed the outcomes of managerial decisions to be observed, even if the motivation for this was somewhat obscured, thus enabling a consideration of employer actions despite lack of access to managers.

The CallCo campaign

The CallCo call centre is an autonomous business unit of the CallCare charity and is managed by its own senior management team with a large degree of operational independence from CallCare's management structure, and day-to-day decisions are largely taken at the business unit. Although it is not a profit-making service, there is emphasis on ensuring that the service is not loss-making. In 2004, CallCo employed just over 350 staff, which reflects a reduction of around 200 staff over the previous five years due to improved technology that allowed the call centre to operate more efficiently. The 350 staff work at two sites in Liverpool. The Communication Workers Union (CWU) began the campaign in 1997 after a local FTO was contacted by a small group of workers there, who were seeking advice about their working conditions. As the CWU was seeking to extend its membership into the rapidly expanding telecommunications industry, CallCo became a target for organising activity. In 1998, in an effort to increase the available organising expertise, it sponsored two trainee organisers through the first year of the TUC Organising Academy, and responsibility for the campaign was handed to one of them under the guidance of an FTO. The initial intention of running a 6–12 month campaign to secure recognition for this group of employees proved extremely optimistic. Recognition was eventually gained in 2000.

Organising phase

In line with the training programme delivered by the Organising Academy, the campaign was deliberately developed in a way to encourage a broad-based workplace activism. CallCo management was initially extremely hostile and denied FTOs workplace access, so an emphasis was placed on building an organising committee of workplace activists broadly representative of the different employee groups. This committee eventually comprised some twenty activists from each of the main shifts, including some part-time staff. The organising committee met regularly, approximately once a month and usually with the organiser and sometimes with another national or local FTO. Meetings involved assessing achievement of recruitment objectives, training activists in campaign skills, dealing with members' concerns, and planning the next period of campaigning. This modus operandi followed much of US experience (see, *inter alia*, Bronfenbrenner and Hickey 2003; Bronfenbrenner and Juravich 1998; Hurd 1993), where this approach decreases the employer's ability to present the union as an outside body seeking to make trouble, and is thus associated with higher success levels in establishing a union presence.

When it became clear that CallCo was not going to grant voluntary recognition without unambiguous evidence of employee support for the union, the organiser and officials decided to meet this objective by demonstrating the union's relevance to the immediate work environment, resulting in key issues being identified to form the basis of the campaign. These issues centred around dealing with abusive service users, unfairness in the bonus payments systems and potential health and safety hazards. In the identification, framing and articulation of these issues, the important role of leaders in organising activity became evident. Kelly (1998) identifies leaders' importance in developing senses of injustice in mobilising groups but he is unclear which persons are in positions of leadership and whether this includes leaders within a group of workplace activists and/or extra-workplace union specialists such as organisers and officials. This case study suggests that the wider definition can shed light on the complex processes of organising.

The role of paid organisers and officials, that is, FTOs, in identifying workplace issues was crucial in the CallCo campaign. Their expertise and professional training allowed the union both inside and outside the workplace to identify, frame and articulate a sense of injustice which, eventually, led to pressures on managers to recognise the union. Organiser training particularly stressed identifying 'winnable issues'. Health and safety was particularly apt here because of its legal underpinnings, even though some health and safety issues did not cause serious day-to-day problems. So, for example, the union quickly identified potential problems related to 'hot-desking', because workstations were not ergonomically adjusted for each worker, and shared equipment such as headphones created the possibility for spreading ear infections and other illnesses. It was not the workers who spontaneously identified these but the organiser, after lengthy discussions with workers about their working lives and using her expertise on legislation and best practice. Once the potential hazards were explained to activists, they were keen to deploy these to develop a campaign in order to improve working conditions by using newsletters and recruitment literature, by encouraging workers to raise these issues with supervisors and drawing attention to any potential industrial injuries. After discussions between the FTO and managers, these issues were addressed by introducing more flexible workstations, ensuring that workers were trained to adjust their workstations to their needs and generally improving awareness of industrial injuries such as repetitive strain injury. The union thus claimed that its involvement had had a positive impact on day-to-day working conditions. Of the process, the FTO organiser commented, '[The organising committee] are great. They're involved and keen but . . . don't know much yet. They . . . sense something's wrong but they don't know what. That's where I can help.'

The FTOs' intervention in identifying issues here contrasted with the situation over bonus payments and abusive callers. Some workers exhibited a spontaneous feeling that there were injustices, with leaders inside and outside the workplace helping to collectivise the grievances and ensure that these were attributed to managers. Calculation of bonus payments was opaque, leading to concerns about potential favouritism and how sick days affected bonuses, particularly if such sick days resulted from industrial injuries. Whether there was any evidence of favouritism or not, the perception of favouritism was sufficient to raise concern, being attributed to management but frequently expressed as an individual concern. After the organiser and lead official explained how the grievance could be developed into a collective workplace campaign issue, the organising committee began identifying evidence of inconsistency of bonus calculations and raising awareness amongst other members and workers. Eventually, management conceded that there was some scope for variability in interpreting the rules relating to bonus payments, improved the advice for supervisors and increased the transparency of the system. Officials and organisers used their expertise to compare the CallCo bonus system with those in other organisations as well as to identify areas where improvements could be made to the bonus system. Although the improvements were not formally negotiated with the union because it was not recognised, these were informed by these discussions. The lead official pointed out, 'That was a real breakthrough. We had finally got [managers] to listen to something we were saying, and they took it on board. They wouldn't admit it, but we knew they were starting to listen to us.'

The issue of abusive callers was more complex. Such calls took three types: where there was evidence of criminal activity which may have left the operator open to the accusation of complicity in the crime; calls where service users were dissatisfied and directed abuse at operators; and calls including sexually explicit language which some operators felt uncomfortable handling. There were no clear guidelines provided by managers about how to deal with such calls. The organiser and officials especially sought to frame this as a collective issue, attributing the existing sense of injustice to management rather than abusive callers. The lead organiser explained,

> They see it as an individual problem. They don't like dealing with a particular call. . . . If one of them passes a call on to another because they don't like it, it doesn't actually solve the problem. . . . The call's still out of order. No one tells the caller it's out of order. We need to look at that. . . . Get them to see that management could change it if they wanted to.

Although this issue constituted the recognition campaign's lengthiest aspect, improvements were eventually made. After initially refusing to enter discussions, because of the view that callers' rights took precedence where a conflict existed with operators' rights, management relented. Improvements were subsequently secured by the union drawing a direct comparison with the policies of similar employers on similar issues that explicitly balanced the rights of callers and operators. Clearer guidelines concerning acceptable and unacceptable use of the service, and how operators should handle such calls, were issued. Whilst not removing all dissatisfaction, these were widely considered an important improvement.

In these examples, the roles of leaders both inside and outside the workplace were important in presenting issues as collective. An important concern relates to the process by which leaders emerge in organising campaigns. CallCo workers recognised the expertise of FTOs (officials and organisers), frequently expecting them to suggest 'solutions' to workplace problems. This suggests two points. Although this might be expected of workers with no experience of trade unionism, it calls into question the extent to which some of the principles of organising that encourage workers to take responsibility for solving their own problems can be applied in practice (Blyton and Turnbull 2004: 167). In turn, this supports Waddington and Kerr's (2000) arguments that organising can create a requirement for officials and organisers to provide support services to members. The divide between 'organising' and 'servicing' work may, then, not be as clearly demarcated as some suggest. Second, this reliance may indicate weaknesses in workplace activism which in turn, and combined with the dependency on FTOs as 'leaders', may weaken the ability of the union structures to adapt during the transition to effective representation.

Language used by leaders is important in helping workers to frame their issues as collective, rather than individual. Where attribution is directed towards a group other than managers, leaders can help workers direct their sense of (perceived) injustice back towards management. The centrality of leaders derives from their skills, training, expertise, experience and access to relevant information to push this process along. All recognition campaigns seek to develop some form of collective response to workplace issues. The point here is that this process and unions' ability to do so are socially constructed. Without such leaders and experts, many of these issues would undoubtedly have remained nebulous and unexplored. Although they worked with workplace activists to develop their skills in the organising phase of the campaign, they were not as successful as they had hoped in developing an organising committee that was able to negotiate directly with management.

Factors leading to recognition

The CWU eventually won recognition in 2000, as a result of its campaigning, the enactment of ERA, and changes in senior CallCo management, whereby the chief executive was replaced by a successor who was familiar with working with unions. By 1999, union membership was approximately 40 per cent of the bargaining unit and far in excess of the 10 per cent threshold necessary for a statutory application. But this figure hides considerable variation between groups. Amongst full-time employees, membership (60 per cent), was much stronger than amongst part-timers (20 per cent). There were several reasons for this. Many part-timers worked fewer than ten hours per week so were difficult to contact, and many expressed support for the union's objectives but were not prepared to pay subscriptions when they worked so few hours. Some felt that they were prepared to cope with, for example, abusive calls because their work at CallCo was only a small part of their week. Others felt that they were prepared to move on to other call centre work if the job at CallCo became difficult or unsatisfactory. These views constrained their decision to join, particularly prior to recognition, but because such views would not inherently prevent these workers from voting in favour of recognition in a ballot, the union was much more optimistic that if a ballot were called, the support would be higher than the extent of membership.

It is reasonable to suppose that senior management was aware of ERA and, having been the target of union organising for two years, may well have sought expert advice. This, combined with a more sympathetic managerial culture after the departure of the chief executive, led to a decision by CallCo to enter into a voluntary recognition agreement. A voluntary agreement was also favoured by the CWU. By the measure of establishing a union presence where there was previously none, this campaign has been successful. But the behaviour of management was at least as important as the CWU's actions in securing recognition. The 'costs' of securing a voluntary agreement, as opposed to making a statutory application involving in all likelihood a ballot, were constraints in the scope of bargaining.

Negotiating recognition

The process of negotiating union recognition demands skill and expertise. As a result, it was undertaken primarily by local and national FTOs, but not without the views and experiences of the workplace activists and organisers helping to define the CWU agenda. The negotiation process took a year, with the agreement finalised in late 2000. It represented a compromise. The union is entitled to negotiate on terms and conditions that are not covered by centralised contracts with CallCare, health and safety matters, and training and development. But it is not entitled to negotiate over the allocation of performance-related pay, nor basic pay, and both parties are committed to use binding arbitration in cases of 'failure to agree'. Whilst this compromise was contested within the wider union, it was, by and large, accepted by workplace activists. Concerns about the restriction on pay negotiations were to some extent mitigated by the fact that the recognition agreement contained a clause that allowed the scope of the agreement to be renegotiated if appropriate.

Representation phase

Since early 2001, the CWU has established workplace representation structures, with six representatives elected to cover constituent groups: two from each of the two workplaces, one for administrative staff and one for team leaders. In the case of the former representatives, it is specified in the recognition agreement that one from each site represents full-time staff, and one part-time staff. The six representatives then appoint a senior representative who becomes the main point of contact between managers and the union. In the three years since, it is notable that there have been four different activists taking on the role of senior representative, all of whom have been men. This indicates that in the representation phase, activists struggled to combine their representation role with their working lives, and the gender balance of the representative structure has shifted away from reflecting the gender split of the workforce. Prior to recognition, the majority of activists were women, as were almost all those on the organising committee, many of whom were in their forties and fifties. CWU organisers remarked upon the ease of contact and relationship-building that this composition facilitated with the predominantly female workers, and this aspect accorded with the organising principle of tactics like 'like-recruits-like' (Heery *et al.* 2000a).

The union's representativeness during the organising phase was, thus, widely seen as an extremely positive characteristic. Since recognition this has shifted significantly. Of the six representatives in 2004, three are men, and a woman has not yet taken on the role of senior representative. Moreover, the union has consistently struggled to fill the requirement that two of the six representatives are part-timers. Instead, where it has not been possible to elect part-time representatives, they have opted to give particular representatives an explicit remit to represent the interests of part-timers, even though they themselves may work on a full-time basis. As with the increasing reliance on FTOs' expertise during the process of negotiating recognition, members accepted the changed profile of activists and there were no formally contested elections for these posts. This points to the relative weakness of workplace organisation despite union efforts to build sustainable structures and campaigns around key issues. Further, membership levels have also declined to around 30 per cent of the workforce. Amongst part-time employees, this figure fell below 10 per cent.

There were several reasons why membership and activism amongst the core of women tailed off. Even with two or three years' experience as workplace activists, the organising committee did not have the necessary expertise to negotiate the recognition agreement. As a result, national and local officials took on this role, but the consequence was to shift the focus of union work away from building workplace collectivism and mobilisation towards an increasing reliance on their professional expertise. This appears to have been accepted by activists, in part, because of the key role of expert officials and organisers in emerging as leaders during the organising phase of the campaign.

The organiser, who was the primary point of contact between the organising committee and the wider union, held a firm view that workplace activists needed to be developed to have the necessary skills and knowledge to negotiate effectively with management. She sought to ensure that they were eventually 'self-servicing', relying less and less on FTO support to undertake representation and negotiating work. Indeed, during one training session prior to recognition, she commented that 'I'm worried that they're still too dependent on us. We really do need to get them servicing themselves, otherwise we won't have achieved anything here.' As the campaign moved into the phase of negotiating recognition and then into the representation phase, the organiser moved on to other campaigns, and responsibility for CallCo members moved to the branch official and, ultimately, a national negotiations officer. In this process of transferring responsibility away from specialist organisers towards generalist officials, some of the focus on building a 'self-servicing' representative structure was lost. Thus, the current senior representative commented that the local official undertook most of the personal casework even where it was relatively routine because 'I haven't got the experience to do stuff like that'. The outcome was that the expert skills of officials and organisers that were so important in helping to build collectivism in the early phases of the campaign have contributed to the inability of the workplace activists to develop 'self-servicing' structures.

Equally, several women who were active in the early phases of the campaign commented that they did not envisage sustaining their activism after recognition because of the different expectations of the roles between the two phases. One commented, 'I don't mind recruiting people to the union. But I don't want to be meeting management – that's not really me.' Another said, 'I wouldn't know where to start [representing members]. I know they'd give you training and everything, but I just can't see it.' Although these views were not universal, they were widely enough held to be of concern to the organiser. She commented:

> I'm not sure they are confident in their skills yet. But I'm not working on the campaign any more so there's nothing I can do. . . . My worry is that they don't have clear expectations about what the union's all about once we get recognised. I don't know how we address that. I think . . . [the officials responsible] may just take over.

But post-recognition reliance on officials, the change of emphasis away from building 'self-servicing' structures and the lack of skills needed to undertake representation work were not the only reasons for the change in activists' willingness to take on the role of representation. A senior national CWU officer with responsibility for organising within the union commented, 'We've learned a lot from the [CallCo] campaign. We've learned that once you eventually get to recognition after such a slog, people are just knackered. They don't want to take on another role with different skills. They just want a break.' If this is true of organising campaigns more widely, it represents a significant challenge for organising activity, namely, how can broad-based participation in workplace unionism be sustained in the transition to developing effective representation structures? This point is discussed further in the conclusion.

The CallCo case study also highlights the challenges to developing activism amongst underrepresented groups in national unions. As CallCo is a very small employer compared to the main groups of members organised by the CWU, it does not form an independent branch. As a result, CallCo members are part of the local 'clerical' branch that mainly covers workers in BT. One of the officials employed at BT but working on full-time secondment to the union is responsible for representing CallCo members. This structure leads to limitations in the engagement of CallCo members in their branch and in the wider union. A senior national official noted, 'There's a bit of a problem with this [structure]. All of the telecom branches have been structured around one employer. So the business at a branch meeting will be the general business of the union. . . . It will all be the local negotiating stuff with BT. Plus a lot of the time, we meet on BT premises. So it's not going to be appropriate for those [CallCo] workers to be welcomed into a BT building, discussing BT business.' Although this is a union-specific challenge, it is not limited to the CWU. Previous research (Simms 2003) has indicated that new members in other unions can encounter similar challenges in engaging with their wider unions, suggesting that there are often structural barriers to newly organised groups of workers participating more widely. At CallCo, three years after the establishment of the representative structures, workplace activists still report that there is little engagement with their branch or wider union. The senior representative reported that CallCo members rarely even send a representative to the local branch meetings. As the structure of the CWU means that engagement with the wider union comes through individual branches, this effectively excludes these members from fuller union involvement. This is not to suggest that this is a deliberate attempt to exclude these workers: rather that existing structures in the CWU, as in many other unions (see, for example, Simms 2003 for a discussion of Amicus-MSF) are ill-equipped to represent new groups of workers. Whilst this may not matter in the short term, it suggests that there are challenges to the stated agenda of the TUC and its constituent unions to broaden the focus of the union movement and to encourage activism amongst underrepresented groups.

Discussion and conclusions

The CallCo case study highlights a number of important aspects of the difficult transition from an organising campaign to establishing an effective representation structure in the workplace once a recognition agreement has been signed. This raises issues that have not been hitherto much addressed in the literature on union organising. Specifically, these relate to the factors that contribute to a successful transition between the organising and representation phases of a campaign, and to the implications of this difficult transition for wider debates about union renewal.

The success of the transition between organising and representation at CallCo can be assessed on two different levels. On the most obvious level, it has been a successful campaign, for it secured recognition. As a result, annual bargaining rounds have addressed issues such as health and safety, the management of sickness procedures and planning of shift systems. Activists and members report that these changes have led to small, but important, improvements in their working lives. Further, individual representation procedures have been significantly improved and managers routinely meet the union representatives to consult on wider issues such as the implications of the introduction of new technology. In other words, channels for employee voice now exist within this organisation that did not exist prior to the CWU's organising efforts. The campaign has also been relatively successful for the union. It has brought in around 150 new members and has allowed the organising department an opportunity to experiment with organising in a small, non-union environment. The experiences in the CallCo campaign have informed organising policy and practice, for example, with regard to the importance of having an effective organising committee. However, the union has been less successful in securing full collective bargaining rights over key issues. Arguably, the ability of the union to represent these members effectively is seriously constrained by its inability to influence central pay awards. A key concern of CallCare in granting recognition was the potential upwards pressure on wages and, therefore, operating costs, reflecting the importance of ensuring that the CallCo service was not loss-making. Similarly, the fact that the union has agreed to binding arbitration may limit its ability to take collective action in future. In general, these limitations reflect the relative lack of strength and organisation at workplace level.

Another level on which an assessment of the degree of success of the campaign can be made is the extent to which it has achieved its objectives of broadening representation amongst underrepresented groups. Although the campaign emerged as an opportunistic response to a call from workers, one of the stated reasons for supporting the campaign was to build activism amongst a group composed predominantly of women, and largely part-time, workers. This reflects the TUC's broader concern to raise membership and activism amongst these groups, and highlights academic debates about the importance of targeting these groups if unions are to regain their influence in the contemporary labour market. One of the ways that unions have attempted to achieve this is by developing organising tactics that allow these groups to engage with the union around issues that are relevant to them and in a way that they are comfortable with (Heery *et al.* 2000a). This is particularly significant as evidence from the USA suggests that these organising tactics may be more effective in securing higher levels of activism amongst women and part-time workers (Hurd 1993). On this measure, we can see that success is much more ambiguous.

The campaign was successful in achieving this objective in the organising phase. The organising committee was largely representative of the group of workers being organised, and although organisers and officials were extremely influential in framing and articulating issues and grievances, all of the issues around which the union campaigned were directly relevant to members' working lives. In the representation phase, not only has membership dropped off significantly but activism is also now limited to the six elected representatives. These representatives are no longer as representative of the group of workers being organised in terms of gender or employment status. The issues around which the CWU can campaign and negotiate are largely dictated by the terms of the recognition agreement, and although the union is continuing to ask for pay issues to be included within this remit, CallCo remains resistant. In all of these senses, the campaign has been less successful than would appear on first examination.

The reasons for this relate to two key factors: the tactics used during the organising phase of the campaign, and the break in the two phases of the campaign presented by the skilled process of negotiating the recognition agreement. Whilst the tactics used in the organising phase had some success in building a workplace union presence that was relevant to the members, they do not appear to have fully prepared the activists for representative roles after recognition. Echoing Markowitz's (2000) findings, this transition has been made more difficult by the shift of emphasis in the two phases of the campaign and the way in which union experts exerted their influence during the negotiation of the recognition agreement. The result has been the development of a workplace representation structure that appears to be less successful at engaging underrepresented groups than the structures used during the organising phase. In part, this illustrates the development of the bureaucratisation of union representation structures as they emerge. And it indicates challenges to the wider debates about union renewal and revitalisation. The kinds of organising methods used in this campaign (organising committees, collective campaigning around workplace issues, like-to-like recruitment, etc.) have been stressed by the TUC's New Unionism initiative and Organising Academy as ways of recruiting and engaging underrepresented groups (Heery *et al.* 2000b). The emphasis of the Organising Academy training has been to encourage organisers to reject formal, bureaucratic representation structures in favour of structures that are more relevant to newly organising workers (Heery *et al.* 2000b). This case study suggests that this may pose problems in the transition to an effective post-recognition representation phase. If these tactics leave activists ill-prepared for this transition, there is evidence that activism can fall away and representative structures can repeat patterns and problems seen in much more established union branches. Supporting Markowitz's (2000) findings, CallCo demonstrates that whilst unions do appear to be able to gain some significant successes during the organising phase of campaigns, the lack of attention paid to the management of the transition to the representation phase, and some of the points conceded during the complex negotiation of this transition, can leave members disengaged. If the union movement is to achieve its stated objective of broadening participation, then further attention needs to be given to how to engage and involve workers after organising campaigns have achieved recognition.

Acknowledgement

My thanks are to Gregor Gall for comments on an earlier version.

11 Does the organising means determine the bargaining ends?

Lisa Jordan and Bob Bruno

In the United States, conventional wisdom amongst many union organisers is that the style of organising campaign waged has a significant impact on both the probability of getting a first contract and the quality of the contract. Yet little research has been done either to support or challenge this. Based on the research that does exist, the card-check process appears to increase the odds of union certification and the likelihood of a first contract. However, our review of successful union organising suggests that the key variable in gaining certification and, ultimately, a first contract rests on the ability of the union to leverage power and to do so in a timely manner. By leveraging power or 'levers of power', we mean ways in which the union brings pressure on a company from within the political, economic and social context that collectively supports production, distribution and exchange. Unions' ability to exercise power in this context is critical to mobilising pressure against hostile employers. Understanding the relationship between organising strategies, bargaining outcomes and worker participation in terms of levers of power draws, in part, from Kelly's (1998) application of 'mobilisation theory' to industrial relations. The validity of his emphasis on the balance of power between capital and labour, and union capacity to mobilise workers' 'collective interests' into forms of oppositional action is borne out in our research. The primary strength of the card-check process is its ability to leverage power on its own timetable, and to limit some of the problems of National Labor Relations Board (NLRB) elections. But unions recognised through NLRB elections, no less than card-check recognition, rely on the capacity to mobilise enough power to compel the employer to agree certification. Unions that successfully win first contracts can usually identify and exploit an employer's inability to resist making a deal. Sometimes employers' vulnerability originates from demand for labour, other times it comes from third parties outside the immediate employment relationship, and on still other occasions the state provides a helpful hand.

This chapter addresses the question: What is the relationship between the method of union organising and the probability of achieving a first contract? In addressing this, we interviewed and surveyed union organisers and representatives from different local unions covering diverse labour markets in which first contracts were negotiated. We examined how the organising and contract campaigns were prosecuted, and identified the key determinants (i.e. levers of power) to union success in gaining an initial agreement. Moreover, we compared the degree of bargaining difficulty experienced by NLRB-certified and card-checked unions. Finally, we explored the state of first-contract bargaining. Ultimately, while unions use a variety of methods to organise (i.e. card-check, neutrality, NLRB elections), they are most effective in negotiating strong first contracts when they have mobilised their members, but mobilised memberships may not be sufficient to win a first contract.

Overview of organising and first contracts in the United States

In contrast to much of the industrialised world, union density has been on a sharp decline in the USA since the 1950s. In 2002, unions represented 13.2 per cent of all workers and only 8.5 per cent of workers in the private sector, whereas in the mid-1950s unions represented 32.5 per cent of all non-agricultural workers (BNA 2003; Lipset and Katchanevski 2001). Private sector union organising occurs under the authority of the National Labor Relations Act (NLRA). The traditional means of certification is through an NLRB election. While in 2000 the NLRB win rate was close to 44 per cent, by 2003 this increased to 57.8 per cent. The figure for 2003 represents the seventh consecutive year that unions have improved their success rate and the highest in twenty years (Cody 2004). Since 1999, 7,391 bargaining units have been certified, representing 441,964 workers (NLRB 2004). Despite successful NLRB elections, union organising remains unconscionably difficult and union wins continue to fail to cover membership losses.

In an effort to increase organising, some unions have turned toward non-traditional forms of organising, including card-checks, neutrality agreements and non-NLRB elections. Where unions are now using card-check and other forms of alternative recognition, it appears to be a strategic response to changes in the external environment and often the result of changes in internalised notions of how unions should function. For example, in 1997 the Hotel Employees and Restaurant Employees Union (HERE) and the United Needletrades and Textile Union Employees (UNITE) combined for 112 representation elections, but in 2003 that figure fell dramatically to just twenty-one elections. According to UNITE, both unions organised 83 per cent of their new 2003 members through card-check recognition (Cody 2004).[1] Between 1997 and 2003, American workers successfully formed at least 511 bargaining units without casting a single NLRB vote (BNA 2004). Card-check recognition is a standard NLRA procedure that allows an employer to forgo the requirement of an NLRB representation election and voluntarily recognise the union. The Supreme Court has affirmed that voluntary recognition has been 'a favored element of national labor policy'

(*NLRB* v. *Lyon and Ryan Ford* 1981) and from the NLRA's inception 'it was recognized that a union did not have to be certified as the winner of a Board election to invoke a bargaining obligation' (*NLRB* v. *Gissel Packing Co.* 1969). On its face, there appears to be good reason for avoiding an NLRB election and insisting on the card-check process. Eaton and Kriesky (2001) found that card-check campaigns were successful in 67.7 per cent of the cases that they examined.

The increased use and success of card-check recognition has been underscored by the NLRB's decision to grant greater scrutiny to voluntary recognition.[2] Not surprisingly, opponents of unionisation have legally and politically challenged the legitimacy of card-check. A measure has even been introduced into the House of Representatives that would outlaw card-check (Union Labor Report 2004). As Delaney *et al.* (1996) and Budd and Heins (1996) pointed out, the legal system has often been called on to stifle labour when its efforts have been productive. If the conservative-heavy NLRB determines that card-check recognition is unlawful, it will take away a powerful tool that unions have increasingly used to avoid the limitations of the NLRB election process. Such a ruling would significantly shift the balance of power further in favour of the employers. While it would be an exaggeration to declare that US unions are doomed to failure if forced to navigate the NLRB process, it does make sense that unions must find ways to innovate or they will not be as effective in recruiting and representing new members.

Gaining union representation, however, does not secure a first contract for the workers. In fact, after successful NLRB elections, less than 70 per cent of units achieve first contracts (Cooke 1984; Bronfenbrenner 1996). In cases mediated and closed by the Federal Mediation and Conciliation Service in 2003, only 56.5 per cent of new bargaining units had achieved a contract within the inaugural year (FMCS 2003 *Annual Report*). Eisenscher (1999) estimated that five years after recognition (in 1987) only 47 per cent of workers were able to win second contracts and, according to Pavy, of the 74,309 workers winning bargaining unit representation in 2003, only 37,000 will still be union members in 2008.[3] In contrast, Eaton and Kriesky (2001) found that, of the neutrality and card-check agreements they examined, about 95 per cent resulted in first contracts.

Perhaps one of the primary advantages of card-check over NLRB elections is in the timing of first-contract negotiations. American labour law provides a twelve-month 'bar' to any formal challenges to the majority representation status of the bargaining unit from the date of NLRB certification. But after the month strikes twelve, if no agreement has been reached, a showing from one-third of the bargaining unit that there are good reasons to doubt the majority claims of the union triggers an NLRB decertification election. Achieving a contract, however, prohibits any party from filing a petition for an election for up to three years, except in the last sixty to ninety day period before a contract expires, and ninety to 120 days in the case of a healthcare institution. Under card-check, much of the power struggle begins before the clock starts ticking. The union must leverage enough power in order to persuade the employer to agree to an alternative form of recognition. Within the NLRB process, the employers can delay recognition by appealing election results, and after certification they can easily stretch negotiations out to one year by 'surface bargaining'.

Determinants of union success

Forming a union either through NLRB elections or alternatives like card-check campaigns is terribly hard, but negotiating a contract and then negotiating another is even harder. If one looks only at the numbers of union certifications and first contracts, it seems clear that card-check campaigns are the route unions should take. However, our findings suggest that it is not the formal means of union certification that matters most in signing an agreement. The key element remains, as it always has, the union capacity to signal to the employer that not signing a contract would be more costly than bargaining in good faith. Eaton and Kriesky (2001) point out that unions gain neutrality and card-check agreements by using various forms of political and economic leverage. The point of leverage is to signal costs to the employer. It is our thesis that those very same leverage points that produce card-check agreements also reduce the employers' resistance to a first contract. Consequently, when unions are strong enough to exercise effective organising pressure against an employer, they are just as likely to achieve a first contract after winning a representation election as after attaining card-check verification. Indeed, Juravich and Hilgert (1999) argued that the choice between NLRB and non-NLRB strategy is not as stark as some have suggested for, if the union's role is to build on the militancy of the workers, that might lead to an NLRB campaign in some instances and not in others. Thus, the choice is as much strategic as it is ideological.

Organising and first-contract outcomes depend upon strategic decisions that unions make to leverage available power. Successful unions play their best hand, signalling that the cost of disagreeing or fighting is ultimately higher than the cost of agreeing and working with the union. Costs are shaped by economic, legal and organisational factors. What alternative recognition processes like card-check provide is a way of establishing that power relationship before the one-year NLRB clock starts to count down. The process of achieving card-check/neutrality reduces the problem of 'limited' information common during first contracts, signalling to the employer that at this point the union has significant power.

A variety of variables have been considered to explain the outcomes of first-contract negotiations: union building strategies, organisers' personality style and percentage of union votes cast in a successful election (Bronfenbrenner 1996; Cooke 1984; Reed 1993). Markowitz (2000) argued that the organising process is not only quantitative but qualitative. Thus, what kind of organisation is being built, and what is the relationship between the organising campaign and the ways in which workers view their union? Answers to these impact upon workers' willingness to stay with the union through procedural delays and employer opposition, and their ability to participate in the negotiations phase in an effective manner. Not surprisingly, timing was also found to be a core determinant. Cooke (1984) found that NLRB procedural delays give the employers more time to reduce majority support and to increase the cost to the union of continuing the fight. Indeed, he found that for every one-month delay during contract negotiations, the chance of getting a first contract is reduced by 4 per cent. Reed (1990) has pointed out that service sector unions win more first contracts, but that the process of organising service sector workers is significantly longer than organising manufacturing workers. Perhaps, the longer process allows for more information-sharing between union and employer, and the employer has a clearer notion of the union's power. Our contention is that alternative forms of recognition, including card-check, shift the timing of the power calculation on the part of employer and thus increase the likelihood of a first contract. Hickey (2002) creates a heuristic model that brings together many diverse variables, where there are basically four determinants in getting a first contract: union organisational strength, impact of external factors, history of the employment relationship and NLRB role. While Hickey's model is useful as far as it goes, he fails to establish that these same variables are the ones that determine union organising success and that rather than being a single determinant of success in a first contract, they are in many instances co-determined.

Method and data

Although we drew on BNA and NLRB data and case studies of organising drives, our primary data derived from a telephone survey during the summer of 2004. We developed a short survey, which included both Likert scale and open-ended questions. Our survey items were designed to answer the following questions. How do organisers understand the role of the organising campaign in obtaining the first contract? Are card-check agreements more likely to lead to first contracts? And what is the relationship, if any, between power-building during the organising campaign and the union's subsequent ability to 'make the employer pay'? Using two databases with identifiable contact information – one from BNA in which card-check recognition occurred and one from the NLRB of elections in which the union was recognised – we contacted more than 100 locals, seeking to speak to either the campaign FTO or the union representative who worked with the members in that unit. This proved problematic, given the schedules of organisers and the difficulty, at times, of finding those who remembered the organising campaign. In the end, we discuss thirty-two organising campaigns: sixteen through card-check and sixteen via NLRB elections.

Is a win simply a win?

Some unions organise in the manner they do out of habit or tradition; for others the method by which they organise is more strategic. Unions like HERE do NLRB elections only as a last resort; others, like the International Brotherhood of Teamsters (IBT), almost always use NLRB elections. Both unions have been successful in organising a significant number of members. In 1997, the IBT logged 30.2 per cent of all NLRB victories, and from 1999 to 2003, 22.7 per cent of NLRB election wins. In comparison, from 1997 to 2003, it organised only fourteen units through card-check. During that same period, HERE successfully card-certified 115 new units, or 22.5 per cent of all units formed through voluntary recognition. Unions committed to card-check argue, as one union organiser from Chicago did, that 'labor law has been written by the ruling class . . . we need to work around that . . . power is about direct action, solidarity, creative actions. [So] we don't do board elections.' This is understandable: union organisers complain of endless delays, worker frustration and unresponsive investigators (Minnesota Organisers Roundtable 2004). At the same time, many organisers seem torn. While all agreed that some contract was better than no contract and that expanding union market share would lead to better contracts in the future, several were concerned that existing card-check agreements allowed for worker apathy. They believed that workers needed the 'organising fight', whether in a card-check or board election to prepare for the contract fight. Some also expressed dismay with the fact that in order to negotiate agreements with employers that insure card-check recognition and/or neutrality (i.e. accretion agreements), the union typically had to give something up in the current contract.

Those who continue to stress the use of NLRB elections argue that they are dealing with intractable employers who would never agree to card-check. They perceive card-check as one that occurs primarily when labour–management relations are good. Moreover, unions like the IBT continue to be quite successful at organising and may well simply not have reason to move to a new process. After all, innovation typically occurs in the face of failure. We use a subset of the cases to consider the diverse relations that exist between employer and union and the range of paths the union can take from organising through first contract. One would expect that unions can most easily unionise and get first contracts when an accretion agreement already exists. Such was the case at Kaiser Permanente in Kansas. When the Service Employees International Union (SEIU) Local 96 decided to organise the facility, the process went easily. The union already had a national card-check/neutrality agreement with Kaiser Permanente and the first contract was easily negotiated using interest-based bargaining. There was little need for the union to think or act strategically, as the union's power had already been signalled on a national level.

Likewise, HERE Local 1 had no problem organising the Raphael and

Tremont Hotels in Chicago. The union already represented four other Starwood properties and had a standing agreement with the company that owned these two small hotels. The union was easily able to get approximately 70 per cent of the workers to sign cards and the properties then became part of the citywide bargaining agreement. The Local expressed its commitment to card-check: 'We don't do Board elections . . . we have a comprehensive strategy of building rank and file leadership.' He said that the union typically works undercover to build a committee and structure within the hotel. Once recognition is gained, a subset of that committee becomes the bargaining committee working with an experienced negotiator from the local. In this case, the union already had significant leverage as a result of their market density, and a contract would have likely been signed in any case. And yet, based on the union's ideology, they chose to do bottom-up organising.

An accretion agreement, however, does not necessarily suggest smooth going. When UNITE began its organising campaign at the Levi's Georgia plant, the union had already negotiated a card-check/neutrality agreement with the corporation. Yet the UNITE representative at the plant called it a 'very difficult' struggle, for local management waged an anti-union campaign. While no unfair labour practice (ULP) charges were filed, local management constantly referred to the area's history of garment and textile strikes. The union was ultimately able to gain majority card status, but was again faced with a difficult struggle to negotiate the local contract. While the contract signed was seen as 'good', it required worker rallies and in-plant strategies to accomplish. Thus, although the union had previously leveraged its power at the national level in order to achieve card-check/neutrality, the union had again to establish a power base at the local level in order to be successful.

We found that the existence of a card-check agreement often signals the existence of a citywide or national pattern agreement. Moreover, unions that principally use card-check tend to be very strategic in their targets. For example, HERE used card-check almost exclusively to organise the Las Vegas strip. It is not surprising then that where card-check agreements exist, first contracts come easily. Typically, the pre-existing agreement or pattern becomes a model for the new contract. Essentially, the contract has been negotiated in previous struggles. What is perhaps more surprising is that 'voluntary recognition' is not always accompanied by easy negotiations. Between 1999 and 2003, FMCS mediators mediated in over 1,500 'voluntary recognition' first-contract disputes (FMCS *Annual Report* 2004). The number of mediated voluntary recognition cases represents 15 per cent of FMCS total caseload since 1999.[4] In Minnesota during the early 1990s, Hilton and Radisson hotels were organised. In only thirty-one days, HERE Local 17 organised the Hilton workers using a card-check process negotiated as part of the hotel's public funding. While the hotel could do little during the organising process, they fought vehemently during the prolonged negotiations stage. The Radisson had been a union house when it closed for renovation. Nearly four years later, when it reopened, management claimed that the union no longer had majority status and forced it to go through card-check again. The union complied but also filed charges with the NLRB. After five years of fighting at the NLRB, the union and company started negotiations, which went on for another two years before a contract was settled. Thus, despite card-check recognition, NLRB delays and management stalling led to a process that took seven years to complete.

Neutrality agreements might also be expected to make organising and getting a first contract easier but, as Eaton and Kriesky (2001) found, these agreements are often ignored. The Amalgamated Transit Union (ATU) Local 998 in Milwaukee found a neutrality agreement with a para-transit firm, Laidlaw, did little to prevent employees from being threatened with discharge for their union activities. The union charged the company with several ULPs, and Laidlaw, in turn, filed seven objections with the NLRB. Local 998 prevailed in the election (47:37). The company's resistance may have actually helped efforts to win recognition. By fighting the organising campaign, the company prepared workers for a tough contract battle. The effect was to create an 'us versus them' mentality among the workers that helped the union to stage a loud, public strike to protest against Laidlaw's intransigence during bargaining. After five months of wrangling, an initial three-year contract was agreed. A second agreement, however, was negotiated without any hostility in less than half the time and made significant improvements in the areas of wages, shift distribution pay and an employer contribution to a pension plan.

Accretion and neutrality agreements essentially signal that some type of power has been leveraged, but unions can also leverage power early in the process of NLRB elections. The United Auto Workers (UAW) campaigned to unionise some 2,300 workers at St Vincent's Mercy Medical Center, Toledo. Healthcare facilities are recognised by union organisers as being one of the most difficult types of workplaces to bring under a union contract in the USA. In 1999, the UAW organised St Vincent's in less than four months in a difficult campaign. While the union did not have a neutrality agreement, the campaign was not hampered by any ULPs and saw only a few customary employer and union objections to the NLRB on bargaining unit determination. What the union did have was leverage created by its political and buying power. Autoworkers are a large consumer of healthcare and heath insurance in the Toledo area and they are a major player in Toledo politics. Wherever large numbers of UAW members congregate with an impact on consumption patterns and electoral outcomes, the union relies on 'top-down pressure campaigns' to create an environment conducive to gaining certification and a first contract. The calculation the UAW makes in these strategic 'markets' is that organising only happens because it will very likely lead to a first contract. In other words, the union had the means to achieve its bargaining objectives during the representation campaign and, ultimately, secured a contract while it was winning NLRB certification.

A similar but more difficult application of strategic market organising leading to a first contract concerns the International Brotherhood of Electrical Workers (IBEW) Local 2150. Cable Locating Services (CLS) had signed contracts with municipal cable companies to detect underground utility lines before the cable provider broke ground to lay cable. When Local 2150 began organising, the firm operated in eleven states and, in the local FTO's terms, was committed to 'keeping Wisconsin union free'. The union quickly formed a committee of workers from each work location. The company used a New York law firm and waged a 'very contentious' anti-union campaign, leading the union to file several ULPs. After winning the representation election with 60 per cent of the vote, the Local had to endure numerous company challenges to the election. Over a year dragged on without an agreement before the union rejected a final company offer and staged a four-week strike. The strike had business implications for the state's cable companies and utility firms. One was WE-Energies, a major purchaser of CLS work, with the effect that WE's service orders became backlogged, causing it to reconsider its relationship with CLS. Under threat of losing WE's business, the cable locator entered into a three-year contract.

Unions like HERE, IBEW and the UAW have taken advantage of segmented market linkages to find vulnerable yet influential employers who can pressure other smaller employers along the product chain to cooperate with unionisation. Over the last few years, the UAW has organised and negotiated labour agreements covering 7,000 workers with Johnson Controls, and ten other large national suppliers to GM, Ford and Chrysler in Detroit. In each case the UAW's influence with GM, Ford and Chrysler helped the union gain either card-check or neutrality agreements from the suppliers, leading to successful organising and first-contract negotiations. In construction and buildings, an even more straightforward style of top-down organising occurs through organising the employers, rather than the contractor, for strategically there is little sense in bottom-up organising because of the short-term nature of the work. The recognition is 'voluntary' on the part of the employer, but it is often leveraged by the availability of a skilled workforce.

Research has suggested that the larger the percentage vote for the union, the greater the probability that first contracts will be signed. Reed (1989: 481) theorised that 'senior managers may believe that the costs associated with not signing a contract will increase as support for the union increases' and consequently, found a positive relationship between the union per cent vote and rates of first contracts. According to Reed (1989: 488), a 1 per cent increase in the per cent vote increased the 'probability of a first contract by five per cent'. Our cases suggest that the relationship is never that simple. IBT Local 493 in Connecticut managed to win not only recognition but also contracts in transportation and manufacturing. In 2001, it 'easily' organised Longwood Manufacturing but had a 'very difficult' time getting a first contract. The Local quietly and quickly gathered signatures from all 86 eligible workers. Standard practice is that the Local will not file for an election without at least 75 per cent of the workers signing NLRB union cards. That may seem extremely cautious, but the Local believed its 'winning margin must be wide enough to send a clear message to the employer'. The union easily won the certification vote (78:6), but within a year it was embroiled in a two-week work stoppage. When the strike ended, Local 493 had secured a three-year deal. In that same year, the Local petitioned the NLRB with 'full carding' (i.e. 100 per cent) on behalf of fifty-five drivers in an educational transport company. Signatures were gained in less than five days and the election won (55:0). But almost a year later, a union–management agreement to submit the contract issues to binding arbitration was required before a contract was reached. It is likely this occurred because the drivers worked indirectly for a publicly funded organisation. In both cases, the near unanimous union support did not result in an easy path to a first contract. With such high victory margins, why did it take so long to negotiate first agreements? Perhaps the short nature of these campaigns failed to give the employer sufficient information about the workers' resolve and the potential cost of not working with the union.

In early 1998, Communication Workers of America (CWA) Local 1032 was approached by a female company driver and told how her boss 'makes demands for sexual favors' in exchange for driving assignments. This led to a year-long effort to compile enough union cards to petition the NLRB for an election to represent the fifty-four drivers at Unique, a taxi service at Newark airport. The election, held in late 1999, was won with 72 per cent support. This should have constituted a strong deterrent to management bargaining resistance. However, Unique dragged out negotiations for two years, repudiated two tentative agreements, was ordered by the NLRB to 'bargain in good faith' and orchestrated an unsuccessful decertification election. For its part, CWA staged around-the-clock, daily demonstrations at the airport, snarling traffic and costing the airport's managing agent nearly $10,000 a day in police overtime. The public protests raised the cost of resistance for Unique and, more importantly, the airport authority. Once the union discovered its influence over airport management, it had the leverage needed to win an agreement. That leverage was unfortunately stumbled upon only after a frustrating and near calamitous bargaining campaign.

The inverse is also true: difficult organising campaigns can lead to easy negotiations. IBT Local 332 in Flint confronted a national management consultant, Management Sciences, in their efforts to represent approximately 800 nurses and technical staff working at four hospitals. Local 332 understood the implications of the hospitals hiring a 'union avoidance' consultant. The hospitals were planning to merge and reorganise as Genesys Hospital. Prior to merger, only one of the facilities was unionised. Local 332 initially formed an 'inside committee' made up people from every building, unit and shift to educate workers about the need for full unionisation. The Local stressed that the committee was important because 'day-to-day communication was essential to combat the union busters'. After a year of hard organising, in mid-1996, the Local petitioned the NLRB and sixty days later won the election 406–305 (56.3 per cent). It then signed a first contract shortly thereafter, and the union has since negotiated two successor agreements. The Local believed that this would not have been possible without the educational work done by the inside committee. The 'difference' for the healthcare workers at Genesys was building rank-and-file support throughout the hospital system to move the union from the election into bargaining. Local 332's experience seems to underscore our thesis and the work of others (Markowitz 2000; Reed 1989) that one of the keys to gaining first contracts is to be found in the union's actions early in the organising stage. The 'deeper' and more thorough the organising effort was, the more likely it was that internal leadership would be developed and, according to internal assessments, the better and more likely the first contract.

Union market share or density also plays a significant role in first-contract outcomes (Hickey 2002). In Milwaukee, IBEW Local 2150 has, since 1999, won fifteen out of sixteen NLRB elections with election margins that exceeded 70 per cent and without neutrality agreements. IBEW's success in the utility industry contributed to its efforts at WE-Energies. Organising 145 workers at WE-Energies followed a surreptitious two-week union campaign to collect enough signatures to petition the NLRB. According to the Local, once the company was aware of the organising drive they 'staged a pretty strong anti-union campaign'. Nonetheless, in the NLRB election the IBEW prevailed by an impressive margin, but its most potent leverage was that it already represented two-thirds of the state's utility workers. Bargaining may have taken a year, but at no time did the union fear that a strike would be necessary to reach a contract.

The struggle to gain recognition and first contracts is seldom easy and it is usually necessary to find appropriate leverage points. Some companies, though, are ideologically hostile and are willing to incur almost any cost to avoid unionisation. Wal-Mart, for instance, announced to their managerial employees, 'staying union free is a full-time commitment' and 'a goal equal to other objectives' (Featherstone 2004). When thwarting worker rights is as important to a firm as making money and selling a quality product or service, then innovation on the part of the labour movement is required.

When HERE Local 17 set out to organise the Four Points Sheraton, a Starwood property in Minneapolis, they planned on an NLRB election. On the national level, HERE had a neutrality agreement with Starwood, but locally the company engaged in interrogation, surveillance, cohesion, bribes and intimidation. Captive-audience meetings were held in rooms where the temperature had been turned up to over 100 degrees. Both the union and management filed ULP charges. The subsequent election was lost, but HERE, which has a 68 per cent market share in Minneapolis and 90 per cent in St Paul, did not give up and immediately began looking for points of leverage. That leverage came from ongoing contract negotiations between HERE and Starwood in Las Vegas and New York. The union made it clear to Starwood: 'you can't be our friend here and our enemy in Minnesota'. The leverage worked. Top management forced local management to abide by the neutrality agreement and to conduct a card-check. The union was allowed into the hotel and as fear among the workers diminished, they began to sign union cards. When the union went to management and asked for recognition, 84 per cent had signed cards. Local 17 believed, 'the fight sets you up better, but it's harder to win the fight. . . . Workers who don't have to fight, don't have enough knowledge to know how to get what they need at the table.' The first contract was gained relatively easily.

The case of International Union of Operating Engineers (IUOE) Local 150 involves an employer willing to give up everything to stay 'union free'. In 1990, the Local represented machine operators working for an on-site contractor at US Steel's flagship works in Gary. But US Steel decided to replace the long-standing unionised contractor with a non-union operator. The new contractor, Koch, immediately fired the incumbent workforce, demanded that they reapply for their now non-union jobs and brought in employees from elsewhere to replace any uncooperative IUOE members. Local 150 set up 24-hour pickets and struck for two weeks. US Steel struck back by suing the union for $250,000 per hour for every hour they held up work on the site. Their treasury threatened, IUOE ended the strike and entered into a confidential settlement. Then in 1995, two employees approached Local 150 with some damaging information that reignited a bottom-up organising campaign. Knowing that US Steel adamantly backed Koch's position, the union decided, with just the bare 33 per cent required minimum of signed cards, to petition the NLRB for an election. IUOE won with 65 per cent of the vote. But Koch, determined never to operate on a union basis, asked US Steel to let it out of its contract. US Steel complied and brought back the original contractor, which in 1996 promptly signed a five-year (union) contract, leading to a second agreement.

One might think a recalcitrant employer would never be a likely target for card-check. But in the late 1990s HERE Local 27 organised the parking lot attendants in Washington, DC. In an eighteen-month battle, the union won card-check recognition from Central Parking. When the campaign began, Central vowed that it would 'never be union', but HERE mobilised worker militancy while searching for other leverage points. By bringing together community support, exposing pension irregularities, filing NLRB charges, pressuring facility owners, sending delegations to managers and picketing and holding community elections, the union was able to force other city parking vendors to recognise it. From the beginning, HERE planned to organise the entire industry. The Local reported, 'Once we won, the national labor relations staff [for the employers] didn't have so much ego, so we could work together' and union and employers have recently completed their third pattern contract.

Peanuts, popcorn, representation: a summary

Four of our cases were in the sports industry. HERE, seeking to organise the concessionaires (i.e. people selling beer, peanuts, team jerseys and programmes, and serving food in private suites) at newly built stadia, was faced with determining how best to organise the workers, a decision that had implications for the quality of the contract. In each, a somewhat different means was used, but the goal in each case was to leverage the power it had to win representation and a first contract. When the Seattle Mariners decided to build a new baseball stadium, it did so primarily as a public venture. As part of a public utility, the city chose a vendor that would agree to card-check/neutrality and assure labour peace. The HERE organising drive was uneventful and in less than a month it had its first contract. Next door, the city's Seahawks were also having a new football stadium built but by largely private finance through Paul Allen, of Microsoft fortune. When the union approached Allen, he refused the same card-check/neutrality agreement that had been agreed next door. But Allen's obstinacy backfired and served to mobilise a now angry group of workers. While it was difficult to organise the workers, the union was eventually able to gain card-check recognition. As with organising, it was difficult to get a first contract. But after four months of negotiations, leaflets, button-up days and threats of pickets, HERE was able to negotiate a contract that was better than the one at the Mariners' field. The fight with Allen was key to mobilising members to get the better contract. This highlights the concern expressed by many of our interviewees that existing card-check agreements reduce expressions of worker militancy and thus lead to contracts that are less than they might otherwise be.

The use of top-down economic and political leverage to force a large employer to avoid interfering with workers' organising rights and efforts to attain a first contract is an approach used in both representation elections and card-check campaigns. While HERE has largely avoided the NLRB process, it has also used many of the tactics plied during its card-check or neutrality agreement campaigns to win selected NLRB elections. The case of Local 10 in Cleveland reveals how successful organising and first-contract negotiations very often unfold simultaneously. In 1990, the Cleveland Indians baseball team announced that it would be opening a new stadium, with 400 concession workers employed by Sports Services, one of the nation's largest sports facilities vendors. Local 10 made a feeble effort in 1994 to protest against the use of non-union labour which Sport Services ignored. But in 1998, it joined with the Cleveland Federation of Labor and the area chapter of Jobs With Justice to build a community coalition to pressure the vendor and the Cleveland Indians to grant recognition. Cleveland Indians did not agree to insist on a card-check, but did pressure Sports Services to 'get a deal done with the union'. Once the Cleveland Indians made it clear that it would not do business with a company that could not guarantee 'in-seat' concessionaires, organising became easier. HERE Local 10 petitioned the NLRB and won an election by 2:1, and negotiated in three months a four-year agreement with significant improvements in worker pay and healthcare benefits. Following this, Local 10, having already leveraged their power at the Indians' stadium and when the city began building a new football stadium, requested a card-check agreement. Remembering the recent 'public battle' with Cleveland Indians, the football team's labour relations council directed two anticipated vendors at the new Cleveland Brown stadium to sign card-check agreements with Local 10. Nearly every concession worker signed cards and HERE Local 10 won recognition rights and a contract for 350 workers. What mattered in these cases was not whether card-check or elections was a better road to a contract, but how the union made strategic choices, developed alliances and used its leverage.

Conclusions

Based on our thirty-two 'positive' cases, union ability to innovate and to find new and effective ways to leverage power is the key to achieving first-contract success. When unions rally workers and use other points of leverage to gain a card-check agreement, they have already signalled their power to employers. In effect, the two-stage process of organising and then winning a contract has in some ways been collapsed into one. On the other hand, when a card-check agreement exists prior to the organising effort, very often the union is left in much the same situation as if an election had occurred. In this situation, workers' ability to leverage their power has not been tested. Thus, while it appears in general that, by using card-check, the union is more likely to get a first contract, the quality of the contract remains dependent on the power of the union to force the employer to pay. It is our contention that the organising and negotiating stages of the collective bargaining process should be viewed as mutually determined. In other words, in order to be most successful, unions should think of the process from organising to second contract as a single process. This includes not only the means of organising, but the structure of the union and the ways in which a unit moves from organising to negotiation mode, as well as the timing and ways in which power is leveraged. Admittedly, however, this perspective is not shared by FTOs. Only one union emphasised continuity of leadership in the transition from organising to negotiating, and in discussions with approximately seventy organisers representing nineteen unions, only three said that their organisations spent time thinking about the best way to ease the transition. In most of the unions, organising and negotiations remain separate functions and seldom are they unified as a strategic plan.

The difficulty US unions face in achieving a first contract often minimises the positive consequences for collective bargaining in those minority cases where initial deals are signed. First agreements are not only necessary for establishing a collective bargaining relationship but ideally for setting a floor for future bargaining improvements. In nearly all the cases we examined, whether NLRB election or card-check, an initial contract was followed by a second, and in some instances, a third agreement. These successive contracts incrementally improved upon the previous one and matured the relationship between union and management. Whether following NLRB election or card-check certification, aggressive management opposition to union recognition typically ceased and a period of accommodation followed. Where first contracts may have been a struggle to attain, successive ones were negotiated in a more businesslike and less adversarial manner. Although this does not assure an enduring partnership – speculative data suggests that less than half of all union workers ever negotiate more than one contract – or even a cessation of all hostilities, first agreements build a bargaining foundation that at least temporarily restructures the labour–management relationship.

While the fact that the recognition process itself led to a first agreement did not have direct implications for how the union–employer relationship evolved, there is some indication that it did correspond to the representational approach of the union. Unions which featured a full-throttle mobilisation of members (i.e. HERE, SEIU) during organising typically lobbied for community and political support during bargaining campaigns and included member representatives on negotiation teams, as well as using committees to conduct union business. Unions like HERE and SEIU that relied heavily on card-check recognition, and to a lesser extent the UAW, also took very public positions on policy questions and actively worked to inspire their members to elect all manner of legislative and executive officials. But card-check is hardly a necessary means to member activism. Unions like the USWA and IBEW which engaged in numerous NLRB elections have created impressive rank-and-file education, organising and political-action programmes. Regardless of the process used to organise, these unions mustered their members' collective strength to pursue bargaining ends. The key seems to be the degree to which the membership is mobilised during the organising and contract phases rather than the particular process followed. While early research points to the benefits of established card-check agreements, the trade-off may well be the degree to which members participate over the long run. At the same time, and as several organisers pointed out, some union representation is better than none.

Mobilising union resources was not, however, always about engaging the full membership in an organising or contract fight. Leveraging power also meant top-down neutrality agreements negotiated by national union leaders, utilisation of union buying power to persuade an employer, and pressure from third-party employers and government officials. In the former cases, workers were mobilised, in Kelly's terms, to 'attribute' a sense of 'injustice' to the employer and to take collective action. But in the latter cases, while injustice may have been felt and attributed, it did not require worker activism. In a number of our examples, union leaders were very successful in tapping into employer vulnerabilities to secure contracts without having to do more than to threaten disruptive behaviour from other concerned parties or their own members.

Where unions did, however, build community coalitions and ask their members to play an active role in organising drives and contract battles, it is likely that group cohesion and identity were more effectively built than in those cases where employer deals were reached without any grassroots push. The increased intra-union member interaction is described by Kelly (1998) as an important premise in helping union leaders to convert individual union members' perceptions of injustice into collective action. And as Markowitz (2000) pointed out, it may well be this sense of self as integral to the union and not just simply a 'win' that is essential to the long-run viability of the labour movement. Organising drives characterised by decentralised decision-making, rank-and-file volunteers, community alliances and linguistic appeals to worker solidarity and class consciousness not only underscore the employer's culpability in committing an injustice, but also in Kelly's (1998) terms, present the union as a 'collective agency' that can 'make a difference' in redressing wrongs. This in turn is likely to increase unions' effectiveness in compelling employers to pay for a first contract.

This research is just a beginning and a more complete analysis of union structure and their organisational decision-making processes is needed. But the cases represent a wide range of union activity as unions move from organising through to first contracts. Unions in the USA will need to continue to innovate and grow increasingly self-reflective if they are to survive. If the NLRB goes against long tradition and bars card-check, an important tool will have been lost. At the same time, recent proposed legislation, like the Employee Free Choice Act, would not only protect card-check recognition, but would provide for first-contract mediation. Whatever the outcome, it will not diminish workers' desire for a union. The ability and willingness of unions to innovate and to empower workers, and the legal and political environment in which they operate, will undoubtedly impact upon workers' ability to make that desire a reality.

Notes

1 In 2004, UNITE and HERE merged.

2 On 7 June 2004, in a 3–2 vote, the NLRB's Republican Party members agreed to solicit amicus briefs on the validity of an election 'bar quality' for voluntary recognition. The Order Granting Review was based on petitions brought by the anti-union National Right-to-Work Legal Defense Foundation in two voluntary recognition cases involving the United Auto Workers (see www.NLRB.Gov/Decisions).

3 The analysis by Gordon Pavy (of the AFL-CIO) was taken from his comments on union organising posted on the Industrial Relations Research Association internet listserve, 15 June 2004.

4 Of course, sometimes card-check agreements never get as far as contract negotiations. A major national neutrality deal between Verison Wireless and the Communication Workers and Brotherhood of Electrical Workers yielded no new union members from the company's roughly 30,000 employees. The pact was in existence from 2000 to 2004 (Union Labor Report 2004).

12 Collective bargaining performance of newly certified unions in Canada

Process and outcomes

Joseph B. Rose

This chapter examines the movement of unions beyond their initial certification as bargaining agents to consider the process for achieving first collective agreements and the substantive outcomes of first-contract bargaining. It begins with an overview of Canadian industrial relations, most notably the processes by which unions organise new members. This is followed by a review of labour policies affecting first-contract bargaining, including process issues such as the duty to 'bargain in good faith', compulsory conciliation and first-contract arbitration procedures. Next, it considers factors influencing the content of first collective agreements, including statutory minima for collective agreements and the jurisprudence pertaining to first-contract arbitration. How well unions do in first-contract bargaining is considered by comparing data on the bargaining process and selected bargaining outcomes in first contracts with bargaining outcomes in Canada as a whole. In the final section, the chapter examines the nexus between local and national unions to assess the degree of national support for collective bargaining, organising and servicing.

Labour policy and collective bargaining

It is generally recognised that certification is the initial step in establishing a meaningful collective bargaining relationship. Many unions experience employer opposition during, and following, the organising process. Accordingly, employer resistance 'is known to affect both the probability of certification success and whether a first collective agreement will be concluded' (Bentham 2002: 167). Labour law is an important factor in explaining differences in union density in Canada and the USA (Godard 2003). Canadian labour laws are more supportive of the right to join a union and bargain collectively than the American law. For example, certification procedures are more streamlined and Canadian labour boards have greater remedial powers to counteract employer unfair labour practices. The evidence also suggests that achieving a first contract is more problematic in the USA than in Canada. A major and frequently cited difference between the two countries has been Canada's adoption of first-contract arbitration to resolve first-contract disputes. Before discussing the details of this procedure, it is useful to highlight other features of labour policy that can influence first-contract bargaining.

The bargaining process

There are three general legal requirements that can come into play in first-contract bargaining. The first is the duty to bargain in good faith and make every reasonable effort to conclude a collective agreement. This obligation is especially important in the context of first-contract bargaining. As described in greater detail below, an unfair labour practice complaint claiming an employer did not bargain in good faith can trigger first-contract arbitration. A second requirement is conciliation. Since the early 1990s, bargaining impasses have been subject to compulsory conciliation, that is, conciliation is a prerequisite for a legal strike or lockout. Although the conciliation process has been modified over time, such intervention has contributed to the prevention and settlement of industrial disputes (Gunderson *et al.* 2001). Third-party intervention in first-contract situations may be especially helpful in overcoming continued employer resistance to collective bargaining and resolving impasses caused by inexperienced negotiators, as opposed to irreconcilable differences (Ponak and Falkenberg 1989). Third, the legal framework limits the ability of employers to use strike replacements to avoid collective bargaining. In Canada, it is illegal to hire permanent strike replacements. Two jurisdictions (Quebec and British Columbia) also prohibit the use of temporary replacements and, in the federal sector, it is an unfair labour practice to use replacements to break a strike (Godard 2003).

The achievement of a first collective agreement can be facilitated in several other ways. For some public sector employees, the right to strike is prohibited. Accordingly, as with contract renewal negotiations, an impasse in first-contract bargaining will automatically be referred to arbitration. Whatever may be the pros and cons of compulsory arbitration, a first collective agreement is assured. Additionally, in some sectors, certification automatically results in collective agreement coverage. For example, in Ontario, only province-wide, multi-employer collective agreements are valid in major building construction. Hence, a newly organised contractor is brought within the ambit of an existing provincial collective agreement. This confers the industry norm for all employment conditions, including the closed shop and the hiring hall procedure (Rose and Wetsel 1986). Finally, in all likelihood, the manner by which unions acquire exclusive bargaining rights will influence the prospect for achieving a first collective agreement. Unions that receive voluntary employer recognition are unlikely to encounter difficulty in obtaining a first agreement.

Statutory requirements for collective agreements

Save certain restrictions on the subjects for bargaining in the public sector (e.g. the organisation of the public service at senior levels of government), there is wide latitude to bargain in the private sector. There is a general requirement that collective agreements comply with labour standards and human rights legislation (e.g. minimum wages, hours of work and overtime, and no discrimination). This is not a constraint, as collective agreements typically exceed the statutory requirements. All jurisdictions establish minimum requirements for collective agreements (G. Adams 2001). Although practice varies somewhat, the norm is that every collective agreement must contain a duration clause for a minimum one-year term, a union recognition clause (recognising the union as the exclusive bargaining agent for the employees in the bargaining unit), a no-strike, no-lockout clause for the duration of the collective agreement, and a grievance arbitration procedure to provide for the final and binding resolution of grievances. Most jurisdictions require a union dues check-off provision. Five jurisdictions establish requirements to bargain over technological change during the life of the agreement and two provinces have 'enacted an on-going consultation duty provision to be included in the collective agreement at the request of either party' (G. Adams 2001: 12–28).

First-contract arbitration: an overview

In 1974, British Columbia became the first jurisdiction to adopt first-contract arbitration. Currently, seven jurisdictions covering over 80 per cent of the workforce provide coverage. Although there are variations in the procedure, 'the common objective is to encourage more frequent and more timely collective bargaining settlements between employers and newly organised workers' (Friedman and Wosniak 1996: 153). The rationale for first-contract arbitration was to deal with 'stubbornly anti-union employers who, in spite of certification, refuse to accept the right of their employees to engage in collective bargaining' (Weiler 1980: 50). Employer interference might involve 'surface bargaining', using delaying tactics and targeting union sympathisers. Faced with employer attempts to undermine their support and win a war of attrition, possibly ending in decertification, unions often felt they had little choice but to go on strike to achieve a first agreement.

First-contract arbitration was seen as a remedy where 'face-to-face negotiations were unworkable and mediation impractical' (O'Brien 2001: 14). It had three purposes. The first and most immediate aim was to bring to an end a first-contract work stoppage. The second purpose was to provide a 'trial marriage', that is, offer the parties an opportunity to experience life under collective bargaining in the hope it would promote enduring bargaining relationships. Third, it was meant to deter other employers from opposing collective bargaining. For example, by awarding generous compensation packages, other employers would be discouraged from interfering with collective bargaining (Weiler 1980). Initially, there were two types of first-contract arbitration. Under the 'fault' system, a labour board finding of bad faith bargaining could lead to a referral to arbitration. Under the 'no fault' system, the procedure could be accessed at either party's request, provided the conciliation process had been exhausted. Following an application for arbitration, any labour dispute in progress must cease. In most jurisdictions, mediation precedes arbitration; the labour board or a private arbitrator has jurisdiction in these disputes and first contracts are imposed for a two-year period.

British Columbia's 'fault' system evolved into what might be called a third model, the 'mediation-supported' system. Introduced in 1993, this model provided for the early appointment of mediators to educate the parties about the collective bargaining process and to encourage bilateral settlements. If mediation is unsuccessful, the mediator can make one of the following recommendations to the labour board: propose terms of settlement, appoint a mediator-arbitrator to achieve a binding agreement, refer the matter to arbitration, or permit the parties to engage in a work stoppage. The labour board's policy is that first-contract arbitration should be used as a last resort and timed to avoid irreparable harm to the collective bargaining relationship. Accordingly, it should be limited to situations where the conduct of one of the parties is impeding a settlement (e.g. bad-faith bargaining), a bitter and protracted dispute has made a settlement unlikely and where only one of the parties has accepted a mediator's recommendations for settlement (O'Brien 2001).

Experience with first-contract arbitration

The evidence indicates that first agreements are imposed infrequently. Between 1974 and 2000, there were nearly 28,000 certifications granted in jurisdictions with first-contract arbitration. First-agreement applications (or referrals) as a proportion of certifications granted was 5.9 per cent. There was considerable variability across jurisdictions, ranging from less than 1 per cent in the federal jurisdiction to 17.5 per cent under Manitoba's no-fault system. Contracts imposed as a percentage of new certifications was 1.4 per cent (ranging from 0.13 per cent in the federal jurisdiction to 7.5 per cent in Manitoba). As these figures suggest, many applications are settled, usually through mediation. British Columbia offers the most extensive documentation of first-contract arbitration. The labour board has established the following guiding principles for the terms of a first contract (O'Brien 2001: 52): (a) it should not contain breakthrough or innovative clauses, nor should it be either status quo or an industry standard agreement; (b) objective criteria such as comparable terms and conditions of similar employees should be used; (c) there must be internal consistency and equity among employees;

(d) the financial state of the employer must be considered if sufficient evidence is presented; and (e) the economic and market conditions of the industry in which the employer competes must be considered.

Given the extensive use of mediation in the British Columbia procedure, these factors have shaped mediators' recommendations for settlements. The jurisprudence reveals that arbitrators are reluctant to depart from mediators' recommendations in the absence of exceptional circumstances, e.g. a change in the employer's financial situation. The labour board also acknowledged the nexus between substantive outcomes and sustaining the collective bargaining relationship:

> In an effort to establish long-term collective bargaining relationships, fundamental collective bargaining rights such as just cause provisions, a fair and accessible grievance procedure, adequate seniority and promotion clauses, layoff and recall rights union security clauses, were to be included in first collective agreements. These types of clauses are 'critical in the establishment of collective bargaining and . . . underline the values of voice, dignity and security', something long recognised by arbitrators. . . . The [labour board] advised arbitrators and mediators to focus on establishing these rights in collective agreements, while at the same time remaining sensitive to the sector or industry in which the collective agreement is to function.
>
> (O'Brien 2001: 52–3)

In most cases, mediators have been able to broker settlements or narrow the issues in dispute. When arbitration is required, it has normally been limited to a few issues, with the emphasis given to 'employees' seniority rights, a grievance procedure and union security' (O'Brien 2001: 66).

There are three criteria for assessing whether first-contract arbitration is an effective policy. The first is whether unions achieve first collective agreements. The second is whether it has had an ameliorating effect on strikes. The third is whether it promotes enduring or long-lasting collective bargaining relationships. It is believed that the procedure succeeds on the first criterion. Bentham (1999) examined the responses of 420 Canadian employers to certification activity between 1991 and 1993, reporting that an estimated 92 per cent of the certifications led to first collective agreements. Bentham (1999) found that the availability of first-contract arbitration increased the probability of third-party assistance reaching a first collective agreement by 39 per cent. The first-contract success rate is considerably lower in the USA and has been estimated at between 66 and 80 per cent (Eaton and Kriesky 2001). The procedure also has an immediate impact on strike activity, since an application for first contract requires the cessation of any work stoppage in progress. However, the incidence of first-contract disputes remains high. Table 12.1 shows that first-contract strikes account for about one in seven disputes, a figure that has remained fairly steady over the

Table 12.1 First-contract work stoppages as a percentage of strike activity in Canada, 1970–98

Work stoppage measures	*1970–79*	*1980–85*	*1986–98*
Work stoppages (%)	11.4	16.0	15.5
Workers involved (%)	1.7	2.1	1.9
Person-days lost (%)	3.4	5.3	4.1

Sources: Anderson and Gunderson (1982, 1989) and Gunderson *et al.* (2001).

last three decades. This reflects lingering and persistent employer opposition to unions and the difficulties attendant on establishing new relationships and substantive terms of employment. Despite their frequency, such disputes involve fewer employees and result in fewer person-days not worked. These results are consistent with the notion that first-contract disputes are associated with smaller employers.

The experience for establishing enduring relationships is mixed. O'Brien (2001: 64) noted that first-contract arbitration can be 'an inadequate remedy when a single-minded employer is willing to go to great lengths to evade collective bargaining'. Indeed, the early experience in British Columbia indicates that in at least half of cases where a collective agreement was imposed, the unions failed to achieve renewal collective agreements and were decertified. Part of the difficulty at that time was the brevity of the 'trial marriage' period (only one-year agreements could be imposed under the law). Although there is insufficient data to assess fully all first-contract procedures in Canada, legislation in Quebec and Manitoba has established enduring collective bargaining relationships. Similar results have been achieved under British Columbia's mediation-supported procedure. The evidence indicates that the decertification rate for unions that applied for first-contract arbitration was not significantly higher than the overall decertification-to-certification ratio. Additionally, preliminary findings of renewal agreement rates provide some support that enduring bargaining relationships are being established (O'Brien 2001).

An analysis of first-contract bargaining patterns

Information on first collective agreements was obtained from the Office of Collective Bargaining Information in Ontario, Canada's largest province. The data provides some descriptive statistics about the characteristics of first agreements (e.g. employees covered) and the stage at which first-contract settlements were achieved (e.g. whether third-party assistance was required, or a strike occurred). It also provides the basis for conducting a content analysis of first agreements stored in the Ministry of Labour's Collective Agreement Library. A comparison of these contract provisions with surveys of Canadian collective agreements provides an opportunity to consider the adequacy of provisions in first agreements. A total of 885 first contracts were negotiated between 1999 and 2002. The average duration of the agreements was 2.5 years. The mean number of employees covered by first agreements was ninety-four employees; the median was twenty-five employees. Approximately 94 per cent of the first agreements covered 200 or fewer employees. The majority of first agreements (76.7 per cent) covered production employees (or a combination of production and other employees). The next largest groups were professional employees (9 per cent) and office employees (or office and other employees) with 8 per cent of the total. The majority of first agreements (61.5 per cent) covered private sector employees.

The data also identifies a number of settlement stages. The first settlement stage is 'direct bargaining', which denotes the parties' ability to reach a settlement without third-party intervention. The next settlement stage is conciliation. As indicated earlier, conciliation is compulsory and a prerequisite for a legal work stoppage. A settlement may be achieved in meetings with a conciliation officer or in post-conciliation negotiations. The parties may mutually agree to refer their impasse to a third stage, mediation. This stage reflects settlements reached with the mediator or in post-mediation bargaining. Taken together, these three stages represent voluntary settlements. Based on the total number of settlements reached in these stages, an overall settlement rate was calculated (i.e. the proportion of settlements reached without proceeding to the final impasse procedure). The failure to achieve a voluntary settlement means that the impasse will proceed to one of the remaining settlement stages – work stoppage or arbitration. These two stages are considered to be mutually exclusive in most cases (e.g. where statutes replace the right to strike with compulsory arbitration), but not all (e.g. a strike might end with the parties voluntarily agreeing to proceed to arbitration). The dispute rate refers to the proportion of all settlements reached at the final impasse procedure.

Table 12.2 provides a breakdown of first-contract settlements by settlement stage for all first-contract settlements and for smaller bargaining units (200 or fewer employees) and larger bargaining ones (over 200 employees). Forty-one per cent of the settlements were reached in direct bargaining and nearly 50 per cent were reached at the conciliation or mediation stage, or negotiations following third-party intervention. This represents an overall settlement rate of approximately 91 per cent. The settlement rate is lower in larger bargaining units (76.3 per cent), principally because non-binding, third-party assistance produces proportionally fewer settlements. Work stoppages accounted for 7 per cent of all settlements and arbitration represented a further 2.5 per cent of settlements. This produced a dispute rate of 9.5 per cent. Larger bargaining units had a dispute rate that was 2.5 times greater (23.7 per cent). This is consistent with previous research, which indicates that larger bargaining units have higher dispute rates (Rose and Picsak 1996).

Do these results indicate anything distinctive about settlement behaviour in first-contract bargaining? Although there are no direct comparisons that

Table 12.2 First-contract settlement rates by settlement stage and bargaining unit size, 1999–2002

Settlement stage	*Total settlements (%) (N = 885)*	*200 or fewer employees (%) (N = 830)*	*200 + employees (%) (N = 55)*
Direct bargaining	41.6	41.4	43.6
Conciliation/post-conciliation*	30.1	30.7	20.0
Mediation/post-mediation**	19.0	19.4	12.7
Work stoppage	7.0	6.3	16.4
Arbitration	2.5	2.2	7.3

Source: Tabulation based on a special data request to the Ontario Ministry of Labour, Office of Collective Bargaining Information.

Note
Percentages may not add up to 100 per cent because of rounding. * Includes post-conciliation bargaining. ** Includes post-mediation bargaining.

control for both size of bargaining unit and time period, two other studies used a similar format for examining settlement behaviour. The first examined major settlements (500 or more employees) in Canada between 1980 and 1998 (Gunderson *et al.* 2001). This study is not directly comparable because it includes a large proportion of legislated public sector settlements resulting from government wage restraint measures. Accordingly, the most direct comparison is with private sector settlements between 1990 and 1998. A second study examined more than 28,000 settlements in three bargaining systems (strike-based systems in the private and public sectors, and public sector arbitration) in Ontario between 1982 and 1990 (Rose and Picsak 1996). It also included an analysis of settlement behaviour in smaller bargaining units (200 or fewer employees) and larger bargaining ones. Given that compulsory arbitration has a chilling effect on bargaining, that is, inhibiting genuine collective bargaining, and produces dependence on arbitration to resolve impasses, it would be more appropriate to make comparisons with strike-based bargaining systems. The study is also useful because it excluded the public sector wage restraint period, thereby providing a better indication of settlement behaviour in the absence of government legislation.

Comparison with the two earlier studies suggests that settlement behaviour is different in first-contract situations. First, there are fewer settlements at the direct bargaining stage in first-contract bargaining (41.6 per cent). The previous Ontario study reported that a majority of settlements (52.6 per cent) were reached in direct bargaining where the right to strike existed. Similarly, the study of major settlements (1980–98) found that just over half of the private sector agreements were reached at this stage. Second, more settlements are reached in first-contract bargaining with the assistance of conciliation and mediation (49.1 per cent). Conciliation and mediation contributed to about 42 per cent of the settlements in the previous Ontario study and only 34 per cent of the major private sector settlements in Canada. Third, as a result mainly of the effectiveness of non-binding procedures, the overall settlement rate in first-contract bargaining (90.7 per cent) is almost comparable to the previous Ontario study (94.6 per cent). It is also higher than for major settlements (about 85 per cent), but this is primarily because of the much smaller size of first-contract bargaining units. Fourth, first-contract bargaining produces a dispute rate about double the previous Ontario study (9.5 per cent versus 4.6 per cent), but lower than for major settlements (14.1 per cent). Nevertheless, the dispute rate of 24 per cent for larger bargaining units engaged in first-contract bargaining (see Table 12.2) was substantially higher than the rate for major settlements.

In general, these results confirm that settlement patterns are influenced by the size of the negotiation unit. Specifically, smaller bargaining units have a higher propensity to settle prior to the final settlement stage and, conversely, larger units typically settle at later stages and have higher dispute rates (Rose and Picsak 1996). In contrast, the parties engaged in first-contract bargaining are less likely to reach a settlement during the initial stage of negotiations and are more likely to benefit from non-binding, third-party assistance. This undoubtedly reflects the specific aspects of first-contract bargaining, including the likelihood of continuing employer opposition to the union, the absence of a mature bargaining relationship and divergent expectations over terms and conditions of employment. The presence of such factors supports the approach of involving mediators early in first-contract bargaining. The relatively high dispute rate in first-contract bargaining confirms that these negotiations are difficult, even though the bargaining units are, on average, relatively small.

Content analysis of first agreements

The assessment of bargaining outcomes is based on a content analysis of selected bargaining issues. Of the 188 first agreements reached in 2002, only 172 contracts are included in the analysis (other files were either missing, incomplete or in French only.) The purpose of this inquiry was to assess the extent to which first agreements included provisions representing the values of voice, dignity and security, e.g. grievance procedures, seniority, union representation and union security. Several other provisions were examined, including health and welfare plans, pensions and contracting out. Wherever possible, comparisons were made between first agreement outcomes and surveys of Canadian collective agreement provisions. Although these surveys are not directly comparable, owing to differences in time periods and bargaining unit size, they offer an opportunity to make some inferences about the content of first agreements. One limitation of the study is that the content analysis does not include wage outcomes. This is because the collective agreements simply record wage rates. As a result, it was not possible to determine the initial percentage increase in wages in first-contract bargaining. Nor was it possible to compare the average annual increase in wages in first agreements with the average wage increase for collective bargaining as a whole. Table 12.3 presents the overall results and findings for the private and public sectors. It was anticipated that unions would achieve better outcomes in the public sector, given the generally lower management opposition to unions and the substantially higher union density rate in the public sector. Accordingly, these factors were expected to result in the adoption of normative terms and conditions of employment in the unionised public sector.

Grievance procedures

As noted above, there is a legal requirement that collective agreements provide for the final and binding resolution of mid-contract disputes.

Table 12.3 Percentage of 2002 first agreements containing selected bargaining outcomes

Bargaining outcomes	*Total (%) (N = 172)*	*Private sector (%) (N = 110)*	*Public sector (%) (N = 62)*
Grievance procedure	100.0	100.0	100.0
Just cause	93.0	91.8	95.2
Initiate at higher step	50.0	37.3	72.6
Union representation	65.1	58.2	77.4
Seniority			
Job posting	81.4	72.7	96.8
Promotion/Transfers	78.5	68.2	96.8
Lay-offs	91.9	89.1	96.8
Recall	89.0	84.5	96.8
Bumping rights	44.8	30.0	71.0
Unpaid leave: union business	69.2	57.3	90.3
Union security			
Rand formula	51.2	43.6	64.5
Union shop/modified union shop	42.4	47.3	33.9
Maintenance of membership	1.7	1.8	1.6
Closed shop	4.7	7.3	0.0
Health and welfare benefits			
Extended healthcare	54.7	45.5	71.0
Dental	48.8	39.1	66.1
Long-term disability	40.1	37.3	45.2
Life insurance	51.7	43.6	66.1
Unspecified	32.0	41.8	14.5
Pensions	59.3	53.6	69.4
Contracting out	27.3	20.9	38.7

Source: Collective Agreement Library, Ontario Ministry of Labour.

Accordingly, it is not surprising that all first agreements contained a grievance procedure. That said, there is considerable variation in grievance procedure characteristics. Given the high priority that unions attach to protecting workers against unjust discipline and dismissal, we examined three issues related to protecting workers' rights. Specifically, we examined whether first agreements included a just cause for discipline provision, established a right to initiate discipline and discharge cases at a higher step in the grievance procedure, and recognised an employee's right to union representation (e.g. a steward) at disciplinary meetings. Regarding the latter provision, the arbitral jurisprudence establishes that a breach of the right to union representation will render the discipline null and void (Brown and Beatty 1993). As shown in Table 12.3, over 90 per cent of the first agreements establish a just cause for discipline provision. Less common are provisions for initiating discipline and discharge grievances at a higher step in the grievance procedure (50 per cent) and the right to union representation (65.1 per cent). These results suggest that employers are more reluctant to expedite grievance handling and extend worker rights to union representation. It is noteworthy that such rights are more prevalent in the public sector, where about 75 per cent of first agreements contain such provisions. Indeed, the right to expedite discipline grievances was nearly twice as prevalent in the public sector as in the private sector (72.6 per cent and 37.3 per cent, respectively).

Seniority

Seniority is, arguably, the most important non-monetary outcome of collective bargaining. As a general rule, unions endorse it to grant longer-service employees 'preferential treatment in job opportunities and security against layoffs', whereas employers generally 'prefer to retain control over such decisions because they believe they are in the best position to judge which employees are the most (or least) deserving' (Giles and Starkman 2001: 301). The analysis examined the relationship between seniority and job rights. In addition to ascertaining whether a job posting provision existed, it examined whether some account of seniority had to be taken in decisions involving job vacancies (promotions and transfers) and job protection (layoffs, bumping rights and recall from lay-off). There are four main findings. First, public sector unions achieved substantially better results. About 97 per cent of first agreements required job posting, and seniority was recognised as a factor in filling job vacancies and lay-off and recall procedures. As well, more than twice as many public sector agreements (71 per cent) established bumping rights, i.e. the right of a worker subject to lay-off to displace another worker with less seniority. Second, private sector employers appear to have greater discretion to fill vacancies, as less than three-quarters of first agreements required job posting and only about two-thirds recognised seniority as a factor to be considered. It is somewhat surprising that the overall results for job posting, promotions and transfers are superior to those in a 1999 Canadian survey of collective agreements in larger bargaining units (200 or more employees). In the latter survey, job posting was found in only 60 per cent of the agreements and seniority was recognised less often as a criterion in promotions (55 per cent of agreements) and transfers (45 per cent of agreements) (Giles and Starkman 2001). In considering these differences, it is recognised that coverage in these areas may have improved since the 1999 survey. Third, seniority assumes greater importance in lay-off and recall decisions (about 90 per cent of first agreements recognise it). Once again, this result compares favourably with the 1999 survey of Canadian collective agreements. The latter survey found 68 per cent of agreements recognised seniority in lay-off decisions and 65 per cent in recall decisions (Giles and Starkman 2001). Fourth, unions were far less successful in establishing bumping rights (about 45 per cent of first agreements), especially in the private sector (30 per cent of agreements). The overall incidence of bumping provisions is marginally lower than reported in the 1999 survey (bumping was found in 48 per cent of the agreements) (Giles and Starkman 2001).

Union representation and security

Provisions establishing unpaid leaves of absence for union business and requiring employees to join a union represent two indicators of the potential strength of first agreements. One might reasonably expect employers who are strongly opposed to unions to resist bargaining demands for time off for union business (e.g. to attend conferences, training or to accept a full-time union position) and mandatory union membership. Table 12.3 shows that almost 70 per cent of first agreements provide for unpaid leaves of absence for union business. Once again, there was a significant difference between sectors: about 90 per cent of public sector agreements recognised such leaves, compared to about 57 per cent in the private sector. As shown in Table 12.3, various union security arrangements exist. Just over half (51.2 per cent) of first agreements establish the Rand formula (employees have the option to join the union, but are required to pay union dues) and another 42.2 per cent contain a union shop (or modified union shop). The Rand formula is more prevalent in the public sector because some bargaining laws require it and some white-collar and professional employees, e.g. nurses, have made it the norm. The results are broadly consistent with the 1999 survey of Canadian agreements. Approximately 49 per cent of first agreements established some type of union membership requirement, compared to about 53 per cent in the Canadian agreement survey. There were, however, two noteworthy differences: the Rand formula was more common in first agreements (51.2 versus 30 per cent) and there were no open-shop arrangements in first agreements (compared to 16.4 per cent of the total in the 1999 survey) (Giles and Starkman 2001).

Benefits

Generally, unionised workers are more likely to be covered by benefit and pension plans than non-unionised workers (Akyeampong 2002). Less certain is whether benefit and pension coverage in first agreements is comparable to Canadian agreements generally. Unfortunately, the figures in Table 12.3 do not provide a complete picture of health and welfare plans. This is because nearly one-third of first agreements fail to specify benefits coverage. In such cases, the agreements either contain a general statement that existing health and welfare plans will continue (i.e. pre-certification coverage is extended) or indicate that benefit coverage shall be in accordance with insurance booklets, which were not attached to the collective agreements. The data reveals that a majority of first agreements provide for extended health benefits and life insurance, 40 per cent to 49 per cent provide dental plans and long-term disability insurance, and 32 per cent provide unspecified health and welfare benefits. Considering the sizeable share of first agreements that fail to specify benefit plans, the percentage of agreements offering extended health, dental, life and long-term disability insurance is likely to be greater than reported in Table 12.3. Based on the percentage of agreements that specified coverage, it is reasonable to assume that an estimated 50 to 60 per cent of first agreements provide the aforementioned health and welfare benefits. Another 59 per cent of first agreements contained pension plans. Consistent with earlier findings, the incidence of non-wage benefits is greater in the public sector. The likelihood of being covered by a benefit plan is greater under established agreements than first agreements. A survey of 1,161 current collective agreements (covering 100 or more employees) found that 90 per cent of the agreements provided for extended healthcare, 84 per cent provided life insurance and dental plans, and 66 per cent provided long-term disability and pension plans (Bedard 2004). As in the case of first agreements, other Canadian collective agreement surveys indicate that benefits coverage is greater in the public sector (Akyeampong 2002).

Overall, it appears that unions were less successful in securing non-wage benefits in first agreements than other bargaining outcomes. It is recognised that such coverage normally increases in relation to the size of the firm. For example, coverage for benefit and pension plans ranges from about 70 per cent of workers in union firms with less than twenty employees to over 80 per cent workers in firms with 100 or more employees. This difference likely reflects higher unionisation among larger firms and the relatively lower costs of administering benefits plans (Akyeampong 2002; Marshall 2003). Even after recognising the relatively small size of the bargaining units in first-contract bargaining, the incidence of non-wage benefit plans is below the norm for collective bargaining.

Contracting out

This issue is often fiercely contested and reflects unions' efforts to protect members' job security versus management's desire to preserve its right to maintain flexibility and operate in an effective and efficient manner. Just over one-quarter of first agreements contained a contracting-out provision, with protection being nearly twice as great in the public sector as in the private sector (38.7 per cent and 20.9 per cent respectively). This finding indicates that there is considerably less protection against contracting out in first agreements than is found in Canadian collective agreements generally. A 1998 study of 1,038 collective agreements (covering 200 or more employees) found that 55.3 per cent of the contracts contained a contracting-out clause. The incidence of contracting-out provisions was higher in the private sector than in the public sector (61.8 and 54.6 per cent respectively) (Jalette and Warrian 2002). It would appear that employers staunchly resist union efforts to restrict their right to contract out work in first-contract bargaining.

Summary

A majority of first agreements contained provisions embracing the values of voice, dignity and security as well as non-wage benefits. At the same time, only a minority of first agreements established bumping rights and protection against contracting out. Compared to Canadian collective agreements as a whole, first agreements were more likely to require some consideration of seniority (except bumping rights) and less likely to include non-wage benefits and a contracting-out provision. Union security arrangements were, on balance, roughly comparable. While first agreements in the public sector provided greater coverage than the private sector, these results suggest that first agreements not only establish fundamental collective bargaining rights, but they likely provide a foundation for long-term bargaining relationships.

National–local union nexus

The starting point for any discussion of the relationship between national and local unions is to recognise that local unions enjoy a high level of autonomy. Nevertheless, the degree of autonomy varies by type of union and bargaining unit size and this, in turn, impacts on servicing arrangements. For craft unions, 'the degree of centralisation is fairly weak and financial control is vested in the local union' (G. Murray 2001: 100). Industrial unions tend to be more centralised. Local unions receive a portion of union dues and are serviced by FTOs from national and international unions (i.e. Canadian sections of unions headquartered in the USA). Public sector unions are a variant of the industrial union model and feature expert services at the head office and fairly weak local structures (G. Murray 2001).

There is evidence that union structures are evolving (G. Murray 1998). Both private and public sector unions have altered structures in response to economic forces (e.g. globalisation, restructuring and privatisation) and the rising demand for specialised services (e.g. pay equity, pensions, workplace restructuring and legal assistance). Increasingly, local unions rely on FTOs to provide such services. A recent study reported that globalisation contributed to the integration of local unions in the larger union structure. Specifically, 'local unions in firms exposed to international markets which have implemented TQM and teamwork are more likely to be integrated into the larger union structure' (G. Murray *et al.* 1999: 187). By the same token, the adoption of new production systems does not always lead to the integration of national–local union structures. The need to access national union support to deal with workplace change depends on the characteristics of national unions, including the breadth of industry and employer coverage, the resources devoted to research on new workplace practices, the extent of education and training provided on new workplace issues, the availability of multiple communication channels to monitor issues faced by local unions and the way local union representation is structured (Frost 2001a).

Other pressures have led to new local union structures and the rationalisation of servicing. In response to the reduction in the average size of certification units, some local unions have moved from the 'one certification unit per local' model to composite local structures comprising multiple certification units. This change represents 'a strategic effort to organise new groups of workers into viable structures, to devolve some basic servicing to the local level, and to achieve new coordinating mechanisms among workers' (G. Murray 1998: 332). For example, the United Steelworkers of America has embraced the 'organising model', a strategy based on recruiting and defending newly unionised workers. According to Murray (2001: 101):

> This represents a conscious organising and servicing strategy designed to better meet the needs of new membership groups in the service sector and small manufacturing units. Indeed, it aims to create union locals that can adjust to the small size of new units being organised. This strategy also allows the union to achieve a financially viable servicing strategy. The union has done this at times by training full-time lay representatives rather than professional business agents or servicing staff. The increased importance of amalgamated locals naturally pushes unions organised on the industrial model towards greater decentralisation in the distribution of services.

FTOs assume a major role in first-contract bargaining for several reasons. First, they bring experience to the bargaining table, including negotiating skills and knowledge of employment conditions in the sector or industry in which the newly certified unit is situated. Because such skills are often absent in a newly certified unit, FTOs will assume the role of chief spokesperson of the negotiating committee. This is especially important considering the probability of post-certification employer opposition to the union, the lower success rates achieving first agreements in smaller units and the relatively high strike rates (Bronfenbrenner 1996; Gunderson *et al.* 2001). Second, FTOs can help develop campaign strategies to increase the first-contract success rate. There is evidence that 'unions can diffuse the negative impact of an adverse bargaining climate and/or an aggressive employer campaign when they use a multi-faceted, rank-and-file intensive campaign that focuses on mobilising the membership to pressure the employer both inside and outside the workplace' (Bronfenbrenner 1996: 166). Third, the central office can also provide research services. For example, some unions maintain collective agreement databases. Public sector unions subject to compulsory arbitration routinely rely on such information to prepare briefs and make submissions at interest arbitration hearings. Finally, FTOs can either supply, or arrange for, legal and technical advice on complex bargaining issues.

Conclusion

In general, Canadian labour law offers substantial protection of the right to organise and bargain collectively. There is legal support for both the bargaining process and the establishment of minimum terms and conditions for all collective agreements. In addition, most Canadian jurisdictions have adopted first-contract arbitration to enhance the probability that newly organised workers will achieve a collective agreement. Although resort to first-contract arbitration is infrequent, the availability of this procedure has contributed to the high percentage of certifications leading to first agreements (estimated at 92 per cent). Data compiled by the Ontario Ministry of Labour allowed an examination of the process and outcomes of first-contract bargaining. The findings reveal that the vast majority of first-contract negotiations are concluded peacefully. However, the first-contract dispute rate of 9.5 per cent was about double that of a previous Ontario study. The relatively high dispute rate combined with the lower incidence of settlements at the direct bargaining stage confirm that first-contract bargaining is often difficult, even though negotiations involve relatively small bargaining units. Bargaining outcomes ranged from adequate to strong for most of the issues examined. The values of voice, dignity and security were clearly recognised in provisions covering grievance procedures, seniority, union representation and union security. Whereas a majority of first agreements provided for non-wage benefits, the incidence of such plans was lower than in Canadian collective agreements as a whole. Unions also had difficulty restricting management rights as evidenced by the modest coverage respecting contracting out and bumping rights.

These findings suggest that first-contract outcomes are sufficient to provide the foundation for long-term collective bargaining relationships.

However, there is a need for further research in a number of areas. One involves the relationship between the bargaining process and bargaining outcomes. At present, little is known about the influence of factors such as employer strategies, union strength and member participation, and employee expectations on first-contract outcomes. In addition, there is a paucity of information about what occurs following the achievement of a first collective agreement, e.g. incidents of decertification and renewal of collective agreements. Research assessing labour relations subsequent to achieving a first agreement would go a long way towards assessing what factors contribute to the establishment of enduring bargaining relationships. The nexus between national and local unions varies and has been evolving in response to economic pressures in recent years. Because newly certified bargaining units often lack the experience and resources to engage in negotiations, it is common for them to request assistance, where unions will typically provide FTOs to carry out negotiations. Considering the high priority unions attach to organising as a means of expanding union membership and strength, it follows that FTOs have assumed a pivotal role in first-contract bargaining and efforts to build enduring collective bargaining relationships.

13 Recognition, bargaining and unions in Australia

Gerard Griffin

For much of the twentieth century, Australian industrial relations were dominated by a strong, centralised arbitration model. This model, enshrined in legislation in 1904, had a number of foundations. Among the most important of these for unions were the formal registration of industrial organisations, including trade unions, and the granting of exclusive jurisdiction over specified segments of the workforce to these registered organisations; the ability of these registered organisations to have a wide range of claims, including claims for improved wages and working conditions, arbitrated by a third-party tribunal external to the employment relationship; and the legal enforcement of decisions of this tribunal, establishing, *inter alia*, minimum wages and conditions for specified classes of employees. Based on this legislative framework, trade unionism in Australia thrived. Density was usually above 50 per cent and its power and influence, both in the polity and in the economy, were widely accepted and supported. Commencing in the 1980s, however, significant changes occurred, with new work methods, new attitudes and new laws severely and adversely affecting unions. Membership has plummeted and union power and influence evaporated. Unions have been slow to respond to these changes. The initial response in the 1980s was to negotiate in 1983 a social contract, known as the Accord, with the federal Labor government. This Accord lasted until the electoral defeat of the Labor government in 1996, but well before then the union movement had realised that this contract was not the response to declining membership and authority. The second major strategic response was a wave of union mergers during the early 1990s. The failure of this strategy to stem the decline led to the third and current strategy of adopting the 'organising model', with an emphasis on organisation and interaction at the workplace level. For many unions, this is a novel experience, not least because of the necessity to share authority and power within the union and, not surprisingly, not all unions have successfully adopted this strategy.

In many ways, Australian unions are now seeking to re-establish their movement without the traditional levels of state support. And they are doing so in an environment where the other parties to the industrial relations system, that is, employers and the state, are increasingly hostile to unionism. For example, legislation passed in 1996 removed much of the traditional state support for trade unionism. Thus, the traditional battles for recognition and acceptance by employers and for input into determining wages and working conditions are being refought in the early twenty-first century. Accordingly, this chapter examines three interrelated issues that are key components of this re-establishment process. The first issue is recognition of unionism, an area in which the state, through its tribunal system, continues to play a major role. As long demonstrated in the US system of industrial relations, recognition does not always lead to collective agreements. Thus, the second issue is the system of bargaining in Australia and the role of unions in that process. The final issue concerns the relative roles, and changes in those roles, of FTOs and members and local activists. The argument advanced is straightforward: unions have retained their traditional state recognition but such recognition is increasingly irrelevant in a bargaining system dominated by employers. In an attempt to change this situation, unions are increasingly adopting the organising model, with its reliance on local activists and members; to date, this strategy has had limited success.

Recognition

Although some nascent form of trade unionism and industrial relations existed prior to the 1850s (Quinlan 1987), it was the discovery of gold in the early 1850s that created an economic environment suitable for the development of trade unionism. Over the next three decades, buoyed by continuing economic growth, employees, in general, continued gradually to improve their working conditions; by 1890, some 350 unions were in existence (Quinlan and Gardner 1995). During these decades, union recognition was achieved through direct bargaining with employers, a status that was easy to win given the prevailing economic conditions. The depression of the 1890s brought an abrupt halt to the march of trade unionism. The loss of a series of strikes during the early 1890s, and de facto derecognition, practically destroyed the union movement. Subsequent and substantial political and social debate (see Macintyre and Mitchell 1989) culminated in 1904 with the passing of the Conciliation and Arbitration Act that was to govern industrial relations in the new Commonwealth of Australia. Importantly, the former colonies, now the states of the Commonwealth, retained their own industrial relations systems and their own industrial law, and continue to do so today. Thus, varying with the class of worker, unions are subject to different legislations within each state. In this chapter, the focus is almost exclusively on the federal legislation; this is the dominant jurisdiction, both in a legal sense following a High Court decision in 1926 that this jurisdiction has precedence, and also in an industrial sense, given that the main industrial issues are largely fought in this arena.

The 1904 Act recreated the Australian union movement. At law, unionism became a creation of the state, which guaranteed it benefits such as exclusive jurisdiction and membership, but heavily regulated its structures, industrial actions and internal affairs. Rather than the bottom-up, market-based movement of the nineteenth century, the union movement of the twentieth century was to be a top-down, state-regulated organism. In effect, many of the contentious issues that help define the character of a union movement were removed from the industrial battleground. Union recognition was to be subsumed within a process of industrial registration and was to be awarded by the bureaucratic pen rather than by struggle at the workplace and interaction with employers. In particular, a successful application to the Office of the Industrial Registrar would result in major benefits, particularly exclusive jurisdiction over a segment of the workforce and enforced recognition on employers. Once an organisation was registered, no competing organisation could subsequently be registered. In effect, if an employee wished to join a union then they had no choice but to join the registered organisation for the specific class of worker to which they belonged. In theory, rival unionism was not possible under this system. In practice, however, some overlap of membership 'was tolerated, for instance, where the applicant covered workers whose trade or industry had a distinctive identity, or who performed supervisory or managerial functions, or who had a history of political or industrial disagreement with the views or actions of the objecting organisation' (Creighton and Stewart 2000: 350). An employer had no choice but to recognise the registered organisation as the appropriate and legally designated representative of their employees. Further, the employer did not have the option of refusing to bargain with that organisation. As discussed later, the employer could be taken before the Australian Industrial Relations Commission (AIRC), the present-day name of the regulatory agency established to implement the new arbitral model, to enforce a bargaining, and ultimately an arbitral, relationship. Derecognition was possible under the 1904 legislation. Envisaged as a punishment for unions that disobeyed the orders of the AIRC, this threat was little used and, for practical purposes, irrelevant.

This reliance of Australian unions on various organs of the state has led a number of commentators, based on the work of Howard (1977), to argue that they are not worthy of the title 'union'. The argument runs that the organisations are so dependent on the state for, among other things, membership and wage increases that they are not unions in the accepted sense of the word. Rather, 'the Australian union can be regarded in general as an institution called into existence by a bureaucratic mechanism (the arbitration system) to enhance the functioning of that mechanism' (Howard 1977: 255). While this claim of dependence has been vigorously contested (see Gahan 1996), there can be little doubt that Australian unions have derived significant succour from the state. And indeed, regardless of any academic criticism, unionism flourished under this state-guaranteed arbitral system. In 1901, membership was less than 100,000 (6 per cent density) in 198 unions. By 1911, the number of unions had risen to 573, membership to

365,000 and density to 28 per cent. The number of registered organisations actually declined to 382 in 1921, largely because of a number of mergers and some structural changes after World War I, but membership had climbed to 700,000 and density to 51 per cent (see Table 13.1). For a union movement that had, for all practical purposes, been wiped out during the 1890s, these tangible rewards from the arbitral system were very attractive. Accordingly, and despite the sometimes onerous obligations imposed by the arbitral model, union strategy for much of the twentieth century revolved around an arbitration system that granted it both recognition and bargaining rights. Overwhelmingly these decades were golden years for the Australian union movement, perhaps best encapsulated by density remaining above 50 per cent between 1920 and 1980 for all but a few of the depression years of the 1930s (see Table 13.1).

Changes started to occur during the 1980s. Factors such as the dismantling of tariff protection, particularly for manufacturing, new forms of work production, massive changes in workforce composition and, particularly, a growing ideology among both employers and the state, questioning the traditional organisation of labour markets, challenged the central role of trade unionism. Over time, these pressures resulted in legislative change, initially fairly cautious in nature in 1988 and in 1993 under Labor Party governments, and then more radical under a conservative coalition government in 1996. As discussed below, this legislation heralded a significantly different bargaining regime. However, it did not affect centrally the existing process of registration and recognition.

This is not to argue that the Workplace Relations Act 1996 did not seek to vary the registration process. Among other issues, the bill had, for

Table 13.1 Membership, density and numbers of unions

Year	*Membership (000)*	*Density (%)*	*No. of unions*
1901	97	6	196
1911	365	28	573
1921	703	52	382
1931	741	45	361
1941	1,076	50	374
1951	1,690	60	359
1961	1,895	57	355
1971	2,452	51	303
1981	2,994	50	324
1991	3,382	42	275
2001	1,902	25	n/a
2002	1,833	23	n/a
2003	1,866	23	n/a

Source: Australian Bureau of Statistics, various years; *Trade Union Statistics*, catalogue no. 6323.0; *Earnings, Benefits and Union Members*, catalogue no. 6310.0; Deery *et al.* (2001).

example, proposed special provisions for enterprise branches of registered organisations, a proposal that was dropped during negotiations aimed at achieving the passage of the bill with the Australian Democrats, a small political party holding the balance of power in the Upper House, the Senate (see Creighton and Stewart 2000: 360). A number of changes to the existing act were passed, including the reduction of minimum membership size to fifty and provisions aimed at facilitating demergers of recently merged unions. However, the core registration and recognition provisions remained. Arguably, major changes in other sections of the 1996 legislation rendered the issue of recognition significantly less important. For example, restrictions on union access to workplaces and the omission of the bargaining in good faith provisions specified in the 1993 legislation meant that, of themselves, registration and recognition were not the key issues for a government aiming to lower the locus of workplace relations to enterprises and to individuals. The new bargaining system introduced under the Workplace Relations Act 1996 means that recognition is much less valuable than hitherto. Prior to the 1990s, recognition was a cornerstone of accessing the arbitral model, and ultimately of compelling employers to bargain or face binding arbitration on a wide range of issues. Post-1996, recognition still has value, not least jurisdictional, but significantly less influence in the bargaining relationship. In this new environment unions are struggling to survive. Membership density had declined to 40 per cent by 1990 and fell to 23 per cent by 2003. In a number of industry sectors, despite having formal recognition, unions are increasingly finding themselves either shut out of the bargaining process or playing only a supporting role.

Bargaining

Until 1993, the traditional arbitration system was the legally superior method of determining the employment relationship. The original legislation in 1904 did make provision for collective bargaining (see McCallum and Smith 1986), but various judicial decisions, particularly those of the High Court over the two succeeding decades, relegated bargaining to an inferior status. Two crucial aspects of this arbitral model were the ability of a registered organisation to have claims for improved wages and working conditions arbitrated by a third party external to the employment relationship, and the subsequent legal enforcement of 'awards', the term for the decisions of this external, third-party tribunal. Bargaining, of course, did not disappear from the industrial relationship and there has been ongoing debate about the respective roles of the arbitral and collective bargaining models, a debate particularly vigorous in the early 1960s (see Hancock 1962; Laffer 1962) and in the mid-1970s, when a special edition of the *Journal of Industrial Relations* (*JIR* 1976) was devoted to it.

In a very broad sense and despite the legalities of the arbitral mode, during periods of economic prosperity, unions, particularly in industries where they were well organised and had sufficient bargaining power, sought to supplement gains made through the arbitral system by engaging in direct bargaining with employers at either the industry or local level. In contrast, a deteriorating economic environment saw unions retreat to the protection of the arbitral model. Thus, the economic boom of the 1960s and early 1970s caused a major surge of bargaining to the extent that it threatened to supplant arbitration. And in New Zealand, similar developments led to legislation in 1972 that formally supported collective bargaining. In Australia, the oil-price shock of 1973 resulted in both rising unemployment and inflation, significant industrial disputation and, in 1975, a return to a centralised wage-fixing system. Accordingly, even in the good economic times, collective bargaining operated in the shadow of arbitration, and unions pursuing the bargaining route were frequently constrained by arbitration strictures, not least monetary fines for operation 'outside the law'. In 1988, the 1904 Act was finally replaced. The 1988 legislation gave some very limited support to collective bargaining: only four pages of the more than 200 pages of legislation were devoted to a bargaining system.

By 1993, however, driven by a range of developments including a deteriorating economy, a continuing decline of unionism and a sharpening of employer enthusiasm for bargaining, the Industrial Relations Reform Act formally enshrined the legal superiority of a bargaining system and relegated the arbitral model to the role of a social safety net. Enacted by a Labor government, unions were particularly horrified by the introduction of a non-union based form of collective bargaining. Titled Enterprise Flexibility Agreements, these provisions allowed non-union employees to band together to negotiate with their employer a collective agreement at the local level. These provisions were little used over the following three years. Arguably, these provisions, and indeed the 1993 Act, have had their major impact as a circuit breaker of the arbitral model, and as a small stepping stone towards the radical changes introduced in the Workplace Relations Act 1996. This legislation formalised two streams of legally sanctioned bargaining systems. It continued the philosophy introduced in the 1993 legislation of making bargaining the legally superior system and enshrined the role of the arbitral system, and particularly that of the AIRC, as a social safety net, albeit a much skimpier net. The AIRC was allowed to arbitrate only on twenty specified 'industrial matters', and all other issues were excluded from its arbitral remit.

The chapter now briefly outlines the current bargaining system, links this system to the remnants of the award-based system, discusses the AIRC's role in fixing minimum wages and its re-emergence as a limited conciliation model, and comments on the role of unions in this bargaining system. The 1996 Act introduced a dual bargaining system: Australian Workplace Agreements (AWAs) and certified agreements. In practice, because certified agreements can be either non-union collective agreements or union-based collective agreements, three different systems operate.

Australian Workplace Agreements

An AWA is an individual agreement, negotiated between an employer and an employee. Either can appoint a bargaining agent to act on their behalf, so, theoretically, a union can represent the employee. The contents of the agreement are largely determined by the parties, subject to the overall constraint that that content must 'pertain' to the employer–employee relationship (s170VF(1) of the Act). The Act does specify some minimum procedural contents, such as a dispute resolution procedure. To oversee this new form of agreement, the Act set up the Office of the Employment Advocate (OEA). The two key roles of the OEA are to approve a proposed AWA and subsequently to register the agreement. Prior to approval, the OEA must apply the so-called 'no disadvantage test'. In effect, this means that the AWA is compared with the relevant AIRC award and that, in that comparison, the employee must not suffer any disadvantage in relation to their terms and conditions of employment. Importantly, this does not mean that all AWA provisions must be equal to or better than award conditions; rather, it is the overall disadvantage that is tested. Thus, as Creighton and Stewart (2000: 174) note, 'the special significance of the AWA concept resides in the fact that for the first time in the history of the federal system, it is possible for an employer and individual employee to "contract out" of an award on terms which are less favourable than those set out in that award'. Equally important, an AWA, except in specific limited circumstances, is also legally superior to certified agreements. Where a proposed AWA passes the 'no disadvantage test' and contains the prescribed clauses, the OEA registers the agreement, thus making it legally enforceable. The agreement is a private agreement between the parties and is not available for public scrutiny, although the parties to the agreement may agree to make it public (for further details of AWAs, see Creighton and Stewart 2000: 174–86).

In practice, AWAs have had a limited but growing numerical impact on Australian industrial relations. From March 1997 to August 2004, 517,000 agreements have been registered by the OEA. Some 253,000 agreements were registered in the two-year period ending June 2004. In view of the three-year maximum length of AWAs, the OEA regards this latter figure as being a good approximation of the agreements currently in force. These 'live' agreements cover less than 3 per cent of the total workforce, a figure swamped by the 39 per cent of the workforce covered by individual contracts of employment. However, over the past twelve months, the number of agreements being registered has risen to around 12,000–15,000 per month, pointing to a growing interest in these individual agreements, particularly in the mining industry. Industry categories in which AWAs are principally found are the retail and the property and business services area (see Table 13.2).

The lack of public scrutiny of AWAs and their wider-spread usage in non-unionised industries, allied with the government's ideological intent in legislating for these individual agreements, have made AWAs a very contentious form of agreement and one much opposed by unions. A rigorous debate has waged between supporters of AWAs, who view them as offering individual choice to employees, and opponents, who regard them as an open invitation to exploit employees (see, for example, proceedings of the ACIRRT 2001 conference). In practice, given the low overall take-up rate of AWAs, while acknowledging that the psychological impact of their availability or threat of usage should not be discounted, these individual forms of bargaining are not mainstream in Australian industrial relations. Rather, certified agreements hold this position.

Certified agreements

These agreements are collective agreements that regulate terms and conditions of employment at individual workplace levels. The bargaining process for these agreements, usually referred to as Enterprise Agreements or Enterprise Bargaining Agreements (EBA), is relatively straightforward: either side can initiate a bargaining period. During this period, negotiations take place and, if successful, the agreement reached can be registered with the AIRC, among other things to give legal effect to the EBA. During the bargaining process, the main parties can call on the assistance of the AIRC to conciliate on matters in dispute. Also during this period, and assuming certain pre-conditions are met, either party can initiate what the Act terms 'protected industrial action', that is, the initiator of the action is protected at law from being sued for damages or similar actions. Importantly, and in marked contrast to the traditional arbitral model, the AIRC, with the exception of disputes affecting the national economy, cannot arbitrate on matters in dispute. This major philosophical change is best summed up in the words used in a decision of the AIRC involving a major dispute in the coal-mining industry. It accepted the legitimacy of varieties of industrial actions by both union and employer and used the term 'all is fair in love and war' (CFMEU 1999).

Once agreement has been reached, the EBA can then be registered with the AIRC. The AIRC has little discretion but to register the agreement once a limited number of conditions are met. In the main these conditions are that a majority of employees have voted in favour of the agreement, that there is a disputes procedure in the agreement and that it passes the no-disadvantage test for employees discussed above. These agreements can last for a period of up to three years. In practice, most agreements have either a two-year or three-year duration, with the average duration gradually lengthening as the parties become more used to the EBA system.

One of the more controversial aspects of certified agreements is that collective agreements can be negotiated, agreed, certified and enforced without the involvement of unions. Building on the more limited provisions in the 1993 Act, the Workplace Relations Act 1996 introduced a fully fledged non-union collective bargaining system. In effect, an employer can negotiate directly with employees, and so long as a valid majority of employees approve the EBA, then the agreement has the same status as one negotiated with a union. At certification, the AIRC is inclined to scrutinise these non-union agreements somewhat more closely to ensure that legislative provisions on consultation and voting have been followed, and that the interests of groups such as young workers or those from a non-English-speaking background, have not suffered. However, once these conditions have been met, then the AIRC must certify the EBA. Non-union EBAs have had a not insignificant impact on the bargaining process. Over the last few years, approximately 15 per cent of all EBAs have been non-union agreements. And given the ongoing decline of density – down to 17 per cent in the private sector in 2003 – the potential for growth of these agreements clearly exists. Non-union EBAs are more likely to exist in manufacturing, government and personnel services (see Table 13.2).

Table 13.2 Certified agreement and AWA employee coverage

Industry sector	*Employees covered by union certified agreements*	*Employees covered by non-union certified agreements*	*Employees covered by live AWAs*
Agriculture, forestry and fishing	4,500	2,700	4,100
Mining	16,000	3,000	19,800
Manufacturing	175,100	25,100	32,800
Electricity, gas and water supply	15,400	100	900
Construction	70,800	6,800	16,000
Wholesale trade	2,900	1,100	4,400
Retail trade	309,000	15,800	43,300
Accommodation, cafés and restaurants	18,500	6,800	23,400
Transport and storage	94,200	5,800	8,500
Communication services	34,600	10,600	19,200
Finance and insurance	100,000	13,600	7,600
Property and business services	28,200	13,800	34,000
Government administration and defence	193,200	16,900	14,000
Education	57,000	6,000	1,400
Health and community services	169,600	12,900	11,800
Cultural and recreational services	34,200	6,200	5,700
Personal and other services	13,100	16,300	6,800
Totals	1,336,300	163,500	253,700

Source: Office of the Employment Advocate (www.oea.gov.au).

Notes
Certified agreement numbers are sourced from unpublished 'Trends in Federal Enterprise Bargaining' data and refer to employees covered. Agreements are current at 31 March 2004. AWAs are sourced from the OEA WorkDesk database, and includes AWAs approved in the past two years up to 30 June 2004.

Unregistered agreements

Once an agreement has been reached between the parties, the option of seeking formal registration in the AIRC becomes available. For most unions and employers, this option is very attractive, not least because of the subsequent legal enforceability of the agreement. For most agreements, however, there is no formal compulsion to seek registration. Both anecdotal and some limited case-study evidence point to a number of agreements not being certified. This seems to be the case in a small number of industries, such as the mining industry, that traditionally had strong workplace bargaining relationships and processes, even under the arbitral model. Furthermore, evidence also points to add-on agreements, agreements reached to resolve a particular issue that arises during an EBA's lifetime, not being registered in the AIRC. Overall, there has been a limited growth in the numbers of unregistered agreements but there is little knowledge of what they contain. Unfortunately, the Australian Workplace Industrial Relations Survey scheduled for 2000/01, a follow-up to the surveys of 1989/90 and 1995, was not carried out. In this absence, the existence of unregistered agreements must merely be noted.

Awards and minimum wages

What happens in workplaces where neither an employer nor employees seek to negotiate an EBA? In effect, the relevant award continues to regulate the employment relationship there. Under the arbitral system, and over time, a complex, interweaving web of awards had emerged that effectively covered all categories and classes of employees. It is against one of these awards that the AIRC conducts its 'no disadvantage' test as part of the EBA certification process. These legally binding documents had wide applicability and tended to cover most workers, whether unionised or not, in the specific segment of the workforce to which they applied. Such widespread coverage was attained through a variety of legal mechanisms, including employer membership of an employer association or the union simply alleging that a number of employers, from industry listings or specialised directories, were parties to an industrial dispute.

In the post-1996 period, awards have become significantly less important for two reasons. First, both certified agreements and AWAs override awards, and second, the Workplace Relations Act 1996 restricted awards to coverage of just twenty 'allowable award matters'. These matters cover the core of the industrial relationship, such as rates of pay, hours of work and leave provisions, but exclude many of the provisions traditionally covered by awards, not least union security mechanisms. This was a deliberate government strategy aimed at forcing employers and employees into enterprise bargaining. The choice offered was: stick with the award system and only twenty core matters would be covered, and thus legally enforced, or move to a bargaining model and the parties themselves determine the range of bargaining subjects. In practice, what has emerged is that coverage under the award system has decreased significantly (see below). It is now found largely in sectors where unions are either very weak or non-existent, and where employees lack bargaining power, in effect producing a second-class system with significant legal limitations.

A key issue that quickly emerged post-1996 was how to determine minimum wages for workers not covered by enterprise bargaining. Australia does not have minimum wage legislation and has traditionally relied on the award system to establish a different wages floor for different groups of workers. The system that emerged drew heavily on the tradition of the arbitral system's national wage cases. Each year, the Australian Council of Trade Unions (ACTU) initiates a so-called 'living wage case' in the AIRC. Acting on behalf of its affiliates, and basing its case on a representative sample of awards, the ACTU submits a claim for a wage increase for those employees covered by these awards. Over time, the AIRC's decision flows on to all awards, including those under state jurisdiction. Importantly, awards specify the minimum hourly rates, and employees receiving rates above these minima – those who have received increases through enterprise bargaining – do not receive any wage increase.

Data from the Australian Bureau of Statistics highlight the extent of change in pay-fixing methods in Australia during the 1990s. Traditionally, awards covered the vast majority of workers: during the 1950s, 1960s and 1970s, coverage varied between 85 and 90 per cent (Dabscheck and Niland 1981: 274). As late as 1990, awards covered 80 per cent, with the remainder covered in the main by contracts of employment (ABS 1990). In 2002, 41.3 per cent of all employees were covered by individual agreements (2.0 per cent registered AWAs and 39.3 per cent unregistered individual agreements, that is, contracts of employment), 38.3 per cent by collective agreements (36.1 per cent registered and 2.2 per cent unregistered), and 20.5 per cent by awards (ABS 2003). The change has been even more dramatic in different industry sectors. The most common method of settling pay in the private sector was unregistered individual agreements (48.5 per cent), while the public sector was dominated by collective agreements (88.5 per cent). In low-pay industries, awards tend to dominate; for example, 61.2 per cent of employees in the accommodation, café and restaurants industry classification had their rates of pay determined by awards.

In practice, the traditional central wage-fixing role of the state, particularly its main judicial arm, the AIRC, has been much reduced at law. Its dispute resolution role in the bargaining process has, however, apparently remained. Forbes-Mewett *et al.*'s (2003) analysis of the AIRC's changing role found that the number of industrial matters referred to it by the two main parties for the first year of the Act's operation was very similar to the equivalent figure for its fifth year of operation. What seems to have occurred is that unions and employers have continued to seek AIRC assistance in resolving industrial disputes, regardless of whether the Commission has the formal power to actually arbitrate these disputes. In effect, the AIRC has, through the wishes of the other parties, continued to play a significant industrial relations role. The legal emphasis here is on conciliation but, in practice, much informal arbitration also occurs. Forbes-Mewett *et al.* (2003: 23) concluded, 'there is a demand for a more [AIRC] interventionist role . . . in the dispute resolution process', that 'the industrial relations practitioner community generally hold very supportive views of the AIRC', and that 'overall, it would appear that regardless of the statutory framework within which it operates the AIRC continues to demonstrate the flexibility and resilience that has been its hallmark of success over many years'.

This continuing role was much to the federal government's chagrin. Forced to concede a role for the AIRC by the negotiations with the Australian Democrats to get their legislation enacted by the Upper House of Parliament, the federal government sought effectively to reduce the AIRC's role by stratagems such as, for a number of years, refusing to replace retiring or resigning members of the AIRC and by advocating, in a Ministerial Discussion Paper, private conciliation as a competitor for the AIRC (Reith 1998). In more recent times, the government has accepted an ongoing role for the AIRC and has instead sought to influence its role indirectly by making appointments to the AIRC largely from the employer side, a significant departure from the traditional balanced appointments. As of mid-2004, some thirteen of the last sixteen appointments came from employer ranks or those identified with them (e.g. lawyers who had represented employers before the AIRC). Only one appointee had a union background. It remains to be seen what impact such appointees have on the bargaining system, and particularly on the AIRC's role. In the past, partisan appointees have not infrequently emerged as respected neutrals.

Overall, and accompanying the state's changed role, there has been a distinct balkanisation of the bargaining system, with the boundaries of each subsystem being determined by factors such as the use of contract workers, union membership and industrial power. In general, employees covered by union-negotiated certified agreements are at the top of the wages ladder. Indeed, in some industries, such as construction, such employees have gained significant increases in real wages over the past five years. The major determinant of this leading role is, simply, bargaining power. Unions here have generally remained active, and reasonably well organised. In some cases, they have resisted major employer onslaughts, such as in the mining industry, or government attack, such as a Royal Commission in the building and construction industry. In a number of cases, unions have had to cede significant bargaining ground, such as on the docks, to remain organisationally intact. Clearly, the locus of control, even in these unionised areas, has swung to employers. Yet the lesson to be drawn is that where unions have survived with reasonable density and where they battle to retain some power in the bargaining process, acceptable outcomes from this process can be achieved. Such bargaining outcomes are achieved, however, solely because of the power of the union and its members, rather than on any formal recognition or legitimacy conferred by the bargaining process. Indeed, the alternative bargaining models arguably make an acceptable outcome more difficult to achieve. As discussed below, the organising model of unionism has facilitated these acceptable outcomes.

On the next rung down are employees covered by non-union certified agreements. On average, wage settlements in non-union EBAs are around 0.5 per cent lower per annum over the past five years. Equally, the range of matters covered by such agreements, particularly those regulating issues of control in the workplace, is usually much narrower than in union agreements. In short, the market power of the employer is reflected in the bargaining outcome. Next in line are employees who have their wages determined through AWAs. While it is difficult to be prescriptive about their contents, on balance, wages rates seem to be lower than those of non-union EBAs and certainly the range of bargainable subjects is narrow, often restricted to core matters, with some conditions being sub-award standard. The lowest rung is occupied by award-covered employees. By definition, awards are restricted to the twenty allowable matters and any slight deviation from this orthodoxy has been challenged through appellate mechanisms by the federal government.

There are, of course, some exceptions. For example, the federal government as an employer insists that all public servants above a specified level of employment sign AWAs, and in the iron ore segment of the mining industry, high-paying AWAs have been used as a deunionisation strategy. Such groups of employees have relatively high salary rates and not infrequently excellent, but not control-threatening, conditions. In general, bargaining outcomes now follow a hierarchy and are closely aligned with market forces. The different processes allow the stronger industrial party to pursue its preferred avenue of bargaining. The post-1996 bargaining system, despite its continued legal recognition of bargaining parties, effectively legitimises bargaining power. The state has withdrawn its support for collectivism and, at best, has retreated to the sidelines. Concepts such as comparative wage justice, salary relativities and equity in pay, historically at the core of wage-fixing in Australia (see Niland 1986) have disappeared. Rather, market power reigns and bargaining outcomes increasingly reflect this change.

Locus of union decision-making

Given both the decentralisation of the bargaining system and the rapid decline in union density, how have unions responded? In particular, has the locus of decision-making within unionism similarly decentralised and have changes emerged in the relative roles, of FTOs and members and local activists? And if so, has new union vibrancy emerged? Perhaps inevitably, the answers to these questions vary from union to union, and are much influenced by the type of strategy being pursued by particular unions. Virtually all unions traditionally followed a dominant arbitral strategy, which served them well for several decades. Under this strategy, power and influence within unionism was concentrated in the hands of FTOs, with the only potential variation between unions being whether these officials were based at the national or at the state level. It should not be surprising, then, that the key union response to declining membership during the late 1980s did not threaten this distribution of power. Indeed, the policy response was directed from the movement's apex, the ACTU, with its power buttressed by a social contract with a federal Labor government. The key strategy was to be a hierarchical, top-down merger of unions, a strategy designed to complement the centralised wage-fixing and social contract systems.

The structural success of this policy – the number of unions dropped from 295 in 1990 to 157 in 1994 – was not matched by membership density, which continued to decline rapidly from 40 per cent to 35 per cent over this period. The recognition that mergers were not, of themselves, the answer to declining union membership led to some rethinking. Changes in the external environment, particularly the growth of enterprise bargaining commencing in the late 1980s, allied with the recognition among major leaders that workplace union structures were a key factor influencing trends in membership levels, dominated this analysis. In 1993, the ACTU led a delegation of FTOs to a number of countries in search of ideas for building membership levels, with a specific brief to examine recruiting methods and techniques. Their report provided the basis for a new strategic response, namely, 'organising'. The 1993 ACTU Congress accepted this report and passed a number of resolutions that enabled the establishment of Organising Works (OW) in 1994. Initially, OW was a small training centre within the ACTU with a twofold purpose. First, to 'recruit, train and support new union recruiters/organisers, who would each be attached to a participating union' (Griffin *et al.* 2003: 82). Second, 'to develop an organising culture' within the union movement (Griffin *et al.* 2003: 82), a much more difficult goal, and time-consuming to define and implement.

The first two years of OW were dedicated to building a base of organisers and fostering an understanding of the concept of organising. What was perhaps not clear at that stage, to the ACTU, the union branches or to OW officials, was that, to achieve the second goal, OW would gradually need to take on more and more responsibility for leading change in organisational culture within union branches themselves. Arguably, it is the extent of this cultural change, allied with the impact of the massive merger wave of the 1990s, that largely determines the relationships between FTOs and lay activists. The effective operation of the organising model requires a more participatory style of official–member interaction, in contrast to the traditionally inactive and passive membership of the arbitral culture (McManus 1997: 31). It requires members to be active in their own workplaces and a workplace delegate structure that represents members and their interests to management. In short, this model demands more from a member in terms of time, effort and input. To move from the centralised approach of the arbitral model to this organising model, OW had to attempt to overturn ninety years of history, a cultural change of huge dimensions. This challenge was not helped by the variable outcomes of the mergers of the 1990s. A number of these were opportunistic, with partners not infrequently determined by political factions and allegiances rather than industrial complementarity. And in some of these marriages of convenience, little post-merger structural or personnel change occurred. Over time, this has changed somewhat, but for some years it was not unusual for different branches of the same union to have different policies and approaches to organising.

It is too simplistic to assert a very strong correlation between policies on organising and the distribution of power within a union. Indeed, one detailed case study argued that centralised leadership was the main factor driving the organising model within a blue-collar manufacturing union (Griffin and Moors 2004). Nevertheless, it remains the case that unions committed to this organising approach and policy must actively seek to involve both lay officials and members in decision-making. At a conference in 2003, which drew 650 officials and delegates, OW officials claimed that no more than twenty unions had adopted a genuine organising model. Further, in only a few of these unions had all mainly state-based branches adopted the model. Arguably, however, these small numbers underestimate the impact of the organising model. At one level, a large number of young union activists have been inducted into the union movement; a key component of the organising model, as in the USA and Britain, is the recruitment of trainees into individual union branches. By 2003, over 400 such trainees had become part of the union movement. A second outcome has been the major debates within unionism about different organisational models and the relevance of these models to the difficult circumstances of the early twenty-first century. Ellem (2002) has chronicled the changing structures and locus of decision-making within unions with members in the Pilbara, a remote mining area in Western Australia where employers have used AWAs effectively to deunionise their workforce. In this case, five unions, covering employees with different trades and skills buried traditional rivalries, including political rivalries, to pool their resources to establish the Pilbara Mineworkers' Union, an organisation with a focus on organising and decision-making at the local level.

A third outcome is the cultural change that has taken, and is taking, place in many unions; indeed the very fact that 650 officials attended a conference on organising is itself a cultural change. Finally, the apparent halt in the decline of both absolute membership as well as density between 2002 and 2003 (see Table 13.1) has boosted the proponents of the organising model. Overall, many union officials now appear to believe that the correct policies and practices are in place, and that the union movement has a realistic chance to remain a viable and vibrant part of the industrial relations system. Perhaps it is this psychological impact of the organising model that, conceivably, is its best asset in bargaining.

A second key factor influencing the relationship between FTOs and lay officials is the growth of enterprise bargaining. With thousands of enterprise agreements being negotiated each year, and with the limited financial and personnel resources of Australian unionism – most dues congregate around 0.5 per cent of gross wages – FTOs, of necessity, have had to seek to enrol and involve at least their activists in the bargaining process and in union decision-making. The dominant system that seems to have emerged in enterprise bargaining is that union activists have become an important part of the bargaining process, but that FTOs become involved at either the final bargaining stage and/or insist on scrutinising the final agreement prior to signing. In practice, a partial transfer of influence has occurred, but FTOs still retain significant control. Some examples of devolved decision-making can be found. However, such examples are rare, and in most unions power and decision-making remain concentrated in the hands of FTOs.

Conclusion

Until recent times, unions enjoyed a core, state-sanctioned, employer-accepted role in the Australian industrial relations system. Recognition was a legal right and the arbitral model underpinned the bargaining relationship to the extent that weak market power was not an inhibitor to achieving satisfactory outcomes. Indeed, for many years a centralised wage-fixing system automatically awarded such outcomes. Within trade unionism, power comfortably resided with FTOs. Commencing in the late 1980s, broad societal changes started to challenge this union role. The changing nature of work, the opening-up of the economy to international forces, the growing acceptance of market deregulation philosophies and a growing support within political parties for a reduced role for all arms of the state in its citizens' lives underpinned this challenge. During the 1990s, unions increasingly lost influence in the economy and polity. Contracts of employment flourished, density declined dramatically, and its traditional ally, the Labor party, passed industrial legislation opposed by unions. Post-1996, with the election of a conservative federal government and new radical legislation, these deleterious pressures have increased.

Currently, despite some limited provisions in the Workplace Relations Act 1996 to encourage company unionism, recognition remains legally guaranteed in most instances. In practice, however, recognition is now much less important. It still guarantees access to the AIRC, but the arbitral powers of that organisation are much reduced. In effect, where an employer decides not to bargain with a recognised union, no longer can that union rely on the AIRC to be the substitute for industrial pressure. The absence of any legal obligation to bargain in good faith means that unions must rely on their own resources to convince the employer to bargain. For their part, employers can choose from a number of bargaining models: offer contracts of employment, offer AWAs, offer non-union collective agreements or offer union collective agreement. Alternatively, they may choose simply to accept the minimum conditions specified in awards. Table 13.2 shows these choices in action and highlights the trend away from union-preferred options. The difficulty for unions attempting to influence the choice of bargaining models is that they have become marginalised in many areas of the economy. Indeed, they are simply absent or only very lightly represented in many workplaces. Thus, the roles of unions vary dramatically across the economy. In some areas, such as the public sector, large companies and skilled areas of employment, they remain important players. In others, particularly small business and relatively unskilled areas, they have no role beyond their involvement in seeking indirectly to increase minimum wages. Increasingly, market power plays a large role in both the bargaining process and its outcomes. In this environment, employers are the dominant force, while the state has abrogated its traditional, pluralist role. The post-1996 bargaining processes have reduced greatly the role of the state and handed the ascendancy to employers. Unions have attempted to respond. Restructuring has occurred and the organising philosophy, with its emphasis on membership involvement in decision-making, has been widely espoused. The rapid decline in density has been halted over the past two years and some high-profile disputes have been won. Yet the crisis remains and further changes in organisation, in operation and in decision-making, including involvement of members and activists, will be necessary if the trade union movement in Australia is to regain some of its former influence.

14 Conclusion

Issues and prospects

Gregor Gall

After years of overt defeat and retreat, coupled with more recent times of underlying inertia and stasis, trade unionists and sympathetic academics and commentators would dearly wish there to be a readily identifiable form of praxis which could credibly serve as model and guide to reinvigorate and expand the trade union movements in Australia, Britain, Canada and the USA. The search for a 'way forward' is still being carried out. In an epoch of the continued dominance of neo-liberalism, the decomposition of social democracy, and the persisting weakness of oppositional social movements, there have been proffered many 'solutions' to return unions to some semblance of their former presence and influence. From the far left, there have been the calls to unionise and mobilise – the 'get off your knees and fight!' school of thought – where rising levels of workers' sectional and class struggle, principally through trade unions, can be voluntarily created through the human agency of the activist and the leader. From the centre-left and centre-right, suggestions of social pact-ism of various hues, at various levels and with various partners as well as of legal minimum regulation have been put forward. Neither of the two broad schools of thought has had much success in achieving its chosen procedural-cum-substantive outcomes.

Aside from any deficiencies in the cogency and credibility of their arguments, the crux of this matter is that neither command the social forces that are capable of compelling workers, unions, political parties, business, government and the state to act as the two schools wish in these regards. Or put another way, the schools do not embody or represent the requisite social forces. Herein lies the '*Catch 22*' situation. In order to create and mobilise the requisite social forces, the cogency and credibility of the arguments must be high with regard to the existing social forces with whom an alliance is sought or with those who are sought to comprise the (new) social force. For both schools of thought, there is objectively a yawning gap between the present and the desired future. For those whom the schools of thought seek to convince, the gap is so big as to make the ideas proffered seem abstract and almost irrelevant.

Where do union 'organising', as a form of praxis, and the new recognition agreements fit into this? One view that is likely to gather pace inside the union movements and associated sympathetic milieus in Australia, Britain, Canada and the USA is that union 'organising' as a method of (and for) rejuvenation and expansion has had its opportunity and has delivered relatively little. In Australia and the USA, 'organising' has been a feature of the union movements there for over a decade while in Britain, for less than a decade. Even taking the counter-factual position of 'how much worse would the situation be without the presence of union "organising"?' does not dramatically alter the aforementioned view, because union 'organising' emerged as a means to stem and reverse the decline. Some, like de Turbeville (2004), question whether union 'organising' is appropriate to the task of rebuilding the unions, either in terms of the scale or the nature of the effort when set against the size of the task faced. Such sceptics ask whether a top-down and bureaucratic initiative can substitute (successfully) itself for a rising social movement. However, that does not mean to say that an alternative mode of organising or operation has yet been conceived of, much less come into practice. Of course, there are other views that tend towards the position that the 'baby shouldn't be thrown out with the bath water', for they believe certain versions or constructions of union 'organising' are, and can be, productive (e.g. Bronfenbrenner and Juravich 1998). And there are others who argue that the medicine should be tried for longer and in bigger doses to see if it produces a recovery. But we can go further in the counter-factual direction by at least posing the question of whether union 'organising' has stymied the possibility of more effective renewal, one source of which might have been the grassroots (see, for example, Clawson 2003).

In Britain in late 2004, due to a financial and membership crisis, both the CWU and GMB unions are reported to have begun moving away from 'organising' because of its expense and its poor results as they batten down their hatches (*Financial Times* 31 August 2004). Meanwhile, the TGWU has now begun moving towards deploying 'organising', with the recruitment of over 100 full-time organisers, and thus away from its previous position of some ambivalence. However, it has already experienced severe difficulties in the first part of its organising drive, the '100% membership campaign' (*Morning Star* 13, 14 September 2004; *Tribune* 10 September 2004). The 100 per cent membership campaign seeks to achieve total density coverage in workplaces where the TGWU has existing members and is recognised by the employer there. USDAW, too, has recently established its own 'Organising Academy'. For many, nonetheless, union 'organising' has 'failed' to live up to the scale of task set for it by itself, its proponents and onlookers. Arguably, the scale of the task was (and still is) too great for an initiative which is neither an epoch-changing social movement nor a product of a social conflagration, but more a technique practised and an appeal disseminated by the upper echelons of national trade unionisms.

Turning to the new recognition agreements, is there any sense in which they represent a harbinger of a 'golden future' for trade unionism, given their newness and novelty? This could be viewed in terms of a model of a further brand of 'new unionism' or as a guide to practice that has a positive demonstration effect. Or is there any sense in which the future for trade unionism can be glimpsed by looking at the new recognition agreements as a prismatic device? By posing these questions in this way, the problems and an array of possible solutions may be starkly illuminated. This is similar to the manner in which Fairbrother (2000) suggested that the circumstances of the past and present vis-à-vis union form and practice may give rise to the possibility of the birth of new forms and practices, i.e. union renewal. In essence, crisis is argued to provide the opportunity of reassessment and changed actions in order to meet the challenges of the new and old in contemporary circumstances.

The evidence presented by the various chapters in this collection suggests that many of the problematic old and existing patterns and practices continue to assert themselves with regard to union form and practice after recent recognition has been gained and representation and bargaining begun. Moreover, there is a symbiosis between, on the one hand, the nature of the workplace union and the impact of the organising prior to the cusp of gaining recognition and, on the other hand, that which exists thereafter. Whilst some instances of relatively positive practices and developments (see, for example, both Holgate and Simms, this volume) have been identified alongside recognition of the continuation of a number of beneficial hitherto existing features and processes, there is little evidence of overall renewal and reinvigoration of existing forms and practices. Indeed, the shaping of union behaviour by the need to play the newly heightened numbers game vis-à-vis the impact of the ERA's membership and support thresholds (see also Gall 2005c) has the effect of running against the key concern of organising, namely, the building of union structures and activities. Neither is there much evidence of new forms and practices. For example, the GMB London region (Holgate, this volume) and the experience of TELCO (The East London Community Organisation) work with the TGWU in gaining union recognition in Canary Wharf (*Morning Star* 6 July 2004; Wills 2004b; Wills and Simms 2004) are examples of but a few instances of the application and success of community or social movement unionism in Britain. Two swallows do not make a summer, no matter how much some may desperately wish otherwise. And no quick fixes exist for long-standing problems. For example, the problems of post-recognition workplace union mobilisation, representation and bargaining may quickly become those of workplace union mobilisation, representation and bargaining per se (cf. Simms, this volume). Moreover, the dead hand of the existing processes of collective bargaining may exert a greater influence on collective bargaining than that of the ERA (cf. McKay *et al.*, this volume). Therefore, and to paraphrase Marx, not only does the influence of the past weigh heavy on the present but it also does so in a nightmarish way.

Consequently, no new efficacious paradigm in the practice of trade unionism has emerged. Neither has the presence and influence of trade unionism entered a new epoch of virility. No (truly) revolutionary rupture in either presence or influence could have been expected here, for the future is always intimately conditioned by its genesis in the conditions of the past. Rather, trade unionism has become physically and psychology hemmed in by its current experiences and by current constraints. Initiatives and novel experiments in both qualitative and quantitative terms to date have been unable to break out of the corral. These conclusions are drawn from the experience of trade unionism in Britain. What of trade unionism in the other countries? Broadly, the same conclusion can be drawn here for Australia, Canada and the USA.

All of this is, of course, rather dispiriting. Understanding the nature of the determinants of the salient processes and outcomes is the first step to turning the situation around. Under capitalism, trade unionism and collective bargaining are highly dependent upon employer and state support for their existence and operation (see, for example, Offe and Wiesenthal 1980). Moreover, neither the terrain on which unions operate nor the compromises and concessions that trade unionism wrests are permanent. Both are part of an unending, unceasing battle. For trade unionists, the issue is the extent and nature of this dependence and the implications these have for unions' actions and behaviours. Conversely, what degree of independence trade unions can create through the generation of their own financial, ideological and organisational resources is the other side of the coin. Again, this has implications for unions' actions and behaviours. Put together, the total resource available to and at the command of the unions is the crux of the matter. In the current period of labour quiescence, both dependent and independent resources are at low ebbs. This configures the balance of power between unions and employers and guides the outcomes of the pursuit of their objective, the nature of their objectives and their interactions. Thereafter, the issue moves to how unions can create more available resource – most obviously independent resource, but with a view to also leveraging dependent resource from employers and state. Although the present situation is frustrating and seems close to hopelessness for those that wish a return to a period of union resurgence and union power, there is an enduring requirement to remember that social change is the sum of the actions of human agencies, and more broadly the interaction of agency, structure and environment. This suggests that trade union power can again be recreated, and without specifying the particular form, lay activists are the central mechanism by which this can be achieved. However, there is a pressing need for a perspective of slow burn by which to set the objectives and context in which these may be attained. There is no substantial evidence that suggests that explosive and rapid penetration and growth are likely. Rather, the course should be set on the course of slow burn, namely, slow and gradual penetration and growth.

Just as the new social movements of the 1990s and after are a long way off becoming a meaningful part of the mainstream within trade unionism, trade unionism is also a long way off becoming an integral part of these movements. Presently, their foci and aims are different, as are their resources for influence. The social movements have both wider and narrower constituencies of interests and members as well as higher and lower level objectives. The average age of the members and participants of the various global social and environmental justice movements (e.g. anti-capitalism, anti-war, anti-poverty and anti-environmental destruction) is considerably younger than the average age of the trade union movements. This lack of crossover and proximity suggests that trade unionism cannot expect a white knight to come riding down the hill to rescue it. In the same regard, a revival in social democracy, the hitherto traditional generator of the ideology and activists of trade unionism, in the foreseeable future also seems unlikely as it continues in its trajectory of decomposition. But if there is any prospect of revival in social democracy, it is hard to see that it could take place without being spearheaded by the trade unions because of their stronger, more immediate and organic link with workers. In Britain, the signs of a political reawakening of a social democratic mould in trade unionism are evident but it has not yet cohered into an intellectual project with a cutting edge and reinforced by social weight.

What implications does this activist-orientated conclusion have for theoretical development? At the most basic level of examining process and outcome, the dialectic between human agency and constructed environment is confirmed as being acute. As Marx might have said, 'Trade unions make their own history but not necessarily in circumstances of their own choosing.' Articulation of interests and relations of power continue to constitute the primary forces that trade unions have to contend, both internally and externally.[1] The underlying contention in this conclusion has been that trade unionism as an organised and socialised form of human agency can potentially shape the social relations around it rather than just be shaped by them. In particular, through exercising strategic choice, trade unionism can pursue the representation of members' interests by developing means of enforcement. However, and for reasons of epochal rather than secular trends, the current ideological and material appeal, and organisational and social form, of trade unionism have become narrowed compared to the scale of the task of revitalisation. Reconstituted and recast through a wider appeal and form such as trade unionism as a social liberation movement of the kind that existed in Brazil, Poland, South Africa and South Korea prior to democratisation may offer a way out of the corral. Members' collective interests would be defined in terms of being producers, consumers and citizens with equality, democracy, social justice and liberty comprising the objectives of the value system. Pursuit and enforcement would necessarily require the construction, and mobilisation, of power resources at various workplace and extra-workplace (community, industry, territorial state) levels. But, of course, we must also recall the salutary lessons of the union movements in these four countries, concerning their great difficulties in making the transition to operating in liberal democracies, focusing on collective bargaining rather than political mobilisation, and fracturing after the common denominator of unity against the 'greater enemy' was removed. Nonetheless, these difficulties are unlikely to completely invalidate the existence of some positive lessons that could be gleaned from the union movements there. Finally, what conclusions can we draw from the union movements elsewhere in France, Greece, Italy, Portugal and Spain, where levels of union densities and political exclusion vary considerably (and in some cases are quite low in the former and high in the latter) but where widespread union and social mobilisations are more common? These mobilisations are far from uniformly effective but they look to be promising mechanisms from the vantage points of union movements in other countries which have a narrower social mobilisation base (see, for example, *European Journal of Industrial Relations* 2003; Frege and Kelly 2004; Milkman and Voss 2004; Verma and Kochan 2004). So whilst the union movements in Britain, Australia, Canada and the USA continued to face (extremely) severe problems, a union future which sets much store by the recreation of lay activist union milieus as part of a wider ideological rebirth of social justice, social democracy and socialism appears to offer significant purchase for union revitalisation.

Note

1 For an extensive review of analyses of union renewal and revitalisation, see Heery (2003) and Heery *et al.* (2004: 1–21). However, valuable as both are, neither provides a foundation for agencies within trade unions in the Lenin-ist way of 'What is to be done?' and 'How is it to be done?' In short, neither is a guide to radical or socialist praxis.

References

ABS (1990) *Award Coverage Australia*, May, catalogue no. 6315.0 (see www.abs.gov.au).

ABS (2003) *Employee Earnings and Hours, Australia*, March, catalogue no. 6306.0 (see www.abs.gov.au).

ACIRRT (2001) 'The AWA experience: evaluating the evidence' Australian Centre for Industrial Relations Research Conference, University of Sydney.

Ackers, P. and Payne, J. (1998) 'British trade unions and social partnership: rhetoric, reality and strategy' *International Journal of Human Resource Management*, 9/3: 529–50.

ACTU (1993) *United States Mission on Recruitment and Organisation*, summary report, ACTU, Melbourne.

Adams, G. (2001) *Canadian Labour Law*, second edition, Canada Law Book, Aurora, ON.

Adams, R. (1994) 'Union certification as an instrument of labor policy: a comparative perspective' in Friedman, S., Hurd, R., Oswald, R. and Seeber, R. (eds) *Restoring the Promise of American Labor Law*, ILR Press, Ithaca, New York, pp. 260–72.

Adams, R. (1995a) *Industrial Relations under Liberal Democracy*, University of South Carolina Press, Columbia, SC.

Adams, R. (1995b) 'A pernicious euphoria: 50 years of Wagnerism in Canada' *Canadian Labour and Employment Law Journal*, 3: 321–55.

Adams, R. (1999) 'Why statutory recognition is bad labour policy: the North American experience' *Industrial Relations Journal*, 30/2: 96–100.

Airey, C., Hales, J., Hamilton, R., Korvovessis, C., McKernan, A. and Purdon, S. (1999) *The Workplace Employee Relations Survey* [*WERS*] *1997–8: Technical Report*, National Centre for Social Research, London.

Akyeampong, E. (2002) 'Unionisation and fringe benefits' *Perspectives on Labour and Income*, Statistics Canada – catalogue no. 75-001-XPE: 42–6.

Allen, V. (1966) *Militant Trade Unionism: a re-analysis of industrial action in an inflationary situation*, Merlin Press, London.

Anderson, J. and Gunderson, M. (1982) 'Strikes and dispute resolution' in Anderson, J. and Gunderson, M. (eds) *Union–Management Relations in Canada*, Addison-Wesley Publishers, Don Mills, pp. 220–44.

Anderson, J. and Gunderson, M. (1989) 'Strikes and dispute resolution' in Anderson, J. and Gunderson, M. (eds) *Union–Management Relations in Canada*, Addison-Wesley Publishers, Don Mills, pp. 287–316.

Anderson, P. (1967) 'The limits and possibilities of trade union action' in Blackburn, R. and Cockburn, A. (eds) *The Incompatibles: trade union militancy and the consensus*, Penguin, London, pp. 263–80.

Arblaster, A. (1994) *Democracy*, Open University Press, Milton Keynes.

Bach, S. and Givan, R. (2004) 'Public service unionism in a restructured public sector: challenges and prospects' in Kelly, J. and Willman, P. (eds) *Union Organization and Activity*, Routledge, London, pp. 89–109.

Batchelor, J. (2001) 'Employment security in the aftermath of the break-up of Rover Group' *Warwick Papers in Industrial Relations*, no. 342, Warwick Business School, Warwick.

Batstone, E. (1988) 'The frontier of control' in Gallie, D. (ed.) *Employment in Britain*, Oxford University Press, Oxford, pp. 218–47.

Bedard, M. (2004) 'Selected provisions in collective agreements – indirect compensation in the workplace' *Workplace Gazette*, 7/1: 33–56.

Bentham, K. (1999) *The Determinants and Impacts of Employer Resistance to Union Certification*, PhD thesis, University of Toronto.

Bentham, K. (2002) 'Employer resistance to union certification: a study of eight Canadian jurisdictions' *Relations Industrielles/Industrial Relations*, 57/1: 159–87.

Beynon, H. (1984) *Working for Ford*, second edition, Penguin Books, London.

Blackburn, R. (1967) *Union Character and Social Class: a study of white-collar unionism*, Batsford, London.

Blanchflower, D. and Bryson, A. (2003) 'Changes over time in union relative wage effects in the UK and the US Revisited' in Addison, J. and Schnabel, C. (eds) *International Handbook of Trade Unions*, Edward Elgar, Cheltenham, pp. 197–245.

Blyton, P. and Turnbull, P. (1998) *The Dynamics of Employee Relations*, second edition, Macmillan, Basingstoke.

Blyton, P. and Turnbull, P. (2004) *The Dynamics of Employee Relations*, third edition, Palgrave, Basingstoke.

Boxall, P. and Haynes, P. (1997) 'Strategy and effectiveness in a neo-Liberal environment' *British Journal of Industrial Relations*, 35/4: 567–91.

Brah, A. (1996) *Cartographies of Diaspora: contesting identities*, Routledge, London.

Brody, D. (1997) 'Labor elections: good for workers?' *Dissent*, 44: 71–7.

Bronfenbrenner, K. (1996) 'Lasting victories: successful union strategies for winning union contracts' *Proceedings of the Forty-Eighth Annual Meeting of the Industrial Relations Research Association*, Industrial Relations Research Association, Madison, pp. 161–7.

Bronfenbrenner, K. (1998) 'Reversing the tide of organising decline: lessons from the US experience' *New Zealand Journal of Industrial Relations*, 23/2: 21–34.

Bronfenbrenner, K. (2003) 'The American labour movement and the resurgence in union organising' in Fairbrother, P. and Yates, C. (eds) *Trade Unions in Renewal: a comparative study*, Continuum, London, pp. 32–50.

Bronfenbrenner, K. and Hickey, R. (2003) 'Winning is possible: successful union organizing in the United States – clear lessons, too few examples' *Multinational Monitor*, June: 9–14.

Bronfenbrenner, K., Friedman, S., Hurd, R., Oswald, R. and Seeber, R. (eds) (1998) *Organising to Win: new research on union strategies*, ILR Press, Ithaca, New York.

Bronfenbrenner, K. and Juravich, T. (1998) 'It takes more than house calls: organizing to win with a comprehensive union-building strategy' in Bronfenbrenner, K., Friedman, S., Hurd, R., Oswald, R. and Seeber, R. (eds) *Organizing to Win: new research on union strategies*, ILR Press, Ithaca, New York, pp. 19–36.

Brown, D. and Beatty, D. (1993) *Canadian Labour Arbitration*, third edition, Canada Law Book, Toronto.

Brown, W., Deakin, S., Hudson, M. and Pratten, C. (2001) 'The limits of statutory trade union recognition' *Industrial Relations Journal*, 32/3: 180–94.

Bruno, R. and Schuls, G. (1998) 'Contract campaigns, union organising and leadership development: the case of Teamster psychologists' *Working USA: The Journal of Labor and Society*, 2/4: 60–7.

Bryson, A. (2001) 'The foundation of "partnership"? Union effects on employee trust in management' *National Institute Economic Review*, 176: 91–104.

Bryson, A. (2002) *The Size of the Union Wage Premium in Britain's Private Sector*, PSI Discussion Paper No. 9, Policy Studies Institute, London.

Bryson, A. (2003) *Employee Desire for Unionisation in Britain*, PSI Discussion Paper No. 12, Policy Studies Institute, London.

Bryson, A. and Gomez, R. (2002) 'Marching on together? Recent trends in union membership' in Park, A., Curtice, J., Thomson, K., Jarvis, L. and Bromley, C. (eds) *British Social Attitudes: the 19th report*, Sage, London, pp. 43–67.

Bryson, A. and Gomez, R. (2003) 'Buying into union membership' in Gospel, H. and Wood, S. (eds) *Representing Workers: union recognition and membership in Britain*, Routledge, London, pp. 72–91.

Bryson, A., Gomez, R., Gunderson, M. and Meltz, N. (2004a) 'Youth–adult differences in the demand for unionization: are American, British and Canadian workers all that different?' *Journal of Labor Research*, 26/1: 155–67.

Bryson, A., Gomez, R. and Willman, P. (2004b) 'The end of the affair? The decline in employers' propensity to unionize' in Kelly, J. and Willman, P. (eds) *Union Organization and Activity*, Routledge, London, pp. 129–49.

Bryson, A. and McKay, S. (1997) 'What about the workers?' in Jowell, R., Curtice, J., Park, A., Brook, L., Thomson, K. and Bryson, C. (eds) *British Social Attitudes: the 14th report – The end of Conservative values?* Ashgate, Aldershot, pp. 23–48.

Budd, J. and Heins, P. (1996) 'Union representation elections and labor law reform: lessons from the Minneapolis Hilton' *Labor Studies Journal*, 20/4: 3–21.

Bureau of National Affairs (2003, 2004) *Card-check Recognition Report*, Washington, DC.

Card, D., Lemieux, T. and Riddell, W. (2003) 'Unions and the wage structure' in Addison, J. and Schnabel, C. (eds) *International Handbook of Trade Unions*, Edward Elgar, Cheltenham, pp. 246–92.

Carter, B. (2000) 'Adoption of the organising model in British trade unions: some evidence from Manufacturing, Science and Finance (MSF)' *Work, Employment and Society*, 14/1:119–36.

Carter, B. (2004) 'Review of Gall, G. (ed.) *Union Organizing: campaigning for trade recognition*' *Work, Employment and Society*, 18/2: 439–41.

CFMEU (1999) *Construction, Forestry, Mining and Energy Union v Coal and Allied Operations*, AIRC, 7 October, Print R9735.

Chamberlain, N. and Kuhn, J. (1965) *Collective Bargaining*, McGraw-Hill, New York.

Charlwood, A. (2004) 'Influences on trade union organizing effectiveness in Britain' *British Journal of Industrial Relations*, 42/1: 69–3.

Chinn, C. and Dyson, S. (2000) *'We Ain't Going Away!' The Battle for Longbridge*, Brewin Books, Studley.

Clawson, D. (2003) *The Next Upsurge: labor and the new social movements*, ILR/Cornell, Ithaca.

Claydon, T. (2000) 'Tales of disorder: the press and the narrative construction of industrial relations in the British motor industry, 1950–79' *Historical Studies in Industrial Relations*, 9: 1–36.

Cockburn, C. (1995) *Women and the European Social Dialogue: strategies for gender democracy*, Equal Opportunities Unit, European Commission, V/5465/95-EN.

Cody, J. (2004) 'NLRB election statistics suggest new organising strategies paying off for unions' Bureau of National Affairs, Washington, DC.

Colgan, F. and Creegan, C. (2002) *Organising and Diversity: reflections on the approach of UNIFI: report to the union*, Centre for Equality Research in Business, University of North London.

Colgan, F., and Ledwith, S. (1996) 'Sisters organising – women and their trade unions' in Ledwith, S. and Colgan, F. (eds) *Women in Organizations: challenging gender politics*, Macmillan, Basingstoke, pp. 152–85.

Colgan, F. and Ledwith, S. (2002a) 'Gender and diversity: reshaping union democracy' *Employee Relations*, 24/2: 167–89.

Colgan, F. and Ledwith, S. (2002b) (eds) *Gender, Diversity and Trade Unions: international perspectives*, Routledge, London.

Colling, T. and Claydon, T. (2000) 'Strategic review and organisational change in UNISON' in Terry, M. (ed.) *Redefining Public Sector Unionism: UNISON and the future of trade unions*, Routledge, London, pp. 79–99.

Colling, T. and Dickens, L. (1989) *Equality Bargaining – Why Not?*, HMSO, London.

Colling, T. and Dickens, L. (2001) 'Gender equality and the trade unions: a new basis for mobilization?' in Noon, N. and Ogbonna, E. (eds) *Equality, Diversity and Disadvantage in Employment*, Palgrave, Basingstoke, pp. 136–55.

Cooke, W. (1984) 'The failure to negotiate first contracts: determinant and policy implications' *Industrial and Labor Relations Review* 38/2: 163–78.

Creighton, B. and Stewart, A. (2000) *Labour Law: an introduction*, third edition, Federation Press, Sydney.

Dabscheck, B. (2001) 'The slow and agonising death of the Australian experiment with conciliation and arbitration' *Journal of Industrial Relations*, 43/3: 277–93.

Dabscheck, B. and Niland, J. (1981) *Industrial Relations in Australia*, George Allen and Unwin, Sydney.

Danford, A. (2004) 'Review of Gall, G. (ed.) *Union Organizing: campaigning for trade recognition*' *British Journal of Industrial Relations*, 42/1: 197–9.

Darlington, R. (2002) 'Shop stewards' leadership, left-wing activism and collective workplace union organisation' *Capital and Class*, 76: 95–126.

Deery, S., Plowman, D., Walsh, J. and Brown, M. (2001) *Industrial Relations: a contemporary analysis*, second edition, McGraw-Hill, Sydney.

Delaney, J., Jarley, P. and Fiorito, J. (1996) 'Planning for change: determinants of innovation in unions' *Industrial and Labor Relations Review*, 49/4: 597–615.

Delgado, H. (2000) 'The Los Angeles manufacturing action project: an opportunity squandered?' in Milkman, R. (ed.) *Organizing Immigrants: the challenge for unions in contemporary California*, ILR Press, Cornell, pp. 225–39.

Department of Trade and Industry (2004) *The UK Contact Centre Industry: a study*, DTI, London.

Diamond, W. and Freeman, R. (2001) *What Workers Want from Workplace Organisations*, TUC, London

Dickens, W. (1983) 'The effect of company campaigns on certification elections: law and reality one again' *Industrial and Labor Relations Review*, 36/4: 560–76.

DiMaggio, P. and Powell, W. (1983) 'The iron cage revisited: institutional isomorphism and collective rationality in institutional fields' *American Sociological Review*, 48:161–73.

Donovan Commission (1968) *Report of the Royal Commission on Trade Unions and Employers' Associations 1965–68*, Cmnd 3623, HMSO, London.

Dundon, T. (2002) 'Employer opposition and union avoidance in the UK' *Industrial Relations Journal*, 33/3: 234–45.

Earls, J. (2002) 'From adversarial to aspirational – a new agenda for trade unions? *Unions 21 Discussion Papers*, no. 9, November.

Eaton, A. and Kriesky, J. (2001) 'Union organising under neutrality and card-check agreements' *Industrial and Labor Relations Review*, 55/1: 42–59.

Eaton, J. and Verma, A. (2004) 'Does "fighting back" make a difference? Strategic choice and bargaining outcomes – a case study of the CAW', mimeo, Centre for Industrial Relations, University of Toronto.

Edwardes, M. (1983) *Back from the Brink: an apocalyptic experience*, Collins, London.

Eisenscher, M. (1999) 'Leadership development and organizing: for what kind of union?' *Labor Studies Journal*, 24/2: 567–81.

Ellem, B. (2002) '"We're solid": union renewal at BHP Iron Ore, 1999–2002' *International Journal of Employment Studies*, 10/2: 123–46.

Employment Committee (1994) *The Future of Trade Unions*, The House of Commons, third report, HMSO, London.

Erickson, C., Fisk, C., Milkman, R., Mitchell, D. and Wong, K. (2001) 'Justice for Janitors: lessons from three rounds of negotiations' *Report of International Conference on Union Growth*, Centre for Industrial Relations, University of Toronto.

European Journal of Industrial Relations (2003) Themed issue on 'Trade Union Revitalisation', 9/1.

Ewing, K., Moore, S. and Wood, S. (2003) *Unfair Labour Practices: trade union recognition and employer resistance*, Institute of Employment Rights, London.

Fairbrother, P. (2000) *Unions at the Crossroads*, Mansell, London.

Farber, H. and Western, B. (2002) 'Ronald Reagan and the politics of declining union organization' *British Journal of Industrial Relations*, 40/3: 385–401.

Featherstone, L. (2004) 'Will labor take the Wal-Mart challenge?' *The Nation*, 28 June.

Federal Mediation and Conciliation Services (2003) *Annual Report*, Washington, DC.

Findlay, P. and McKinlay, A. (2002) 'Bargaining alone? Social capital and new unionism' *Renewal*, 10/2: 21–9.

Findlay, P. and McKinlay, A. (2003a) 'Organizing in electronics: recruitment, recognition and representation – shadow shop stewards in Scotland's "Silicon Glen" in Gall, G. (ed.) *Union Organizing: campaigning for trade union recognition*, Routledge, London, pp. 114–32.

Findlay, P. and McKinlay, A. (2003b) 'Union organising in Big Blue's backyard' *Industrial Relations Journal*, 34/1: 52–66.

Fine, S. (1969) *Sit-Down: the General Motors strike of 1936–1937*, University of Michigan Press, Ann Arbor.

Fiorito, J. (2003) 'Union organising in the United States' in G. Gall (ed.) *Union Organizing: campaigning for union recognition*, Routledge, London, pp. 191–210.

Forbes-Mewett, H., Griffin, G. and McKenzie, D. (2003) 'The Australian Industrial

Relations Commission: adapting or dying?' *International Journal of Employment Studies*, 11/2: 1–24.

Forth, J. and Millward, N. (2002) 'Union effects on pay levels in Britain' *Labour Economics*, 9/4: 547–62.

Freeman, R. (1985) 'Why are unions faring poorly in NLRB representation elections?' in Kochan, T. (ed.) *Challenges and Choices Facing American Labor*, MIT Press, Cambridge, MA, pp. 45–64.

Freeman, R. and Diamond, W. (2003) 'Young workers and trade unions' in Gospel, H. and Wood, S. (eds) *Representing Workers: union recognition and membership in Britain*, Routledge, London, pp. 29–50.

Freeman, R. and Medoff, J. (1984) *What Do Unions Do?*, Basic Books, New York.

Frege, C. and Kelly, J. (2004) (eds) *Varieties of Unionism: strategies for union revitalisation*, Oxford University Press, Oxford.

Friedman, S. and Wosniak, R. (1996) 'First contract arbitration: the Canadian experience' *Proceedings of the Forty-Eighth Annual Meeting of the Industrial Relations Research Association*, Industrial Relations Research Association, Madison, pp. 153–60.

Frost, A. (2001a) 'Creating and sustaining local union capabilities: the role of national unions' *Relations Industrielles/Industrial Relations*, 56/2: 307–35.

Frost, A. (2001b) 'Reconceptualising local union responses to workplace restructuring in North America' *British Journal of Industrial Relations*, 39/4: 539–64.

Fürstenberg, F. (1998) 'Employment relations in Germany' in Bamber, G. and Lansbury, R. (eds) *International and Comparative Industrial Relations*, Sage, London, pp. 201–23.

Gahan, P. (1996) 'Did arbitration make for dependent unionism? Evidence from historical case studies' *Journal of Industrial Relations*, 38/4: 648–98.

Gall, G. (1992) 'The NUJ: a union in crisis' *Capital and Class*, 48: 7–15.

Gall, G. (1993) 'The employers' offensive in the provincial newspaper industry' *British Journal of Industrial Relations*, 31/4: 615–24.

Gall, G. (1995) 'HRM in practice: a case study revisited' *Personnel Review*, 24/3: 43–55.

Gall, G. (1997) 'Developments in trade unionism in the financial sector in Britain' *Work, Employment and Society*, 11/2: 219–35.

Gall, G. (1998a) 'Industrial relations and the local press' in Franklin, B. and Murphy, D. (eds) *Making the Local News: local journalism in context*, Routledge, London, pp. 91–102.

Gall, G. (1998b) 'Resisting the rise of the non-union employer: the case of the press workers' *Capital and Class*, 64: 43–61.

Gall, G. (1998c) 'The prospects for workplace trade unionism today: evaluating Fairbrother's union renewal thesis' *Capital and Class*, 66: 149–57.

Gall, G. (1999) 'What is to be done with organised labour?' *Historical Materialism*, 5: 327–43.

Gall, G. (2000a) 'Employment relations and the labour process in the newspaper industry: is there the potential for the return of the NUJ?' *New Technology, Work and Employment*, 15/2: 94–107.

Gall, G. (2000b) 'Debating mobilisation, class struggle and the left: a response to a reply by Kelly' *Historical Materialism*, 7: 175–80.

Gall, G. (2001a) 'Industrial relations under new ownership: the case of the provincial newspaper industry' *Personnel Review*, 30/1: 22–41.

Gall, G. (2001b) 'Back on terms' *People Management*, 13 September, pp. 40–2.
Gall, G. (2002) 'The return of the National Union of Journalists to the provincial newspaper industry in Britain?' *Media, Culture and Society*, 24/5: 673–92.
Gall, G. (ed.) (2003a) *Union Organizing: campaigning for trade recognition*, Routledge, London.
Gall, G. (2003b) Introduction in Gall, G. (ed.) *Union Organizing: campaigning for trade recognition*, Routledge, London, pp. 1–18.
Gall, G. (2003c) 'Employer opposition to union organisation' in Gall, G. (ed.) *Union Organizing: campaigning for trade recognition*, Routledge, London, pp. 79–96.
Gall, G. (2003d) 'Conclusion – drawing up a balance sheet' in Gall, G. (ed.) *Union Organizing: campaigning for trade recognition*, Routledge, London, pp. 228–43.
Gall, G. (2003e) 'Organizing in the offshore oil and gas industry in Britain, *c.*1972–1990: a long flame burning or spark that has gone out?' in Gall, G. (ed.) *Union Organizing: campaigning for trade recognition*, Routledge, London, pp. 39–55.
Gall, G. (2003f) *The Fruits of Our Labour? The outcomes of the new recognition agreements*, New Unionism Project, Trades Union Congress, London.
Gall, G. (2003g) 'Trade recognition in Britain: developments, issues and prospects' *Human Resources and Employment Review*, 1/4: 196–202.
Gall, G. (2004a) 'British employer resistance to trade union recognition' *Human Resource Management Journal*, 14/2: 36–53.
Gall, G. (2004b) 'Trade recognition in Britain, 1995–2002: turning a corner?' *Industrial Relations Journal*, 35/3: 249–70.
Gall, G. (2004c) 'The new trade union agreements in Britain: processes and outcomes' *Human Resources and Employment Review*, 2/2: 76–81.
Gall, G. (2005a) *Trade Unionism in the Financial Services Sector*, Ashgate, Aldershot.
Gall, G. (2005b) 'The outcomes of the new recognition agreements' unpublished paper, University of Stirling.
Gall, G. (2005c) 'Organising non-union workers as trade unionists in the "New Economy" in Britain' *Economic and Industrial Democracy*, 26/1: 43–65.
Gall, G. and McKay, S. (2001) 'Facing "Fairness at Work": union perception of employer opposition and response to recognition' *Industrial Relations Journal*, 32/2: 94–114.
Gall, G. and Murphy, D. (1996) 'Journalism in changing times: the changing relationship between trade unionism and professionalism in the British provincial newspaper industry' in Fincham, R. (ed.) *New Relationships in the Organised Professions*, Avebury, Aldershot, pp. 225–46.
Giles, A. and Starkman, A. (2001) 'The collective agreement' in Gunderson, M., Ponak, A. and Gottlieb Taras, D. (eds) *Union–Management Relations in Canada*, fourth edition, Toronto, Addison Wesley Longman, pp. 272–313.
Godard, J. (2003) 'Do labor laws matter? The density decline and convergence thesis revisited' *Industrial Relations*, 42/3: 458–92.
Godard, J. (2004) 'Trade union recognition: statutory unfair labour practice regimes in the USA and Canada' *Employment Research Series*, no. 20, Department of Trade and Industry, London.
Gollan, P. (1999) 'Non-union forms of employee representation in the United Kingdom and Australia', Research Colloquium, Loughborough University, Loughborough, January.
Gollan, P. (2000) 'Non-union forms of employee representation in the United Kingdom and Australia' in Kaufman, B. and Taras, D. (eds) *Non-union Employee*

Representation: history, contemporary practice, and policy, M.E. Sharpe, Armonk, New York, pp. 410–52.

Gollan, P. (2001) 'Tunnel vision: non-union employee representation' *Employee Relations*, 23/4: 376–400.

Gospel, H. and Willman, P. (2002) 'The right to know: disclosure of information for collective bargaining and joint consultation in Germany, France and Great Britain', Discussion Paper No. 453, Centre for Economic Performance, LSE, London.

Gospel, H. and Willman, P. (2003) 'The coming of workplace information sharing and consultation: what it means for employee representation in Britain' *Perspectives on Work*, 7/1: 38–9.

Gospel, H. and Wood, S. (eds) (2003) *Representing Workers: trade recognition and membership in Britain*, Routledge, London.

Greenfield, P. and Pleasure, R. (1993) 'Representatives of their own choosing: finding workers' voice in the legitimacy and power of their unions' in Kaufman, B. and Kleiner, M. (eds) *Employee Representation: alternatives and future directions*, Industrial Relations Research Association, Madison, Wisconsin.

Griffin, G. and Moors, R. (2004) 'The fall and rise of organising in a blue-collar union' *Journal of Industrial Relations* 46/1: 39–52.

Griffin, G., Small, R. and Svensen, S. (2003) 'Trade union innovation, adaptation and renewal in Australia: still searching for the holy membership grail' in Fairbrother, P. and Yates, A. (eds) *Trade Union in Renewal: a comparative study*, Continuum, Sydney, pp. 78–101.

Gunderson, M., Hyatt, D. and Ponak, A. (2001) 'Strikes and dispute resolution' in Gunderson, M., Ponak, A. and Gottlieb Taras, D. (eds) *Union–Management Relations in Canada*, fourth edition, Toronto, Addison Wesley Longman, pp. 314–58.

Hancock, K. (1962) 'Compulsory arbitration versus collective bargaining: three recent assessments' *Journal of Industrial Relations*, 4/1: 20–31.

Haque, R. (2002) *Migrants in the UK: a descriptive analysis of their characteristics and labour market performance*, Department of Work and Pensions, London.

Healey, D. (1989) *The Time of My Life*, Michael Joseph, London.

Heery, E. (1996) 'The new new unionism' in Beardwell, I. (ed.) *Contemporary Industrial Relations: a critical analysis*, Oxford University Press, Oxford, pp. 175–202.

Heery, E. (2001) 'Learning from each other: a European perspective on American labor' *Journal of Labor Research*, 22/2: 307–19.

Heery, E. (2002) 'Partnership versus organising: alternative futures for British trade unionism' *Industrial Relations Journal*, 33/1: 20–35.

Heery, E. (2003) 'Trade unions and industrial relations' in Ackers, P. and Wilkinson, A. (eds) *Understanding Work and Employment: industrial relations in transition*, Oxford University Press, Oxford, pp. 278–304.

Heery, E., Conley, H., Delbridge, R. and Stewart, P. (2004) 'Seeking partnership for the contingent workforce' in Stuart, M. and Martinez-Lucio, M. (eds) *Partnership and Modernization in Employment Relations*, Routledge, London, pp. 171–87.

Heery, E., Healy, G. and Taylor, P. (2004) 'Representation at work: themes and issues' in Healy, G., Heery, E., Taylor, P. and Brown, W. (eds) *The Future of Worker Representation*, Palgrave, Basingstoke, pp. 1–36.

Heery, E. and Simms, M. (2003) *Bargain or Bust? Employer responses to union organising*, Trades Union Congress, London.

Heery, E., Simms, M., Simpson, D., Delbridge, R. and Salmon, J. (2000a) 'Organising unionism comes to the UK' *Employee Relations*, 22/1: 38–57.

Heery, E., Simms, M., Delbridge, R., Salmon, J. and Simpson, D. (2000b) 'The TUC's Organising Academy: an assessment' *Industrial Relations Journal*, 31/5: 400–15.

Heery, E., Simms, M., Delbridge, R., Salmon, J. and Simpson, D. (2000c) 'Union organising in Britain: a survey of policy and practice' *International Journal of Human Resource Management*, 11/5: 986–1007.

Heery, E., Simms, M., Delbridge, R., Salmon, J. and Simpson, D. (2003) 'Trade union recruitment policy in Britain: form and effects' in Gall, G. (ed.) *Union Organizing: campaigning for trade union recognition*, Routledge, London, pp. 56–78.

Hickey, R. (2002) 'Strategic contract campaigns at multinational corporations' *Labor Studies Journal*, 27/1: 71–91.

Holgate, J. (2004a) *Organising Black and Minority Ethnic Workers: trade union strategies for recruitment and inclusion*, PhD thesis, University of London.

Holgate, J. (2004b) 'Black and minority ethnic workers and trade unions: strategies for organisation, recruitment and inclusion' SERTUC working paper, London.

Howard, W. (1977) 'Australian trade unions in the context of union theory' *Journal of Industrial Relations*, 19/3: 255–73.

Hurd, R. (1993) 'Organizing and representing clerical workers: the Harvard model' in Cobble, D. (ed.) *Women and Unions: forging a partnership*, Cornell University Press, Ithaca, New York, pp. 316–36.

Hyman, R. (1983) *Industrial Relations: a Marxist introduction*, Macmillan, London.

Hyman, R. (1989) *The Political Economy of Industrial Relations: theory and practice in a cold climate*, Macmillan, London.

Hyman, R. (1997) 'The future of employee representation' *British Journal of Industrial Relations*, 35/3: 309–36.

Hyman, R. (2001a) 'Trade union research and cross-national comparison' *European Journal of Industrial Relations*, 7/2: 203–32.

Hyman, R. (2001b) 'Voice, security and citizenship', Mimeo, London School of Economics.

Hyman, R. (2001c) *Understanding European Trade Unionism: between market, class and society*, Sage, London.

Income Data Services (2000) *Report*, 811, June.

Industrial Relations Services (1992) 'Lean Production – and Rover's "New Deal"' *IRS Employment Trends* 514: 12–15.

Industrial Relations Services (1996) 'Turning the tide: new unionism in finance' *IRS Employment Trends* 619: 12–16.

Jacobi, O. (2003) 'Union recognition in Germany: a dual system of industrial relations with two recognition problems' in Gall, G. (ed.) *Union Organizing: campaigning for trade union recognition*, Routledge. London, pp. 211–27.

Jalette, P. and Warrian, P. (2002) 'Contracting-out provisions in Canadian collective agreements – a moving target' *Workplace Gazette*, 5/1: 64–76.

Jarley, P. (2002) 'American unions at the start of the twenty-first century: going back to the future?' in Fairbrother, P. and Griffin, G. (eds) *Changing Prospects for Trade Unionism: comparisons between six countries*, Continuum, London, pp. 200–37.

Jefferys, S. (2003) *Bank Union Activists: who they are and what makes them tick?*, Working Lives Research Institute, London Metropolitan University.

Journal of Industrial Relations (1976) Symposium on Bargaining and Arbitration in Australia, 19/4.

Juravich, T. and Bronfenbrenner, K. (1998) 'Preparing for the worst: organizing and staying organized in the public sector' in Bronfenbrenner, K., Friedman, S., Hurd, R.W., Oswald, R.A. and Seeber, R.L. (eds) *Organizing to Win: new research on union strategies*, ILR Press, Ithaca, New York, pp. 261–82.

Juravich, T. and Hilgert, J. (1999) 'UNITE's victory at Richmark: community-based organising in communities of color' *Labor Studies Journal*, 24/1:27–36.

Kahn-Freund, O. (1979) *Labour Relations: heritage and adjustment*, Oxford University Press, Oxford.

Kaufman, B. (2001) 'The employee participation/representation gap: an assessment and proposed solution' *University of Pennsylvania Journal of Labor and Employment Law*, 3/3: 491–561.

Kaufman, B. and Kleiner, M. (1993) (eds) *Employee Representation: alternatives and future directions*, Industrial Relations Research Association, Madison.

Kelly, J. (1988) *Trade Unions and Socialist Politics*, Verso, London.

Kelly, J. (1996) 'Works councils: union advance or marginalisation?' in McColgan, A. (ed.) *The Future of Labour Law*, Mansell, London, pp. 46–63.

Kelly, J. (1998) *Rethinking Industrial Relations: mobilization, collectivism and long waves*, Routledge, London.

Kelly, J. (1999) 'Social partnership in Britain: good for profits, bad for jobs and unions' *Communist Review* 30/3–10.

Kelly, J. (2000) 'Mobilisation and class struggle: a reply to Gall' *Historical Materialism*, 7:167–74.

Kelly, J. and Badigannavar, V. (2004) 'Union organizing' in Kelly, J. and Willman, P. (eds) *Union Organizing and Activity*, Routledge, London, pp. 32–50.

Kelly, J. and Heery, E. (1989) 'Full time officers and trade union recruitment' *British Journal of Industrial Relations*, 27/2: 196–213.

Kelly, J. and Heery, E. (1994) *Working for the Union: British trade union officers*, Cambridge University Press, Cambridge.

Kelly, J. and Willman, P. (eds) (2004) *Union Organizing and Activity*, Routledge, London.

Kirton, G. (1999) 'Sustaining and developing women's trade union activism: a gendered project?' *Gender, Work and Organisation*, 6/213–23.

Kittner, M. (1997) *Arbeits- und Sozialordnung*, Bund Verlag, Koln.

Kochan, T. (2003) 'A US perspective on the future of trade unions in Britain' in Gospel, H. and Wood, S. (eds) *Representing Workers: union recognition and membership in Britain*, Routledge, London, pp. 166–77.

Kumar, P. and Murray, G. (2003) 'Strategic dilemma: the state of union renewal in Canada' in Fairbrother, P. and Yates, C. (eds) *Trade Unions in Renewal: a comparative study*, Continuum, London, pp. 200–20.

Labour Research Department (1992) 'The union derecognition bandwagon' *Labour Research*, 77/4: 6–8.

Laffer, K. (1962) 'Compulsory arbitration and collective bargaining' *Journal of Industrial Relations*, 4/2: 146–51.

LCTUC (1979) *British Leyland, the Edwardes Plan and Your Jobs*, Leyland Combine TU Committee, Birmingham.

Leys, C. (1983) *Politics in Britain: from Labourism to Thatcherism*, Verso, London.

Lipset, M. and Katchanovski, I. (2001) 'The future of private sector unions in the U.S.' *Journal of Labor Research*, 22/2: 239–244.

Lloyd, C. (1999) 'What do employee councils do? Representation in non-union firms', BUIRA Conference, De Montfort University, Leicester, July.

Locke, R. and Thelen, K. (1995) 'Apples and oranges revisited: contextualised comparisons and the study of comparative labor politics' *Politics and Society*, 23: 337–67.

Logan, J. (2001) 'Is statutory recognition bad news for British unions? Evidence from the history of North American industrial relations' *Historical Studies of Industrial Relations*, 11: 63–107.

Logan, J. (2002) 'Consultants, lawyers and the "union-free" movement in the USA since the 1970s' *Industrial Relations Journal*, 33/3: 197–214.

Lyddon, D. (1996) 'The car industry 1945–79: shop stewards and workplace unionism' in Wrigley, C. (ed.) *A History of British Industrial Relations 1939–1979*, Edward Elgar, Cheltenham, pp. 186–211.

Mantsios, G. (1998) *A New Labour Movement for the New Century*, Monthly Review Press, New York.

McCallum, R. and Smith, G. (1986) 'Opting out from within: industrial agreements under the Conciliation and Arbitration Act 1904' *Journal of Industrial Relations*, 28/1: 57–85.

Macintyre, S. and Mitchell, R. (eds) (1989) *Foundation of Arbitration*, Oxford University Press, Melbourne.

McManus, S. (1997) 'Gender and union organising in Australia' in Pocock, B. (ed.) *Strife, Sex and Politics in Labour Unions*, Allen and Unwin, Sydney, pp. 26–44.

Marchington, M., Goodman, J. Wilkinson, A. and Ackers, P. (1992) 'New developments in employee involvement' *Employment Department Research Series*, no. 2, London.

Marchington, M., Wilkinson, A., Ackers, P. and Dundon, T. (2001) 'Management choice and employee voice' Research Report, Chartered Institute of Personnel and Development, London.

Markovitz, A. (1986) *The Politics of the West German Trade Unions: strategies of class and interest representation in growth and crisis*, Cambridge University Press, Cambridge.

Markowitz, L. (2000) *Worker Activism After Successful Union Organizing*, M.E. Sharpe, Armonk, New York.

Marks, G. (1989) *Unions in Politics: Britain, Germany and the United States in the nineteenth and early twentieth centuries*, Princeton University Press, New Jersey.

Marshall, K. (2003) 'Benefits of the job' *Perspectives on Labour and Income*, May, Statistics Canada, catalogue no. 75-001-XIE:5–12.

Marston, S. (2001) 'Geography and social movements' *Political Geography*, 20:7: 925–8.

Metcalf, D. (2004) *British Unions: resurgence or perdition?*, Centre for Economic Performance, LSE, London.

Metcalf, D., Hansen, K. and Charlwood, A. (2001) 'Unions and the sword of justice: unions and pay systems, pay inequality, pay discrimination and low pay' *National Institute Economic Review*, 176: 61–75.

Milkman, R. (2000) (ed.) *Organizing Immigrants: the challenge for unions in contemporary California*, ILR Press, Ithaca, New York.

Milkman, R. and Voss, K. (2004) (eds) *Rebuilding Labor: organizing and organizers in the new union movement*, ILR/Cornell, Ithaca.

Millward, N., Bryson, A. and Forth, J. (2000) *All Change at Work? British employment relations, 1980–98, as portrayed by the Workplace Industrial Relations Survey Series*, Routledge, London.

Minnesota Organisers Roundtable (2004) South St Paul, Minnesota, July.

Mitchell, D. (1996) *The Lie of the Land: migrant workers and the California landscape*, Regents, University of Minnesota.

Mönnich, H. (1991) *The BMW Story: a company in its time*, Sidgwick and Jackson, London.

Moore, S. (2004) 'Union mobilization and employer counter-mobilization in the statutory recognition process' in Kelly, J. and Willman, P. (eds) *Union Organization and Activity*, Routledge, London, pp. 7–31.

Moore, S., McKay, S. and Bewley, H. (2004) 'The content of new voluntary trade union recognition agreements 1998–2002: volume one – an analysis of new agreements and case studies' *DTI Employment Relations Research Series*, no. 26, Department of Trade and Industry, London.

Morris, T., Storey, J., Wilkinson, A. and Cressey, P. (2001) 'Industry change and union mergers in British retail finance' *British Journal of Industrial Relations*, 39/2: 237–56.

Murray, A. (2003) *A New Labour Nightmare: the return of the awkward squad*, Verso, London.

Murray, G. (1998) 'Steeling for change: organisation and organising in two USWA districts in Canada' in Bronfenbrenner, K., Friedman, S., Hurd, R., Oswald, R. and Seeber, R. (eds) *Organising to Win: new research on union strategies*, ILR Press, Ithaca, New York, pp. 320–38.

Murray, G. (2001) 'Unions: membership, structures, actions and challenges' in Gunderson, M., Ponak, A. and Gottlieb Taras, D. (eds) *Union–Management Relations in Canada*, fourth edition, Toronto, Addison Wesley, pp. 79–116.

Murray, G. (2002) 'Unions in Canada: strategic renewal, strategic conundrums' in Fairbrother, P. and Griffin, G. (eds) *Changing Prospects for Trade Unionism: comparisons between six countries*, Continuum, London, pp. 93–136.

Murray, G., Levesque, C., Roby, N. and Le Queux, S. (1999) 'Isolation or integration? The relationship between local and national union in the context of globalisation' in Waddington, J. (ed.) *Globalisation and Patterns of Labour Resistance*, Mansell, London, pp. 160–91.

National Labor Relations Board (2004) *CATS Elections Fiscal Year 2004*, Washington, DC.

National Union of Journalists (2003) *Review of the Employment Relations Act 1999: the NUJ response*, NUJ, London.

Niland, J. (ed.) (1986) *Wage Fixation in Australia*, Allen and Unwin, Sydney.

Noon, M. (1993) 'Control, technology and the management offensive in newspapers' *New Technology, Work and Employmen*, 8/2: 102–10.

Noon, M. and Ogbonna, E. (2001) *Equality, Diversity and Disadvantage in Employment*, Palgrave, Basingstoke.

O'Brien, J. (2001) 'First collective agreement legislation: from exceptional remedy to routine solution', project submitted in partial fulfilment of the requirements for the degree of Masters of Business Administration, Simon Fraser University.

Offe, C. and Wiesenthal, H. (1980) 'Two logics of collective action: theoretical notes on social class and organizational form' *Political Power and Social Theory*, 1: 67–115.

Oxenbridge, S. (1997) 'Organizing strategies and organizing reform in New Zealand service sector unions' *Labor Studies Journal*, 22/3: 3–27.

Oxenbridge, S., Brown, W., Deakin, S. and Pratten, C. (2003) 'Initial responses to the statutory recognition procedure of the Employment Relations Act 1999' *British Journal of Industrial Relations*, 41/2: 315–35.

Palmer, T., Grainger, H. and Fitzner, G. (2004) *Trade Union Membership 2003*, DTI, London.

Pateman, C. (1970) *Participation and Democratic Theory*, Cambridge University Press, London.

Pavy, G. (1994) 'Winning NLRB elections and establishing collective bargaining relationships' in Friedman, S., Hurd, R., Oswald, R. and Seeber, R. (eds) *Restoring the Promise of American Labor Law*, ILR Press, Ithaca, New York, pp. 110–21.

Peterson, R., Lee, T. and Finnegan, B. (1992) 'Strategies and tactics in union organising campaigns' *Industrial Relations*, 31/2: 370–82.

Ponak, A. and Falkenberg, L. (1989) 'Resolution of interest disputes' in Sethi, A. (ed.) *Collective Bargaining in Canada*, Nelson Canada, Scarborough, pp. 260–93.

Quinlan, M. (1987) 'Early trade union organization in Australia: three Australian colonies, 1829–1850', *Labour and Industry*, 1/3: 61–95.

Quinlan, M. and Gardner, M. (1995) 'Researching industrial relations history: the development of a database on Australian trade unions 1825–1900' *Labour History*, 66: 90–113.

Ramsay, H. (1977) 'Cycles of control: workers' participation in sociological and historical perspective' *Sociology*, 11/3: 481–506.

Ramsay, H. (1983) 'Evolution or cycle? Worker participation in the 1970s and 1980s' in Crouch, C. and Heller, F. (eds) *Organisational Democracy and Political Processes: International Yearbook of Industrial Democracy*, Wiley, London, pp. 203–26.

Reed, T. (1989) 'The impact of the union organiser on the probability of securing a first contract' *Industrial Relations Research Association Series, Proceedings of the Forty-Second Annual Meeting*, pp. 478–91.

Reed, T. (1990) 'Union attainment of first contracts: do service unions possess a competitive advantage?' *Journal of Labor Research*, 11/4: 425–35.

Reed, T. (1993) 'Securing a union contract: impact of the union organiser' *Industrial Relations*, 32/2: 188–204.

Reith, P. (1998) *Workplace Reform in Australia: a compendium of ministerial papers*, vol. 1, Canberra.

Rose, J. and Chaison. G. (1996) 'Linking union density and union effectiveness: the North American experience' *Industrial Relations*, 35/1: 78–105.

Rose, J. and Picsak, M. (1996) 'Settlement rates and settlement stages in compulsory interest arbitration' *Relations Industrielles/Industrial Relations*, 51/4: 643–64.

Rose, J. and Wetsel, K. (1986) 'Outcomes of bargaining structures in the Ontario and Saskatchewan construction industries' *Relations Industrielles/Industrial Relations*, 41/2: 256–80.

Rose, R. (1991) 'Comparing forms of comparative analysis' *Political Studies*, 39: 446–62.

Rothstein, R. (1996) 'Toward a more perfect union? New labor's hard road' *The American Prospect*, 26: 47–54.

Rover Worker (1998) 'Onslaught at Rover' in Cohen, S. (ed.) *What's Happening??*

The Truth about Work ... & The Myth of "Partnership", Trade Union Forum, London, pp. 60–2.

Rundle, J. (1998) 'Winning hearts and minds in the era of employee-involvement programs' in Bronfenbrenner, K., Friedman, S., Hurd, R., Oswald, R. and Seeber, R. (eds) *Organizing to Win: new research on union strategies*, ILR Press, Ithaca, New York, pp. 213–31.

Safford, S. and Locke, R. (2001) *Unions on the Rebound: social embeddedness and the transformation of building trades locals*, Sloan Working Paper 4175-01, MIT Sloan School of Management, Boston, MA.

Savage, L. (1998) 'Geographies of organising – Justice for Janitors in Los Angeles' in Herod, A. (ed.) *Organizing the Landscape: geographical perspectives on labor unionism*, University of Minnesota, Minneapolis, pp. 225–62.

Scarbrough, H. and Terry, M. (1996) 'Industrial relations and the reorganisation of production in the UK motor industry: a study of the Rover Group' *Warwick Papers in Industrial Relations*, no. 58, Industrial Relations Research Unit, Warwick.

Sciacchitano, K. (1998) 'Finding the community in the union and the union in the community: the first-contract campaign at Steeltech' in Friedman, S., Hurd, R., Oswald, R. and Seeber, R. (eds) *Restoring the Promise of American Labor Law*, Ithaca, ILR Press, New York, pp. 150–63.

Simms, M. (2003) 'Union organizing in a not-for-profit organization' in Gall, G. (ed.) *Union Organizing: campaigning for trade union recognition*, Routledge, London, pp. 97–113.

Simms, M., Heery, E., Delbridge, R., Salmon, J. and Simpson, D. (2000) 'Organising women: the dual challenge for British unions' British Universities Industrial Relations Association annual conference, Warwick.

Smith, P. and Morton, G. (1990) 'A change of heart: union exclusion in the provincial newspaper industry' *Work, Employment and Society*, 4/1: 105–24.

Smith, P. and Morton, G. (1993) 'Union exclusion and the decollectivisation of industrial relations in contemporary Britain' *British Journal of Industrial Relations*, 31/2: 97–114.

Snape, E. (1994) 'Union organizing in Britain: the views of local full-time officials' *Employee Relations*, 16/8: 48–62.

Snape, E. (1995) 'The development of "managerial unionism" in Britain: the view from below' *Work, Employment and Society*, 9/3: 559–68.

Streeck, W. (1995) *German Capitalism: does it exist? Can it survive?* Max-Planck-Institut Für Gesellschaftsforschung, Köln.

Streeck, W. (1998) *The German Model of Co-determination and Cooperative Government*, Bertelsmann Foundation/Hans-Böckler Foundation, Gütersloh.

Surowiecki, J. (2004) *The Wisdom of Crowds: why the many are smarter than the few and how collective wisdom shapes business, economies, societies and nations*, Random House, New York.

Sweeney, E. (2000) Address to UNIFI conference, February.

Taylor, P. and Bain, P. (2003) 'Call centre organizing in adversity: from Excell to Vertex' in Gall, G. (ed.) *Union Organizing: campaigning for trade union recognition*, Routledge, London, pp. 153–72.

Taylor, P., Hyman, J., Mulvey, G. and Bain, P. (2002) 'Work organisation, control and the experience of work in call centres' *Work, Employment and Society*, 11/1: 133–50.

Taylor, R. (1994) *The Future of Trade Unions*, Andre Deutsch, London.

Terry, M. (1996) 'Negotiating the government of Unison: union democracy in theory and practice' *British Journal of Industrial Relations*, 34/1: 87–110.

Terry, M. (1999) 'Systems of collective representation in non-union firms in the UK' *Industrial Relations Journal*, 30/1: 16–30.

Terry, M. (2003) 'Partnership and trade unions in the UK' *Economic and Industrial Democracy*, 24/4: 485–507.

Thelen, K. (1991) *Union of Parts, Labour Politics in Post-War Germany*, Cornell University Press, Ithaca, New York.

Towers, B. (1997) *The Representation Gap: change and reform in the British and American workplace*, Oxford University Press, Oxford.

Towers, B. (2003) 'Comparisons and prospects: industrial relations and trade unions in North America and Britain' in Gall, G. (ed.) *Union Organizing: campaigning for trade union recognition*, Routledge, London, pp. 173–90.

Trade Union Congress (2003) *Review of the Employment Relations Act 1999 – TUC response*, TUC, London.

Turbeville, S. de (2004) 'Does the "organizing model" represent a credible renewal strategy?' *Work, Employment and Society*, 18/4: 775–94.

Turner, L., Katz, H. and Hurd, R. (eds) (2001) *Rekindling the Movement: labor's quest for relevance in the 21st century*, ILR Press, Ithaca, New York.

UNIFI (1999a) 'Birth of a new and great union' *Fusion*, July, pp. 8–9.

UNIFI (1999b) *Partnership: principles and problems*, Position Paper No. 4, BIFU/NWSA/UNIFI, London.

UNIFI (2000a) *Organising for Growth and Development*, UNIFI, London.

UNIFI (2000b) *Call Centres: UNIFI in your workplace*, UNIFI, London.

UNIFI (2001a) 'Financial services sector, the labour market and UNIFI membership' *Research Factsheet*, UNIFI, London.

UNIFI (2001b) *The Future of the Finance Sector: influences on the next decade*, UNIFI, London.

UNIFI (2001c) *Organising Young Workers*, UNIFI, London.

UNIFI (2001d) *Report to Annual Conference*, UNIFI, London.

UNIFI (2001e) *UNIFI Staff 2001 Conference*, Daventry, February 2001.

UNIFI (2001f) *UNIFI at a Glance*, UNIFI, London.

UNIFI (2002a) *Participation in UNIFI*, UNIFI, London.

UNIFI (2002b) *Report to Annual Conference*, UNIFI, London.

UNIFI (2004a) 'Finance workers to get super union' UNIFI press release, London.

UNIFI (2004b) 'Can you believe what they say? Globalisation and Project Monsoon', www.unifi.org.uk/hsbc/jobrisk/2004-aug17a.htm.

UNIFI (2004c) *Report to Annual Conference*, UNIFI, London.

Verma, A. and Kochan, T. (2004) (eds) *Unions in the 21st Century: an international perspective*, Palgrave, Basingstoke.

Virdee, S. (2000) *Racism, 'Racial Formation' and the Class Struggle: a study of 'race' and organised labour in England*, unpublished PhD thesis, University of Warwick.

Waddington, J. (1999) *Membership Retention and Trade Union Organisation: the case of unions in banking*, UNIFI Inaugural Congress, Blackpool, May.

Waddington, J. and Kerr, A. (2000) 'Towards an organising model in Unison? A trade union membership strategy in transition' in Terry, M. (ed.) *Redefining Public Sector Unionism: Unison and the future of trade unions*, Routledge, London, pp. 231–62.

Wajcman, J. (2000) 'Feminism facing industrial relations in Britain' *British Journal of Industrial Relations*, 38/2:183–201.

Walton, R. and McKersie, R. (1965) *A Behavioural Theory of Labour Negotiations*, McGraw-Hill, New York.

Watling, D. and Snook, J. (2003) 'Works councils and trade unions: complementary or competitive? The case of SAGCo' *Industrial Relations Journal*, 34/3:260–70.

Watson, D. (1988) *Managers of Discontent: trade union officers and industrial relations managers*, Routledge, London.

Weiler, P. (1980) *Reconcilable Differences*, Carswell, Toronto.

Whisler, T. (1999) *The British Motor Industry, 1945–94*, Oxford University Press, Oxford.

Whiting, R. (1983) *The View of Cowley: the impact of industrialisation upon Oxford 1918–1939*, Oxford University Press, Oxford.

Whittall, M. (2000) 'The BMW European works council: a cause for European industrial relations optimism?' *European Journal of Industrial Relations*, 6/1: 61–83.

Whittall, M. (2003) *European Works Councils – A Path to European Industrial Relations? The Case of BMW and Rover*, PhD thesis, Nottingham Trent University.

Whittall, M. (2004) 'European labour market regulation: the case of European works councils' in Vosko, L. and Stamford, J. (eds) *Challenging the Market*, McGill-Queens University Press, Toronto, pp. 151–74.

Wilks, S. (1984) *Industrial Policy and the Motor Industry*, Manchester University Press, Manchester.

Williams, K., Haslam, C., Johal, S. and Williams, J. (1994) *Cars: Analysis, History, Cases*, Berghahn, Providence.

Willman, P. and Kelly, J. (2004) 'Introduction' in Kelly, J. and Willman, P. (eds) (2004) *Union Organizing and Activity*, Routledge, London, pp. 1–6.

Wills, J. (2000) 'Great expectations: three years in the life of a European works council' *European Journal of Industrial Relations*, 6/1: 85–107.

Wills, J. (2002) *Union Futures: building networked trade unionism in the UK*, Fabian Ideas 602, Fabian Society, London.

Wills, J. (2003) 'Organizing in transport and travel: learning lessons from TSSA's Seacat campaign' in Gall, G. (ed.) *Union Organizing: campaigning for trade union recognition*, Routledge, London, pp. 133–52.

Wills, J. (2004a) 'Trade unionism and partnership in practice: evidence from the Barclays–UNIFI agreement' *Industrial Relations Journal*, 35/4: 329–43.

Wills, J. (2004b) 'Organizing the low paid: London's living wage campaign as a vehicle for change' in Healy, G., Heery, E., Taylor, P. and Brown, W. (eds) *The Future of Worker Representation*, Palgrave, Basingstoke, pp. 264–82.

Wills, J. and Simms, M. (2004) 'Building reciprocal community unionism in the UK' *Capital and Class*, 82: 59–84.

Witt, M. and Wilson, R. (1999) 'The Teamsters' UPS strike of 1997: building a new labor movement' *Labor Studies Journal*, 24/1: 58–73.

Womack, J., Jones, D. and Roos, D. (1990) *The Machine That Changed the World*, Rawson Associates, New York.

Wood, S. and Godard, J. (1999) 'The statutory recognition procedure in the Employment Relations Bill: a comparative analysis' *British Journal of Industrial Relations*, 37/2: 203–44.

Wood, S., Moore, S. and Willman, P. (2002) 'Third time lucky for statutory union recognition in the UK' *Industrial Relations Journal*, 33/3: 215–33.

Wood, S., Moore, S. and Ewing, K. (2003) 'The impact of the trade union recognition procedure under the Employment Relations Act 2000–02' in Gospel, H. and

Wood, S. (eds) *Representing Workers: union recognition and membership in Britain*, Routledge, London, pp. 119–43.
Wrench, J. and Virdee, S. (1996) 'Organising the unorganised: race, poor work and trade unions' in Ackers, P., Smith, C. and Smith, P. (eds) *The New Workplace and Trade Unionism: critical perspectives on work and organization*, Routledge, London, pp. 240–78.
Yates, C. (2000) 'Staying the decline in union membership: union organising in Ontario, 1985–1999', *Industrial Relations/Relations Industrielles*, 55/4: 640–71.
Yates, C. (2003) 'The revival of industrial unions in Canada: the extension and adaptation of industrial union practices to the new economy' in Fairbrother, P. and Yates, C. (eds) *Trade Unions in Renewal: a comparative study*, Continuum, London.

Index